THE
USAAF
HANDBOOK

1939–1945

THE
USAAF
HANDBOOK
1939–1945

MARTIN W. BOWMAN

SUTTON PUBLISHING LIMITED

First published in 1997 by
Sutton Publishing Limited · Phoenix Mill
Thrupp · Stroud · Gloucestershire · GL5 2BU

British Library Cataloguing in Publication Data
A catalogue record for this book is available from the British Library

ISBN 0 7509 1280 4

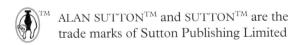 ALAN SUTTON™ and SUTTON™ are the
trade marks of Sutton Publishing Limited

Typeset in 10/12 pt Plantin Light
Typesetting and origination by
Sutton Publishing Limited.
Printed in Great Britain by
Butler & Tanner, Frome, Somerset.

CONTENTS

Introduction

It is asking the impossible for a book of this size to cover, in depth and in detail, every single aspect of the seventeen United States Army Air Forces during the period 1939–45, and to address the whole range of equipment, personnel, units, weapons and characteristics associated with each one. Most of these topics warrant a book in their own right, and in many cases publications detailing aircraft, armament, clothing and equipment, medals and awards, personnel and personalities, and so on, have already been produced. Few are definitive, and even fewer have attempted, in a single volume, to cover the whole gamut of issues involving every air force.

This handbook is designed not only to inform, but also to dovetail with all existing (and future) works, and furthermore, to fill in some of the gaps and clarify some misconceptions. Many of the photos have not been published before, and those that have are included in this volume to illustrate a specific point in the text or because they contain details not considered relevant before. The casual reader and the serious researcher should both find this book invaluable as, I hope, it will obviate the need to thumb through several sources – many of which are difficult to obtain – to find the identity of a Medal of Honor winner, the date of a battle or mission, the names of the commanders, their units and their aircraft, or to determine the identity of a squadron or group (squadron codes have been included where possible). I ask the reader to excuse any oversights and omissions, as space is at a premium, and hope that the majority of questions will find an answer within the pages of this volume.

Many people have contributed information, photos, books, advice and time to help increase the book's accuracy and scope. I would particularly like to thank: Steve Adams; Mike Bailey, who painted the superb side views featured herein; Patricia Everson, 448th Bomb Group Collection; and Truett Woodall, for their gracious and never-ending support in making available rare wartime books, photos and data. I am especially grateful to Mike for the loan of many important photos and his most valuable on-the-spot technical assistance. Charles Warren also provided much valuable information on flight clothing and equipment. Phyllis Dubois, Lesley Fleetwood and Christine Snowden were most helpful during my many forays to the US 2nd Air Division Library in Norwich, and provided much willing assistance with research.

I am also most grateful to the following individuals, companies and organizations for the kind loan of photos and for supplying further information: John Archer; Joe Boder, USAF (Retd); Beech Aircraft Co.; Boeing Aircraft; Col. Bill Cameron, USAF (Retd); Cessna Aircraft Co.; Abe L. Dolim USAF (Retd); Aldon P. Ferguson; J. Wallace Fields USAF (Retd);

Kenneth W. Fields; Robert M. Foose; the Ford Archives; Larry Goldstein; Sol Greenberg; the late Russ D. Hayes; the late Alan Healy; Claire Johns; Myron Keilman; Jack Kings; Jack Krause; Lockheed-California Aircraft Co.; John Mason; Dave Mayor; Ian McLachlan; John McClane; Merle Olmsted; McDonnell Douglas Aircraft; Northrop Aircraft Co.; Francie Meisner Park WASP (Retd); Connie, Gordon and Lloyd Richards; David H. Rust; Col. Albert J. Shower USAF (Retd); Derek Smith; Steve Snelling; Gen. George W. Sweeney USAF (Retd); the Thorpe Abbotts Memorial Museum; Gen. Paul W. Tibbets USAF (Retd); Elmer Vogel USAF (Retd); Paul Wilson.

Martin Bowman
1996

Glossary

AAC	Army Air Corps
AAD	Army Air Depot
AAF	Army Air Forces, US Army
AAFFTD	AAF Flying Training Detachment
AAFSAT	AAF School of Applied Tactics
ABC–1	USA/UK agreement of March 1941 stipulating that these nations would exchange military missions and that when the USA entered the war it would furnish naval, ground and air support for the campaign against the Axis powers.
AEF	American Expeditionary Forces
AF	Air Force
Air Corps	Army Air Branch 1926–41
Air Service	Army Air Branch 1920–6
AM	Air Medal
ARGUMENT	Joint operation against German aircraft industry by 8th and 15th AFs, February 1944.
ATC	Air Transport Command
ATG	Air Transport Group
AVG	American Volunteer Group
AWPD	Air War Plans Division
Bomb Group (BG)	Bombardment Group
Bradley Plan	Adopted for the expansion of the USAAFs in the UK, September 1943. Formulated in the spring of that year by a group of WD officers headed by Major-General Follet Bradley.
CBI	China-Burma-India theatre
CLARION	Comprehensive plan for co-ordinated air attacks on German transportation facilities from 22 February 1945.
CROSSBOW	Allied bombing against German V-1 and V-2 sites
DFC	Distinguished Flying Cross
DSC	Distinguished Service Cross
EAME	European–African–Middle East Theatre
EM	Enlisted Men
ETO	European Theatre of Operations
FEAF	Far East Air Forces
FG	Fighter Group
Flak	*Fliegerabwehrkanonen*. German anti-aircraft forces.
FRANTIC	Code-name for shuttle bombing attacks beginning 2 June 1944.
GHQAF	General Headquarters Air Force

GP	General Purpose
HUSKY	Allied invasion of Sicily, summer/autumn 1943.
IP	Initial Point
LS	Liaison Squadron
MAAF	Mediterranean Allied Air Forces
MARKET GARDEN	Allied airborne and land operations in Holland, September 1944.
MATTERHORN	Plan approved in April 1944 for the bombing of Japan by B-29s based in the Calcutta area and staging through advanced fields in the Chengtu area.
MIA	Missing In Action
MP	Military Police
MPI	Mean Point of Impact
MTO	Mediterranean Theatre of Operations
NAAF	North African Air Forces
NFS	Night Fighter Squadron
NO-BALL	Site for V-1 and V-2 rockets
OD	Olive Drab
OTU	Operational Training Unit
OVERLORD	Allied invasion of German-held Europe, which began on D-Day, 6 June 1944.
POINTBLANK	US strategic bombing effort before the cross-Channel invasion, June 1943–May 1944.
POM	Preparation for Overseas Movement.
RTU	Replacement Training Unit
SAD	Strategic Air Depot
SHAEF	Supreme Headquarters Allied Expeditionary Force
SOP	Standard Operating Procedure
STARKEY	Deception plan to force the appearance of the Luftwaffe over the English Channel in September 1943.
STRANGLE	Air operation to interdict movement of enemy supplies in Italy.
TCG	Troop Carrier Group
TIDALWAVE	Ploesti bombing mission, 1 August 1943.
TORCH	Allied invasion of Axis-controlled French North Africa which began on 8 November 1942.
USAFBI	US Air Forces in the British Isles
USASTAF	US Army Strategic Air Forces in the Pacific
USSTAFE	US Strategic Air Forces in Europe
VARSITY	Crossing of the Rhine operation near Wesel, 24 March 1945.
VHBG/W	Very Heavy Bomber (B-29) Group/Wing
VLR	Very Long Range
WD	War Department
ZOI	Zone of the Interior

CHAPTER ONE

Background to War

US aviation began in 1898, when the US Army invested $50,000 in the development of a man-carrying aeroplane. It failed, and it was not until 1908 that the Army accepted a tender for $25,000 from the Wright Brothers to build a military biplane capable of carrying two airmen at 40 mph. The US Army established an Aeronautical Division in the Signal Corps on 1 August 1907, and acquired its first aircraft in August 1909, when it accepted the Wright Model B. It remained the only aircraft on the inventory for two years. Army personnel learned to fly, but for some years they were not organized into units for operations.

As a result, in 1913, when relations between the USA and Mexico were strained as a result of a revolution in Mexico, there was no aviation unit available for service along the border. The Army, however, despatched some of its aviators and aircraft to Texas, and on 5 March 1913 these were formed into the 1st Aero Squadron, a provisional organization consisting of two companies, equipped with Curtiss R-2 biplanes. In December, after the provisional unit had moved to San Diego for training, it was organized officially as an Army squadron.

On 18 July 1914 the Aviation Section of the Signal Corps was vested with all responsibilities for US Army flying. Meanwhile, following Pancho Villa's raid on Columbus, New Mexico, in March 1916, the 1st Aero Squadron joined the force that Brig.-Gen. John J. Pershing organized to try to capture the Mexican bandit. Thus the 1st Aero Squadron, which provided communication and reconnaissance services during the Mexican expedition, was the first US aviation unit to take the field for a military campaign.

Meanwhile, although war had broken out in Europe, little progress had been made towards expanding the Army's air arm. Congress created an Aviation Section in the Signal Corps by an Act approved on 18 July 1914, but the legislators provided little money for the new service. Moreover, the Signal Corps naturally used the meagre resources to develop aviation as a means of communication, observation and reconnaissance, rather than as an instrument for combat. One company of the 2nd Aero Squadron was organized in 1915 and sent to the Philippines. By early 1917 only seven squadrons were located in the whole of the USA. The 7th was formed in February 1917 for duty in the Panama Canal Zone, the 6th was organized in Hawaii in March 1917, and three others, the 3rd, 4th and 5th, were in the process of being formed when the USA entered the First World War on 6 April 1917.

At the time, the USA's military air services and aircraft industry were in an even more parlous state than those of most of the European powers in

1914. The Army Aviation Service comprised just 65 officers and 1,120 other ranks, originally part of the Signal Corps, with only around 300 aircraft, none of which were suitable for combat on the Western Front. In fact, of all the aircraft flown by US pilots in the First World War, only a few Curtiss H4 twin-engined biplane flying boats were operated on maritime duties and the Standard E1 and Morse S4 single-seat biplane fighters were only suitable for training. The British-designed de Havilland 4 (DH4) became the standard combat aircraft, while several other British and French types were also used, the most famous being the SPAD and the Sopwith Camel. However, the USA moved quickly, designing and developing the reliable 'Liberty' engine and making plans for expansion of its ailing aircraft industry. About half of the almost 7,900 aircraft in service by the time of the armistice were US-built (although less than 800 of them were at the front), and almost three-quarters of the engines. The DH4 and the Handley Page and Caproni night bombers were built under licence, but the 'Liberty' engine proved too powerful for the Bristol Fighter.

Pershing, who became commander of the American Expeditionary Forces, soon developed a plan for the deployment of 260 combat squadrons to France. Later the plan was revised, with the number of squadrons reduced to 202, all of which were to be at the front by 30 June 1919. On 29 May 1918 Pershing separated the Air Service from the Signal Corps and made his 1886 West Point classmate, Maj.-Gen. Mason M. Patrick, Chief of Air Service and in charge of all US air elements of the AEF. Lt.-Col. Benjamin D. Foulois was appointed Chief of Air Service of the 1st Army and Assistant Chief, and Col. William Mitchell was appointed Chief of Air Service of the 1st Corps.

British and French instructors helped produce more than 11,400 aircrew by the armistice, of whom 4,300 were overseas but only about 1,250 were at the front. Groups were slow to be deployed in the field, and only fifteen squadrons had arrived by July 1918. In Gen. Pershing's opinion, the main functions of the AEF's Air Service were to drive off hostile aircraft and to obtain information about German movements. Therefore, half of the 202 squadrons were to be observation units assigned to three armies and sixteen corps. Of the remainder, 60 were to be pursuit squadrons, but the plan also provided for 27 night bombardment and 14 day bombardment squadrons.

The first US aviation unit to reach the Western Front was the 1st Aero Squadron, an observation organization, which sailed from New York in August 1917 and arrived at Le Havre on 3 September. As other squadrons were organized in the USA, they too were sent overseas, where they continued their training. In the USA the Chief Signal Officer was responsible for organizing, training and equipping aviation units until 21 May 1918. At that time President Woodrow Wilson created a Bureau of Aircraft Production and made it responsible for aeronautical equipment; training of personnel and units was the responsibility of the Division of Military Aeronautics, which had been created by the War Department on 27 April 1918. Although the bureau and division were recognized by the War Department on 24 May 1918 as forming the Army's Air Service, no Director of Air Service was appointed until 27 August 1918.

It was February 1918 before any US aviation squadron entered combat. On 3 April the 94th Pursuit Squadron, resplendent with its famous 'Hat-in-Ring' insignia, became the first US-trained pursuit squadron in action on the Western Front. Also in April, the 1st Corps Observation Group was organized, and in May the 1st Pursuit Group was formed. In July 1918 the AEF organized its first wing, composed of the 2nd and 3rd Pursuit Groups, and later, the 1st Day Bombardment Group.

During the war the aero squadrons played important roles in such famous battles as the Aisne–Marne, St Mihiel, when 1,481 aircraft took part, and the Meuse–Argonne, when more than 250 bombers and 100 pursuit planes took part, dropping 32 tons of bombs. Some, like the 94th Squadron, commanded by Capt. Edward V. Rickenbacker, or the 27th, which had 2nd Lt. Frank 'balloon-buster' Luke Jr (whose total was 14 balloons and 4 aircraft) as one of its aviators, developed distinguished records in combat. Rickenbacker, who had joined the squadron in March 1918, finished the war as the USA's top 'ace', with 21 aircraft and 4 balloons destroyed. He was awarded the Medal of Honor. Luke was killed in a shoot-out on 27 September 1918 after crash landing. In 1919 he was awarded a posthumous Medal of Honor.

Some airmen, Brig.-Gen. William 'Billy' Mitchell among them, were advocating the formation of an air force that would concentrate military aviation on inflicting heavy blows against the enemy. In September 1918, for the Allied assault against the German salient at St Mihiel, Mitchell brought together almost 1,500 US and French aircraft for co-ordinated operations in which observation and pursuit squadrons supported ground forces, while the other two-thirds of the air force bombed and strafed behind the lines. Later, during the Meuse–Argonne offensive, Mitchell used a somewhat smaller concentration of air power to keep the enemy on the defensive.

By Armistice Day, 11 November 1918, 45 combat squadrons (20 pursuit, 18 observation and 7 bombardment) in 14 groups (7 observation, 5 pursuit and 2 bombardment) had been assigned to the front. The USA had 45 Army squadrons and 200,000 personnel under arms.

After the war the Army quickly demobilized most of its air arm, including the wing, all of the groups and most of the squadrons. Little progress was made in military aviation as the US Army created new organizations for peacetime service. In most cases these had no connection with those that had been active during the war, but gradually the Army reconstituted many active First World War organizations, such as the 1st Pursuit Group, which meant that old units could consolidate with active units. This policy has continued ever since.

On 4 June 1920 an Act of Congress, the Army Reorganization Bill, created an Air Service (which by this time numbered just 10,000 personnel), with a planned complement of 1,514 officers and 16,000 EM, as a combatant arm of the US Army. However, the Air Service and the Air Corps, created by the Air Corps Act of 2 July 1926, which replaced it were not responsible for the combat units. Their training and operations came under the control of ground forces. The Air Service and Air Corps were responsible only for personnel matters and for materiel logistics, particularly training individual pilots and other specialists, and developing, procuring, storing and distributing aeronautical equipment.

The Air Corps Act of 1926 initiated a five-year expansion programme for 1,514 officers, 16,000 EM and 1,800 serviceable aircraft. The composition, organization and command of the combat elements of the air arm throughout the 1920s and early 1930s were based on principles laid down by the War Department General Staff in 1920. These were reflected in a war plan that called for the following aviation organizations as part of an expeditionary force: one observation squadron for each of fifty-four divisions and one for each of eighteen corps; one observation group (four squadrons), plus one attack wing (one attack and two pursuit groups), for each of six armies; one attack wing, one observation group, and one bombardment group for General Headquarters. Thus the war plan placed the greatest emphasis on observation aviation. It gave lesser roles to pursuit aviation (whose function was to destroy enemy aircraft and assist in attacking enemy troops and other objectives) and to attack aviation (whose function was to harass the enemy's ground forces). It assigned a minor place to bombardment aviation, with the mission of destroying military objectives in the combat theatre and in the enemy's zone of interior. In addition, it placed aviation under the command of ground officers at division, corps, army and GHQ levels.

Within the air arm there was conflict between air and ground officers over the composition, organization and command of military aviation. Billy Mitchell and other Air Service officers wanted aviation units organized as an air force under the command of airmen. Mitchell and other officers desired a greater proportion of pursuit units dedicated to counter-air operations. They knew that observation aviation was no longer as important as establishing more pursuit units. Most importantly of all, they wanted to increase the number of bombardment groups. Bombardment, they felt, was now the major instrument of warfare and deserved priority above all else. In 1921 the Army, led by Mitchell, set out to prove the Admirals of the Fleet wrong when they said that a bomber could not sink a battleship. Mitchell had wanted to bomb one of Germany's largest First World War battleships, the *Ostfriesland*, at anchor off the Capes of Virginia after the surrender. It had widely been proclaimed as unsinkable, but on 21 July 1921 Mitchell's eight Martin MB-2 bombers needed to drop only seven bombs to capsize and sink it and two other warships. It was a milestone in US Army aviation history. The feat was repeated in 1923, when two obsolete US battleships suffered the same fate.

Feeling vindicated, Mitchell continued his uncompromising campaign on behalf of strategic bombing. Following the loss of the Navy dirigible *Shenandoah* in 1925, he publicly accused the high command of the Army and the Navy of being guilty of 'incompetency, criminal negligence and almost treasonable administration of the national Defense'. In December 1925 Mitchell was court-martialled, found guilty, and suspended from the Air Service for five years. He resigned his commission in 1926. (Ten years after his death from a heart attack in 1936, Mitchell was posthumously awarded the Medal of Honor.)

During the isolationist period between the two world wars, the US's air

Capt. Ira C. Eaker, in breeches and tunic with the distinctive Sam Browne, pictured on 26 February 1929 beside a Boeing P-12, one of the best-known AAC pursuit fighters between the wars. Eaker was chief pilot during the endurance record flight over Los Angeles on 1–7 January 1929, when air-to-air refuelling was used successfully. (Boeing)

defences relied on a small peacetime organization that would be capable of rapid expansion in war. For several years the striking force based in the USA therefore consisted of just three groups: the 1st Pursuit, the 2nd Bombardment and the 3rd Attack. There was also one observation group (the 9th), and there was one observation squadron for each of the Army corps. During the same period there were three composite groups overseas: the 4th in the Philippines, the 5th in Hawaii and the 6th in Panama.

During the period 1927–32, just eight new groups were activated. Five of them were pursuit, with one observation. In 1929 ninety Boeing P-12s were ordered, the largest single Army order for fighters since 1921. Deliveries of the P-12B began in the first half of 1930. The standard bomber from 1928 to 1932 was the Keystone series, closely followed by the Curtiss B-2 Condor. The Keystone could only achieve just over 100 mph, and the Condor's performance was even poorer. Significantly, only two of the eight new groups in Army service during 1928–32 were bombardment: these were the 7th in 1928 and the 19th in 1932. This took the total number of groups by the end of 1932 to fifteen. However, 13 of its 45 squadrons were observation (only one less than ten years previously), while in the same period the number of attack squadrons remained just four (although five more were activated in 1933). The number of bombardment squadrons increased from seven to twelve.

It was not until 1 March 1935 – when the War Department established General Headquarters Air Force to serve as an air defence and striking force – that an air officer was at last appointed to command. Brig.-Gen. Frank M. Andrews was appointed Commander (while Brig.-Gen. Oscar Westover became Chief of the Air Corps on 24 December that year). Some observation units remained assigned to corps areas, but all the pursuit, bombardment and attack units in the USA became part of the new combat organization.

Boeing XP-936 No.3, one of three company-financed prototypes, which led to the P-26A, the first all-metal production fighter for the Air Corps, in 1933. (Boeing)

The combat elements of GHQAF were organized into three wings: the 1st Wing (with headquarters at March Field, California) had two bombardment groups, one attack group and three observation squadrons; the 2nd Wing (Langley Field, Virginia) had two bombardment and two pursuit groups, plus three observation squadrons; the 3rd Wing (Barksdale Field) had an attack and a pursuit group, plus one bombardment, one attack and two pursuit squadrons. The commanding general of GHQAF, who reported to the Army's Chief of Staff and was to report to the command of the field force in time of war, was responsible for the organization, training and operations of this air force. The Chief of the Air Corps still retained responsibility for personnel and materiel logistics.

The change of function of the 9th Group from observation to bombardment in 1935, and the inactivation of the 12th Observation Group in 1937, finally signalled the decline in observation and the growth of bombardment aviation. However, there were no other significant changes (apart from the 10th Transport Group, the first of its type, being activated), and the number of groups remained at 15 (10 in the USA and 5 abroad) until 1939. Capt. Claire Chennault – the most outspoken advocate of pursuit aviation between the wars, and head of pursuit instruction at the Army Air Corps Tactical School at Maxwell Field, Alabama – fought, in vain, for more pursuit groups. Chennault retired on the grounds of ill health in 1937, and later led a volunteer US pursuit group, the American Volunteer Group, known as the 'Flying Tigers', for the Nationalist Chinese forces opposing the Japanese.

During the 1930s the accepted theory was that a formation of unescorted bombers could get through to their target if they were properly arranged and armed sufficiently. After air manoeuvres in 1933, Brig.-Gen. Westover had wanted to eliminate pursuits altogether because of their repeated failure to intercept the bombers. This theory was discussed and taught at the Army Air Corps Tactical School at Maxwell Field, Alabama. Bombing operations at the Tactical School Bombardment Section at Maxwell Field had largely adopted a strategic bombing doctrine – mainly through the instigation of its Chief, Capt. Harold L. George – since 1931. Bomber aircraft development during the late 1930s also took the new strategy into account.

Usually, Air Corps officers attended the fourteen-week school at the mid-point of their careers. There, a small, influential group of officers, led by Maj. Harold L. George, Maj. Donald Wilson, 1st Lt. Kenneth L. Walker, and 2nd Lt. Haywood S. Hansell Jr, developed a set of concepts about air power. They believed that air power could directly influence the course of future wars by having strategic air forces fly long-range missions and destroy an enemy's industrial infrastructure. Further, they taught that these long-range bombers, if properly equipped with defensive fire-power and organized into massed formations, would be capable of penetrating an enemy's defences and striking directly at the enemy's will to resist. As the 1940s dawned, these teachings developed into an unofficial doctrine of air power that was put into practice in the Second World War.

Funds for new aircraft were very limited, and it was often left to manufacturers to fund their own developments in the hope that they would attract orders from the Army. Boeing and Martin used their own funds to produce the first all-metal monoplane bomber designs, the B-9 and B-10

Boeing Y1B-9A (Model 246), one of five service test aircraft, in flight with a P-26A in 1933. The B-9 was the first Boeing bomber design. Only seven examples were built, the AAC opting instead for the equally revolutionary Martin B-10. (Boeing)

Curtiss P-36 Mohawk. The red 'meatball' in the the national insignia was deleted after the Japanese entered the war, to avoid confusion with the enemy marking. (USAF)

respectively. A service test order for five Y1B-9As was all Boeing received for its troubles, but the Army did buy the two prototypes.

On 17 January 1933 Martin received an order for forty-eight B-10A production models. During trials in 1932, the XB-907A prototype, at 207 mph, was faster than any US fighter then in service. Boeing had better fortune with the Model 248, the first all-metal monoplane fighter. Between January and March 1932 Boeing built three prototypes at its own expense. After testing as the XP-936, the Army purchased these and ordered 136 P-26 production models.

The Curtiss P-36, and the P-35, designed by Alexander P. de Seversky, meanwhile, were the first single-seat Army pursuit monoplanes to feature a retractable undercarriage and enclosed cockpit. Although neither type was produced in large numbers, they did represent a quantum leap in performance. The P-35 had a top speed of 290 mph and a range of 950 miles. The US Army Air Corps purchased 77 P-35s and 60 P-35As in 1935–6 from Seversky (which became Republic Aviation in 1937).

In 1934 the Army ordered a design study to determine the feasibility of an extremely heavy bomber. Boeing designed the XB-15, a massive, four-engined bomber weighing over 70,000 lb and armed with six machine-guns. It was so large that passageways were built inside the wing to enable the crew to carry out minor engine repairs in flight. Unsuitable for combat, it was converted to a cargo carrier. In August 1934 the Boeing Company was invited to participate in a US Army competition for a new multi-engine bomber. The aircraft had to be capable of carrying a bomb load of 2,000 lb

The Model 299 outside the final assembly hangar at Boeing Field, Seattle, on the afternoon of 17 July 1935. Eleven days later it made its maiden flight. (Boeing)

for between 1,020 and 2,200 miles, at a speed of 200–250 mph. The US Army stipulated that a flying prototype had to be available for trials in August 1935. The term 'multi-engine' had generally been used to indicate two engines, but Boeing were already working on a new concept for a four-engined bomber, and the XB-15 was currently under development for an Army contract, so after obtaining assurances that it could submit an aircraft with additional engines for the competition, design work and construction of a four-engined aircraft were rushed ahead.

While the role of later versions was to be offensive, the Model 299 was conceived for a purely defensive mission: the protection of the US coastline from foreign surface fleets. It was this designation, and not the later, formidable, defensive machine-gun armament, which suggested the famous name, 'Flying Fortress'. Unlike its predecessor, the B-9, all bombs were carried internally, and defensive armament consisted of four streamlined machine-gun blisters on the sides, top and bottom of the fuselage and a nose gunner's station. The prototype was powered by four 750 hp Pratt & Whitney 'Hornet' engines. Rushed to completion in only a year, the Model 299 was flown for the first time on 28 July 1935 by Boeing test pilot Leslie Tower.

The Model 299 was flown from Seattle to Wright Field at Dayton, Ohio, only a month after it was rolled out. Average speed for the 2,100 mile flight was an unbelievable 233 mph. The competitive testing was almost completed when, on 30 October 1939, the Model 299 crashed following take-off with the controls inadvertently locked. Leslie Tower and Maj. Ployer Hill (chief of Wright flight testing) were killed, but three other crew in the rear fuselage escaped. Before the crash the US Army had been considering an order for 65 bombers. This was now reduced to a service test order for 13 flight articles and a static test model under the designation YB-17. This was changed to Y1B-17 shortly before the first one was ready for test flying on 2 December 1936. The major significant change from the Model 299 was the substitution of Wright 'Cyclone' engines of 1,000 take-off horsepower for the earlier 'Hornets'.

The first Y1B-17s went into service during January–August 1937 with the 2nd BG. Meanwhile, the US Army ordered the static test aircraft completed as a high-altitude bomber with turbo-supercharged engines. This was delivered as the Y1B-17A and resulted in a production order for 39 B-17Bs. These were delivered to the 2nd and 7th Bomb Groups during October 1939–March 1940.

When civil war erupted in Spain in 1936, the Luftwaffe and the Regia Aeronautica took advantage of the situation to test their new aircraft in combat. A few US types, like the Grumman GE-23, took part, but Martin B-10s, Curtiss BT-32 Condors and Hawk III biplane fighters were among those which participated in the Sino–Japanese conflict on the Chinese side when full-scale war broke out in 1937.

On 14 November 1938, the day the USA recalled its ambassador from Berlin, President Franklin D. Roosevelt chaired a meeting at the White House with senior government colleagues and Maj.-Gen. Henry H. 'Hap' Arnold (who had been appointed Chief of the Air Corps on 22 September), to discuss the worsening situation in Europe. Arnold had been appointed Chief of the Army Air Corps in September 1938, following the death of Gen. Westover in an aircraft accident. F.D.R. was aware of the weaknesses in US defence forces, and pointed out that Hitler had a reported air strength almost twice that of the British and French forces *combined*. F.D.R. therefore wanted an Army Air Corps of 20,000 aircraft, with a production capacity of 2,000 aircraft a month. F.D.R. knew that Congress would not pass such a request, and instructed the War Department to plan for an additional 10,000 aircraft a year.

Three days after the White House meeting, Arnold tasked Lt.-Col. Carl A. 'Toohey' Spaatz, Air Corps Chief of Plans, and Col. Joseph T. McNarney and Col. Claude Duncan at the GHQAF at Langley to draw up a plan to meet the President's request. Spaatz and his team did just that, but the target could not be achieved. By the autumn of 1938 the AAC had a strength of just 1,600 aircraft and production was only fractionally over eighty-eight planes a month. However, the Air Corps plan did serve as a blueprint for further expansion of the Air Corps.

In January 1939 Roosevelt asked Congress to strengthen the USA's air power, which the President described as 'utterly inadequate'. After much wrangling and horse trading, in April 1939 Congress passed the expansion bill authorizing the Air Corps ceiling of 5,500 aircraft. By June that year the AAC had barely thirteen operational B-17s and just 22,287 personnel – only twice the number of cavalry personnel! On 1 September 1939 Hitler attacked Poland, and the Second World War began. In the months that followed, as

Axis forces won one victory after another, the Army's air arm was deprived of vast numbers of B-17, B-24, B-25, B-26, A-20 and P-40 aircraft which went to the UK, much to the chagrin of senior AAC officers (there were just thirty active groups in 1940). Fortunately for the USA, it had two years' breathing space before it too entered the global war. It developed aircrew oxygen supply, superchargers to boost high-altitude engine performance, and the costly but effective Norden bombsight. When the time came, these innovations would be invaluable, while other technological advances – notably airborne radar and jet engine development – would be passed on to US industry by the UK.

Meanwhile, the US aircraft industry geared up to build the new aircraft whose technical development was improved by the experience gained by the RAF in combat in Europe. US fighter development in particular benefited greatly from events in Europe. The P-51 Mustang was designed from the outset to meet British requirements as a long-range wing mate for the Spitfire and Hurricane after North American Aviation at Inglewood, California, was approached by the British Purchasing Commission in April 1940 to produce the Curtiss H-87 (P-40D). North American's suggestion that they build a brand new and infinitely superior fighter instead, using the same 1,150 hp Allison V-1710-39 engine, was accepted, but a 120-day limit for the construction of a prototype was imposed. Undeterred, German-born chief designer Edgar Schmued got to work, and North American succeeded in delivering the NA-73X prototype in just 117 days.

The prototype NA-73X was flown for the first time on 26 October 1940 by Vance Brese, but it crashed on a subsequent flight, on 30 November. However, success was assured. The first Mustang I production NA-73 was flown on 23 April 1941 (and the USAAC's first XP-51 was flown to Wright Field on 24 August for evaluation). The first of 150 production models (originally called 'Apache', later Mustang) for the RAF, made its maiden flight on 1 May 1941. The new fighter was armed with four .30 in and two .5 in machine-guns.

Early in 1939 the USAAC had drawn up a requirement for a new heavy bomber of vastly superior performance to the B-17, then in production, with a greatly improved range of 3,000 miles, a top speed in excess of 300 mph and a ceiling of 35,000 ft. The Consolidated Company of San Diego, California, submitted the LB-30, a landplane version of their Model 29 flying boat (PB2-Y), which had been developed as a result of a specification issued in May 1938 by the French government for a heavy bomber. The chief architect was Isaac Machlin Laddon, who was responsible for the Catalina flying boat.

By 20 January 1939 preliminary specifications of the Model 32 were ready. Among the more unusual features was a tricycle undercarriage and the fact that the main gears had to be long to exceed the tall bomb bays and were retracted outwards by electric motors. Roller-shutter doors were fitted to protect the 8,000 lb bomb load, which was stowed vertically in the two halves of the bomb bay. The twin-finned empennage used on the company's Model 31 flying boat (P4Y-1) was another feature.

In September 1939 France followed up its tentative order with a production contract for 139 aircraft under the original LB-30 designation. On 26 October David R. Davis's high-aspect ratio wing was married to the fuselage for the first time. Consolidated had to carry out almost thirty

"It's Cadet Schmaltz, sir – he's hopeless!"

Experienced bombardiers could place their practice bombs within yards of the target from as high as 20,000 ft – which led to claims that bombs could be placed in a pickle barrel from such heights.

changes before the Air Corps would issue a contract for the XB-24 prototype, which flew for the first time on 29 December 1939. William A. Wheatley was at the controls as it took off from Lindbergh Field, next to the Consolidated plant in San Diego. The XB-24 had hand-held .30 in Browning machine-guns in the nose, waist, dorsal and ventral positions and in the tail.

In 1940 a US contract was placed for seven YB-24s for service trials in the autumn. These aircraft were similar to the XB-24, but the gross weight had been increased by 5,400 lb to 46,400 lb. The wing leading edge slots were deleted, and de-icing boots were fitted to the wings and tail. The YB-24s proved successful during service trials, and an order was placed for thirty-six of the initial B-24 production version. However, only nine aircraft were completed to B-24A standard, which now weighed 53,600 lb and had .5 in machine-guns in the tail in place of the .30 in guns of previous models. Six YB-24s and twenty B-24As were diverted to the RAF, and after the fall of France, the UK took over the French contract for 139 LB-30s. As a result of experience gained in Europe with other combat types, the XB-24 was fitted with self-sealing fuel tanks and armour plate.

In 1940 the 2nd and 7th Groups, equipped with Boeing B-17B high-altitude bombers, practised precision bombing using the top secret Norden bombsight until experienced bombardiers could place their practice bombs within yards of the target from as high as 20,000 ft – which led to claims that bombs could be placed in a pickle barrel from such heights. Precision bombing called for attacks in daylight, but the ideal conditions prevailing on the ranges at Muroc Dry Lake in California's Mojave Desert were not to be found in Europe, where first the Luftwaffe and then RAF Bomber Command discovered that day bombing was too hazardous. During the first few months of the war, unescorted RAF bombers on daylight raids fell easy victim to the Luftwaffe's Messerschmitt 109s and 110s and forced the British heavies to operate only at night.

Both the B-17 and the B-24 were greatly improved as a result of RAF experience gained in Europe. The B-17C, which flew for the first time on 21

By 1940 the B-18A was standard equipment in the USSAC, and some were still in front-line service in Hawaii and Alaska at the time of the Japanese attack on Pearl Harbor, 7 December 1941. (McDonnell Douglas)

July 1940, was a more combat-worthy model following recommendations made by the UK as a result of experience in air combat. Limited-vision cupolas on the side of the fuselage were replaced with streamlined Plexiglas coverings, and a single .50 in machine-gun was installed in the under gunner's position. In the spring of 1941, 20 aircraft of a 1939 contract for 38 B-17Cs were diverted to the UK, where the type was converted for service as the Fortress I. By September 1941, after twenty-four high-altitude operations, it was decided that the Fortress was unsuitable for further operations with Bomber Command. Operational experience revealed that its defensive firepower of five .303 in machine-gun, was totally inadequate for flights over heavily defended targets in Europe. As a result of the RAF's experience, the forty-two B-17Ds built had self-sealing fuel tanks and armour plate.

On 21 June 1941 the Army Air Corps was renamed the Army Air Forces and took on the task of co-ordinating the activities of the Air Force Combat Command (formerly GHQ Air Force) and the office of the Chief of the Air Corps. Maj.-Gen. Henry H. Arnold was named Chief of Army Air Forces, Maj.-Gen. G.H. Brett, Chief of the Air Corps, and Lt.-Gen. D.C. Emmons, Commanding General, Air Force Combat Command. On 1 July the North Atlantic Transport Service, for aerial transport of passengers and freight, was inaugurated by a B-24 piloted by Col. C.V. Haynes, in flight from Bolling Field.

When the Japanese attacked Pearl Harbor and the USA entered the war on 7 December 1941, all US aircraft production from newly constructed manufacturing capacity was destined for the UK. The Lend-Lease Act made US funds available for Allied aircraft contracts, which were given Army designations. The Air Corps' aim to have fifty-four groups in service by the time the USA entered the war was therefore delayed. Sixty-seven active groups were in the Air Corps' inventory, but many of them were still in the process of being organized. Few had aircraft suitable for combat.

CHAPTER TWO

Strategy for the Global Mission

Overall command structure

In June 1941 President Roosevelt approved the plan for the formation of a new, autonomous army division: the Army Air Forces (although the Air Corps and Air Force Combat Command remained in existence until 9 March 1942). Maj.-Gen. Henry H. 'Hap' Arnold was given overall command. Arnold was a known supporter of Billy Mitchell's ideas about strategic bombing, and his open support of Mitchell had led to him being promoted sideways for several years by the Chiefs of Staff.

The Army Air Forces constituted one of the three elements of the Army of the USA, the other two being the Army Ground Forces and the Army Service Forces (initially the Services of Supply), all of which came under the auspices of the War Department. The structural organization of this huge element is shown on page 16. The Air Corps may be regarded as the flying component of the Army Air Forces, although this is an inexact definition. However, it is true that the Air Corps was an arm of the service as well as a part of the Army Air Forces. Centralized planning and decentralized execution of directives became features of the new organization when the Army Air Forces were reorganized on 9 March 1942. The air element was already in existence after June 1941, but it now took on a more streamlined appearance, ready for war.

In 1941 four American air forces were concentrated in the continental USA. Two more air forces, the Philippine Department Air Force and the Hawaiian Department Air Force, were stationed in the Pacific area, while the Panama Department Air Force (later the Caribbean Air Force) was stationed in the Caribbean. An equally small Alaskan Air Force guarded the vast Alaskan wastes and the Aleutian island chain stretching into the Bering Sea.

The basic organization for the continental defence of the USA centred on the tactical air forces, of which, at the outbreak of the Second World War, there were four: the 1st AF (HQ Mitchel Field, Long Island, New York), 2nd AF (HQ Geiger Field, Spokane, Washington State), 3rd AF (HQ MacDill Field, Tampa, Florida) and 4th AF (HQ March Field, Riverside, California). All originated as Air Districts under the old GHQAF in the winter of 1940–1. Set up as air combat organizations, each was assigned a certain area of the USA in which to operate: 1st AF, eastern seaboard; 2nd AF, north-western and

Gen. 'Hap' Arnold, Chief of the AAF, seen here at a medal ceremony in England in 1943. (USAF)

mountain areas; 3rd AF, south-eastern; and the 4th AF, along the west coast and in the south-west. Their original function was the provision of units and aircraft for the defence of the continental USA, and participation with Army Ground Forces in combat training and manoeuvres, but later they mainly organized and trained bomber, fighter and other units and crews for assignment overseas.

Establishment dates of the air forces from October 1940 to 28 December 1942 were as follows:

Panama Canal AF (19 October 1940) 20 November 1940 (re-designated Caribbean AF August 1941)

Hawaiian AF (19 October 1940) 1 November 1940

1st AF (Northeast Air District, 19 October 1940) 16 January 1941

2nd AF (Northwest Air District, 19 October 1940) 16 January 1941

3rd AF (Southeast Air District, 19 October 1940) 16 January 1941

4th AF (Southwest Air District, 19 October 1940) 16 January 1941

Philippine Dept Air Force (6 May 1941) 20 September 1941 (re-designated Far East AF from 28 October 1941)

Alaskan Air Force (28 December 1941) 15 January 1942

Organization of the ARMY AIR FORCES

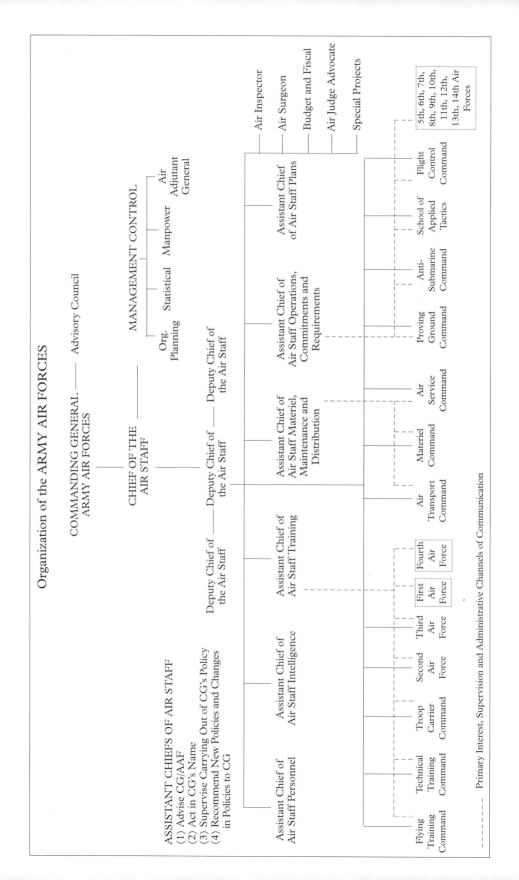

COMMANDING GENERAL —— Advisory Council
ARMY AIR FORCES

CHIEF OF THE
AIR STAFF

MANAGEMENT CONTROL

Org. Statistical Manpower Air
Planning Adjutant
General

Deputy Chief of —— Deputy Chief of
the Air Staff the Air Staff

ASSISTANT CHIEFS OF AIR STAFF
(1) Advise CG/AAF
(2) Act in CG's Name
(3) Supervise Carrying Out of CG's Policy
(4) Recommend New Policies and Changes
in Policies to CG

Deputy Chief of
the Air Staff

Assistant Chief
of Air Staff Plans

Air Inspector

Air Surgeon

Budget and Fiscal

Air Judge Advocate

Special Projects

Assistant Chief of
Air Staff Personnel

Assistant Chief of
Air Staff Intelligence

Assistant Chief of
Air Staff Training

Assistant Chief of
Air Staff Materiel,
Maintenance and
Distribution

Assistant Chief of
Air Staff Operations,
Commitments and
Requirements

Flying
Training
Command

Technical
Training
Command

Troop
Carrier
Command

Second
Air
Force

Third
Air
Force

First
Air
Force

Fourth
Air
Force

Air
Transport
Command

Materiel
Command

Air Service
Command

Proving
Ground
Command

Anti-
Submarine
Command

School of
Applied
Tactics

Flight
Control
Command

5th, 6th, 7th,
8th, 9th, 10th,
11th, 12th,
13th, 14th Air
Forces

—————— Primary Interest, Supervision and Administrative Channels of Communication

Gen. H.H. Arnold in Washington, DC, headed the Air Staff. In addition to the duties of his command, he was a member of the Combined Chiefs of Staff and the Joint Chiefs of Staff, which determined the strategic objectives and plans of the Allied armed forces. The Air Staff was the arm of the Commanding General, which enabled him to direct and control all the parts of the AAF world-wide. Apart from Arnold, the headquarters of the AAF included the Deputy Commander and Chief of Air Staff, the Air Staff, comprising four Deputy Chiefs, six Assistant Chiefs of Air Staff (each responsible for plans; operations, commitments and requirements; personnel; intelligence; training and materiel, maintenance and distribution) and several special officers, each a specialist in a particular field. These included:

Chief, Management Control, who advised on organizational, administrative and procedural matters, prepared recommendations to obtain the most efficient utilization of AAF manpower, and obtained and maintained statistical information relative to all AAF activities;
Air Inspector, who developed plans and policies for all AAF inspections, and conducted periodic and special inspections of AAF activities for the Commanding General;
Air Surgeon, who planned and directed all medical facilities and personnel of the AAF, including aero-medical research;
Chief, Budget and Fiscal Office, supervised and administered all AAF budget and fiscal matters;
Air Communications Officer, who determined policies and programmes for air communications activities, including radio, radar, teletype and carrier pigeons, etc.;
Air Judge Advocate, who acted as legal counsel of the AAF;
Chief, Office of Legislative Services, who handled matters involving relationships with Congress, including proposed legislation;
Special Assistant for anti-aircraft, who advised on all anti-aircraft activities affecting the AAF;
Chief, Special Projects, who performed such special projects as the Commanding General from time to time assigned;
Chief, Office of Flying Safety, who developed and carried out a flying safety programme for the prevention of aircraft accidents, and developed and enforced procedures for the control of military air traffic;
Chief, Office of Technical Information, under direction of the AAF Public Relations Board, who planned and supervised relations and related activities.

Commands and the Army Air Forces

Six commands were created to support and supply the numbered air forces: Technical Training Command, Flying Training Command, Proving Ground Command, Materiel Command, Air Service Command and Ferry Command (re-designated Air Transport Command on 30 April 1942, I Troop Carrier Command from 20 June 1942). Technical Training and Flying Training Commands, which on 7 July 1943 were combined into Training Command, are covered elsewhere.

Proving Ground Command (Eglin Field, Florida) had been organized as Air Corps Proving Ground on 15 May 1941, and was re-designated Proving Ground Command on 1 April 1942. Its function was to carry out operational tests and studies of aircraft and aircraft equipment.

Materiel Command (Wright Field, Dayton, Ohio) had been organized as Air Corps Materiel Division on 15 October 1926, and was re-designated Materiel Command on 9 March 1942. Its function was to research, develop and procure aircraft and related equipment.

Air Service Command (Patterson Field, Fairfield, Ohio) had been organized as Air Corps Provisional Maintenance Command on 15 March 1941, and became Air Corps Maintenance Command on 29 April 1941, being re-designated Air Service Command on 17 October 1941. Its function was the distribution of equipment and supplies to AAF units, maintenance and repair of aircraft, and training of service, supply and maintenance units for assignment overseas.

The number of separate items required to arm, service and repair aircraft was phenomenal. Approximately 80,000 items were listed in 1940; by 1944 they amounted to 500,000. Between January 1942 and August 1945 some 19 million tons (760,000,000 cu. ft) of supplies were conveyed overseas by ship. Approximately 47,500 primary fighters also reached the theatres of war by sea.

The nucleus of the wartime Troop Carrier Command organization existed in the air transport services established in 1931 at each of the four air supply depots in the continental USA. On 29 May 1941 a new Air Corps Ferrying Command was evolved to deliver aircraft built in the USA to RAF crews operating with the British Purchasing Commission in the USA. By July 1941 the ACFC had begun a transatlantic service using B-24 Liberator aircraft. The ACFC also ferried new US aircraft from factory to US front-line units all over the world, as well as providing a world-wide air transport service for personnel, supplies and mail. I Troop Carrier Command, at Indianapolis, Indiana, was organized as Air Transport Command on 30 April 1942 and re-designated I Troop Carrier Command on 20 June 1942, under Brig.-Gen. Harold L. George. George enlisted private aircraft owners, barnstormers and even cropdusters to be re-trained in large, multi-engine aircraft. In 1942 operations began with 11,000 men, rising to over 200,000 by the end of the war. Its function was the organization and training of troop carrier, glider and medical air evacuation units and crews, and joint training with Army Ground Forces of airborne units. Ultimately, I Troop Carrier Command operated about 3,700 aircraft, carrying men and materiel some 935 million miles. It also delivered 250,000 aircraft to all combat theatres, losing 1,000 aircraft as a result of accidents or enemy action. Its peak wartime strength was 2,400,000 personnel.

Strategy for Europe

Air War Plans Division

In July 1941 the President asked the Secretaries of War and of the Navy to produce estimates for bringing their forces to an effective war footing. Arnold seized the opportunity to gain permission for the AAC's Air War

Plans Division to prepare their own report, forcing the War Plans Division to concentrate solely on the needs of its land forces.

Arnold's staff officers at the AWPD, headed by Col. Harold L. George, and including Lt.-Col. Kenneth Walker, Maj. Haywood Hansell and Maj. Laurence S. Kuter, formulated a policy (AWPD/1) of relentless air attacks against Germany, strategic defence in the Pacific Theatre and air operations in defence of the Western hemisphere. If Japan entered the war, it too would be subjected to aerial bombardment after Germany had surrendered. The planning team listed 154 targets for its strategic bombing concept. The principal targets were the German airframe assembly plants and associated metal production, some 50 electrical generating or switching stations, 47 key points in the German transportation network, and all of the 27 synthetic petroleum plants in Germany. It was proposed that six months' strategic bombing of these targets, together with the neutralization of the Luftwaffe, submarine and naval facilities, might render a land campaign unnecessary.

AWPD/1 calculated that to achieve these objectives, using precision bombing as its weapon, 1,060 B-25 and B-26 medium bombers, 3,740 B-17, B-24 heavy and B-29 and B-32 very heavy bombers, and 3,412 P-40, P-47 and P-51 fighters would have to be deployed against Germany from bases in the UK and Egypt, together with 3,740 intercontinental B-36 bombers, based in the USA. Gen. George and his team were convinced that 6,800 medium, heavy and very heavy bombers based in Europe and North Africa could bring about the downfall of Germany. Even if this were true, building new and existing aircraft of this magnitude was impossible in the time allotted for victory by aerial bombardment alone.

In the summer of 1941, for instance, the US Air Forces had on hand less than 700 bombers of all types. The B-32 never entered full-scale production, and the sheer enormity of the B-36 project prevented the bomber reaching wartime production. A specification issued on 11 April 1941 had called for a very long-range bomber capable of 10,000 miles range without refuelling and able to carry a 10,000 lb bomb load at least half the distance. It also had to have a maximum speed of 400 mph and an operational ceiling of 35,000 ft. In order to reach the original range specification it would have to carry 21,116 gallons of fuel in the wings. If all this were not enough, the sheer size of the aircraft would require a 5,000 ft runway – almost an impossibility at the time.

It would not be until September 1944 that Convair flew the first XB-36, and by then production deliveries, scheduled to begin in March 1945, were no longer critical because when the order was confirmed on 19 August 1944, the capture of the Mariana Islands allowed B-29s to be based there to attack the Japanese mainland.

AWPD/1 concluded that the Army Air Forces needed to expand to 61,799 aircraft (37,051 of which would be trainers) and 2,100,000 men. It predicted also that the AAF could mount a campaign in less than a year; half the time the Army needed to prepare for war in Europe. By early September 1941 Gen. George Marshall, the Army Chief of Staff, reacted favourably to the plan and sent it straight to the Secretary of War, Henry

Stimson, without first submitting it to the Army–Navy Joint Board. Stimpson rubber-stamped AWPD/1, but circumstances prevented the plan reaching Roosevelt. Significantly, though, AWPD-1's statistics formed the basis for levels of new aircraft production and training schedules for the AAFs, and a strategic bomber offensive against Germany became accepted as both AAF and US government policy.

Distribution and composition of forces (including initial replacement and initial replacement reserves), AWPD/1, 1941				
Type	ETO Groups/ Planes	Asia/Far East Groups/ Planes	ZOI Groups/ Planes	Total (USA) Groups/ Planes
Medium/Heavy/Very Heavy/Very Long-Range/Light/Bombers:				
B-25/26	10/1,1060			10/1,060
B-17/24	20/1,700	2/170	25/2,125	47/3,995
B-29/32	24/2,040			24/2,040
B-36	44/3,740			44/3,740
A-20				13/936
Fighters:				
P-40/47/51	21/3,412	1/162	32/5,200	54/8,748
Dive-bombers:			13/1,248	
Transports:				
C-47/46/54				19/1,064
Observation:				27/1,917
Trainers:				37,051
Total	119/11,952	3/332	57/7,325	251/61,799

Unit equipment and depot reserves, including initial replacements				
Groups	Unit Equipment	Reserves	%	Total
Medium Bombardment	57	49	96	106
Heavy Bombardment	35	50	150	85
Very Heavy Bombardment	35	50	150	85
Very Long-Range Bombardment	35	50	150	85
Fighter	80	82	100	162
Light Bombardment	37	35	100	72
Dive-Bomber	57	39	70	96
Transport	52	4	8	56
Observation	52	19	36	71

AWPD/1, of course, would be overtaken by events. Generating plants in the enemy power grid would be difficult to locate and bomb accurately, while hydro-electric dams needed special bombs so big that they could not be carried inside the bomb bays of B-17 and B-24s, and in any event, they would need to be dropped from just 50 ft, a suicidal height. Even so, AWPD/1 concluded that German industry could be destroyed by daylight precision bombing because, in theory, 90 per cent of the bombs dropped on a clear day would explode within 1,250 ft of the MPI.

Only oil supply provided a weak spot in the enemy's infrastructure, but attacks on this and the German transportation system would not begin until late in the war. AWPD/1 did take into account civilian morale in the face of heavy bombing, and concluded that it would not collapse. Events in Europe had already shown that, and US observers had seen it with their own eyes during the Battle of Britain. In the UK in 1940 there existed the same jealousy between the Army and the RAF. The latter's sentiments, 'It takes close co-ordination with the Army to obtain maximum misuse of air power', echoed those of Billy Mitchell, Arnold and others. Arnold and other high-ranking officers – such as Gen. Spaatz, Lt.-Col. Grandison Gardner (an ordnance, armaments and bombing technical expert), Maj. Franklin O'Carroll (an expert in aircraft engines), Maj.-Gen. G.H. Brett (Chief of the AAC), Ira C. Eaker, Gen. R. Royce, Gen. Saville, Lt.-Gen. D.C. Emmons and Marriner – were sent to the war-ravaged UK as observers. Lessons could be learned by studying the tactics employed by the RAF and the Luftwaffe, and could help the AAC to plan ahead for the time when its airmen would be called upon to fight.

Spaatz, for instance, saw for himself what RAF Fighter and Bomber Commands were made of, and he was persuaded that any German invasion of the UK could be defeated. However, he saw no evidence that suggested night bombing was a war-winning weapon, and he therefore had no reason to question the US daylight precision bombing doctrine. The RAF had abandoned its daylight bombing campaign in February 1940 in favour of a night offensive, albeit on a small scale, aimed at German cities. During 1941 more and more bombs began falling on built-up areas, mainly because pin-point bombing of industrial targets was rendered impractical by the lack of navigational and bombing aids. Bombing by day, though, was certainly not the panacea US commanders such as Spaatz seemed to think it was. How could US day bomber missions survive when those of the RAF and Luftwaffe blatantly could not? The question of survivability of US day bombers in modern warfare, and the need for an effective long-range fighter to protect them on missions, were not addressed. Plans for building up the AAC and the daylight precision bombing policy went ahead without question.

Between 27 January and 27 March 1941, secret meetings between the US and UK armed forces staff committees determined a course of action whereby the US and the UK and its Commonwealth could defeat Germany and the Axis powers. These sessions closed with the signing of an agreement which came to be known as ABC-1. It stipulated that the USA and the UK would exchange military missions (see Chapter Three). Also, it provided that when the USA entered the war it would furnish naval, ground and air support for the campaign against the Axis powers. The British-US offensive needed to be directed against the Axis powers of Germany and Italy in the European Theatre of War, and then, when the situation in Europe allowed, the attack against Japan would begin. The USA, the UK and its dominions could assemble the Allied invasion force needed to open a second front in Europe.

The final report, American-British Staff Conversations No 1 (ABC-1), of 27 March 1941, said: 'The Atlantic and European Area is considered to be the decisive theatre.' Both the UK and the USA agreed a policy of defeating Germany first, and, if necessary, Japan second. ABC-1 foresaw the day soon when joint US-RAF air operations would be used to operate offensively, primarily against Germany. As a result of the ABC-1 agreement, a Special US Army Observer Group, headed by Maj.-Gen. James E. Chaney, a veteran airman who had been an air observer in the UK in 1940, was activated in London on 19 May 1941. Seventeen officers comprised his staff, the Chief of which was Brig.-Gen. Joseph T. McNarney, while his Air Staff consisted of Col. Alfred J. Lyon, AC, and Maj. Ralph A. Snavely, AC. Three days later, on 22 May, Chaney and McNarney met the British Chiefs of Staff Committee, including Air Marshal Sir Charles Portal.

McNarney addressed the British War Cabinet Conference on 27 May 1941. He informed them that the Special Observer's mission was:

1. to co-ordinate all details relative to the reception, location and accommodation of US Army and US AAC personnel sent to British areas under ABC-1;
2. to assist in the co-ordination of the allocation of equipment from the USA;
3. to advise the Chief of Staff of the US Army as to the manner in which the air and ground forces should be employed in the UK;
4. to deal with any problems which might arise in connection with the execution of War Plan ABC-1.

Following these initial meetings, there were conferences between the members of the staff of Maj.-Gen. Chaney and their counterparts in the British Army. On 13 June Col. Lyon held a conference with Air Vice-Marshal Ralph Sorley on the equipment and aircraft to be used against the 'German military power'.

In June 1941 Germany invaded the Soviet Union, but Operation BARBAROSSA had ground to a halt by December that year. Most importantly, a start could be made on building up a strategic daylight precision bombing force in the UK, and later in North Africa and Italy, that could bomb and ultimately cripple the Axis war industry. US strategists were convinced that enemy targets could be destroyed by daylight precision bombing. They believed that heavily armed B-17 and B-24 fleets could fight their way to their targets without incurring prohibitive losses. The RAF operated differently. Air Chief Marshal (later Sir Arthur) Harris, appointed head of RAF Bomber Command on 22 February 1942, was directed by Marshal of the RAF, Sir Charles Portal, Chief of the Air Staff, to break civilian morale by the use of night area bombing rather than precision bombing, and the targets would be civilian, not just military. The infamous 'area bombing' directive, which had gained support from the Air Ministry, and Prime Minister Winston Churchill, had been sent to Bomber Command on 14 February, eight days before Harris assumed command.

On 28/29 March, 234 bombers, mostly carrying incendiaries, went to Lübeck, a historic German city on the Baltic; its thousands of half-timbered houses were an ideal target for a mass raid by RAF bombers carrying incendiary bombs. About half of the city, some 200 acres, was obliterated. For four consecutive nights, beginning on 23/24 April, Rostock was attacked with incendiary bombs. By the end, only 40 per cent of the city was left standing. Then, on the night of 30/31 May 1942, 1,046 bombers, in the first of three RAF 'Thousand Bomber' raids on German cities, raided Cologne. More than 600 acres of the city were razed to the ground. The fires burned for days, and almost 60,000 people were made homeless. The fact that these raids severely reduced the Germans' ability to produce war materials by killing the workforce was not lost on many senior officers in the US Air Forces. Later, they would also resort to fire-bombing raids on German and Japanese cities, but with even more deadly effect.

On 25 August 1942 President Roosevelt requested a complete reassessment of future air requirements, and as a result, a new AAF plan, AWPD/42, was issued. The original AWPD/1 team had dispersed, but Maj.-Gen. Haywood S. Hansell Jr was brought from England to oversee the preparation of AWPD/42. The directive remained the same as that adopted in AWPD/1. It was optimistic in its assumption that US bombers would enjoy low loss rates while inflicting high losses on the enemy fighters because of their superior firepower. In essence, AWPD/42 differed little from the original AWPD/1, but bombing priorities had shifted to the Atlantic U-boat pens because of the alarming losses of Allied shipping.

Unit composition

The principal AAF unit for administrative and control purposes was the *group* (roughly comparable to an Army regiment). AAF groups were composed of a single type of aircraft, and were designated by arabic numerals: 376th BG, 56th FG, etc. Normally, they were commanded by lieutenant-colonels or full colonels. Within the AAF operational structure, groups ranked between *wings* and *squadrons*. There were several types of fighter and bomber groups, but all were known as fighter or bomber groups. Fighter groups normally had three squadrons, and bomber groups four.

The strength of a typical heavy bomb group (B-17/B-24) comprised a group HQ with 25 officers, 1 W/O and 57 EM, and four squadrons, each with 67 officers, 360 EM and 12 aircraft. The total complement (for 48 combat crews) would be 293 officers, 1 W/O, 1,487 EM and 48 aircraft.

The strength of a typical medium bomb group (B-25/B-26) comprised a group HQ with 25 officers, 1 W/O and 57 EM, and four squadrons, each with 67 officers, 310 EM and 16 aircraft. The total complement would be 293 officers, 1 W/O, 1,297 EM and 63 aircraft.

The strength of a typical single-engined or fighter-bomber group (A-36/P-39/P-40/P-47 or P-51) comprised a group HQ with 27 officers, 1 W/O and 70 EM, and three squadrons, each with 39 officers, 245 EM and 25 aircraft. The total complement would be 144 officers, 1 W/O, 805 EM and 75 aircraft. A typical twin-engine or fighter-bomber group (P-38) would share the group HQ with a single-engined group, and would comprise three squadrons, each with 39 officers, 274 EM and 25 aircraft. The total complement would be 144 officers, 1 W/O, 892 EM and 75 aircraft.

Force requirement for deployment overseas (without 50 per cent reserves), AWPD/42

	Groups	Aircraft		Groups	Aircraft
UK:			**Far East:**		
Heavy bombers	42	2,016	Heavy bombers	3	144
Medium bombers	15	960	Medium bombers	2	128
Light bombers	5	320	Night Fighters	3	300
Fighters	25	2,500	Photo-reconnaissance	1	52
Observation	8	672	Transports	1	52
Dive-bombers	4	384	Totals	10	676
Troop carrier	8	416			
Totals	107	7,268			
North Africa:			**India-Burma-China:**		
Heavy bombers	3	144	Heavy bombers	2	96
Medium bombers	4	256	Medium bombers	2	128
Light bombers	1½	96	Dive-bombers	1	64
Fighters	1	100	Fighters	½	50
Observation	1	72	Fighters (multi-seat)	3	300
Photo-reconnaissance	½	–	Transports	6	312
Troop carriers	3	156	Totals	14½	950
Totals	14	824			
Middle East:					
Heavy bombers	4	192			
Light bombers	3	192			
Medium bombers	1	64			
Totals	8	448			

Note: The grand total of these forces was 153½ groups. By the end of 1942, the AAF had approximately 70 groups (heavy bomber, medium/light bomber, fighter, troop carrier and reconnaissance) in the war theatres, including 8 in Latin America and Atlantic bases. By the end of 1943, it had 136 groups. The AWPD/42 figure was surpassed in February 1944, by which time the AAFs totalled 160½ groups in the combat theatres (including Latin America and Atlantic bases). At the end of 1944, there were 214 groups, including 105 in the ETO (reaching a peak of 109 groups in April 1945), 43 in the MTO, 7 in the Pacific, 30 in the FEAFs.

By February 1945 the normal allocations of aircraft and personnel to AAF groups were as shown:

Type of Group	Aircraft	Personnel
Very Heavy Bombardment (B-29)	45	2,078
Heavy Bombardment	72	2,261
Medium Bombardment	96	1,759
Light Bombardment	96	1,304
Single-engine fighter	111–26	994
Twin-engine fighter	111–26	1,081
Troop Carrier (C-47)	80–110	1,837
Combat Cargo (C-46/C-47)	125	883

In addition, there were several other specialized groups in the AAF, including air commando, air depot, air service, emergency rescue, glider, observation, photo-reconnaissance and service.

Integration of air forces within Allied air commands

As the strategic picture in each theatre changed, US Air Forces became a fundamental part in the formation of strategic and tactical air forces within the Allied chain of command. Often, as in the case of the ETO and MTO, these included the British and French air and naval forces. The first example of the formation of joint Allied forces was in 1942–3, with the formation of the Northwest African Air Forces following the successful TORCH operation in November 1942. Air forces in the MTO comprised the 12th AF, commanded by Brig.-Gen. Jimmy Doolittle, which included the bomber, fighter, air support, service commands and troop carrier wing, and Eastern Air Command, which comprised the British Army Co-operation Command, as well as coastal defence, photo-reconnaissance and service units.

On 18 February 1943 all the Allied air elements in North Africa were reorganized into a strategic air force on the basis of types to tasks to be performed rather than types of aircraft employed. The NAAF now consisted of no less than six main air components under Lt.-Gen. Carl A. Spaatz, namely, the Northwest African Strategic Air Force, Air Service Command, Training Command, Tactical Air Force, Coastal Air Force and the Photographic Reconnaissance Wing.

Lt.-Gen. Dwight D. Eisenhower, theatre commander, had overall control of all air force and British, French and US Army units, and Royal Navy forces (see page 26) at his disposal. Experience in North Africa in 1942–3 established the pattern for the build-up to the Normandy invasion, when all Allied forces, including the US and RAF air components, were commanded by Gen. Dwight D. Eisenhower, Supreme Commander, SHAEF.

By the end of 1943 Gen. 'Hap' Arnold and the AAF sought to install a single Allied Strategic Air Force Commander in overall charge of the US Air Forces in Europe and RAF Bomber Command. This would make him independent of the ground forces leaders, and overall bombing operations in Europe could be planned in a truly strategic manner. This would became an even more important consideration with the arrival in Italy, on 19 February 1944, of the 15th AF. Arnold obtained the US Chief's agreement for the formation of a new US headquarters in London to command and control all US strategic bomber forces in Europe. A new organization, known as the US Strategic Air Forces in Europe, was activated at Bushey Park, and on 1 January 1944 Gen. Carl A. Spaatz assumed command. The USSTAF gave Spaatz operational control of both strategic air forces, and administrative control of the US air forces in the UK (the 8th and 9th). Lt.-Gen. James H. Doolittle assumed command of the 8th AF in place of Gen. Ira C. Eaker, who left to command the Mediterranean Allied Air Forces.

As of 30 December 1943 the AAFs in England comprised 4,618 aircraft, 4,242 of them combat aircraft, divided into 45¾ groups (26¾ heavy bomber, 12

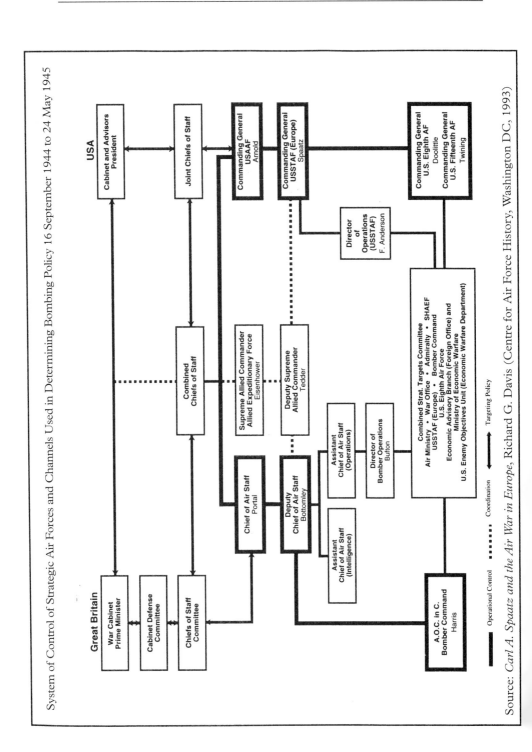

System of Control of Strategic Air Forces and Channels Used in Determining Bombing Policy 16 September 1944 to 24 May 1945

Source: *Carl A. Spaatz and the Air War in Europe*, Richard G. Davis (Centre for Air Force History, Washington DC, 1993)

fighter, 4 medium bomber, 2 troop carrier and 1 reconnaissance).* The arrival of the 15th AF committed an additional 12 heavy bomber groups and 4 fighter groups to operations in Europe. Strategic bombing was limited from the outset because of the need to bomb V-1 sites in France (Operation CROSSBOW), and the first major campaign involving both the 8th and 15th AFs against a common objective did not take place until February 1944, during 'Big Week' (20–25 February 1944), when the 8th and 9th AFs in England and the 15th AF in Italy mounted an intensive air campaign against German industry.

During 'Big Week' over 3,800 bomber sorties were flown by the 8th and 15th AFs in Operation ARGUMENT, a co-ordinated attack on the German aircraft industry; 10,000 tons of bombs were dropped for the loss of 226 bombers and 28 fighters. Germany had planned that its production of aircraft should have reached about 48,000 by 1944, but it only produced 32,000. The Combined Bomber Offensive by the RAF and AAF saw 1.4 million tons of bombs dropped on Germany. The AAF flew 400,000 heavy bomber sorties and dropped approximately 1 million tons. About 75 per cent of all bombs dropped by the 8th AF fell on Germany, and 25 per cent on France. One-third of bombs dropped by the 15th AF fell on Germany and Austria, with 29.4 per cent falling on Italy. About 43 per cent of the 8th AF's and 24 per cent of the 15th AF's tonnage was directed at oil targets, aircraft factories and other industrial targets: 260,000 tons of bombs fell on oil targets and factories, and 280,000 tons on land transportation in Germany. According to the USSBS *Statistical Appendix to Overall Report (European War)*, February 1947, the AAF Strategic Air Forces dropped 603,000 tons on land transportation.

Strategy: Pacific, CBI and Alaska

Pearl Harbor and the Japanese attack on the Philippines

At the time of the Japanese attacks on Hawaii (7 December 1941) and the Philippines (8 December) which brought the USA into the Second World War, the brunt of the early operations fell on the Air Force units in the Hawaiian, Philippine and Alaskan Departments. (By 1942 the USA held part of the Aleutian chain, with the Japanese at the other end, on Attu and Kiska, which they used as a defence against any US invasion of Japan through the Aleutian chain and the Kuriles.)

Shortly before 0800 hours on Sunday 7 December 1941, 350 Japanese aircraft, which had been launched from carriers 275 miles north of Hawaii, attacked the naval base at Pearl Harbor and bombed and strafed airfields on the islands. The raid was a complete surprise. The USA had broken the Japanese 'Purple Code' and knew that Japan was preparing for war, but expected that the first bombs would fall on the Philippines or Malaya. The trainee operators on a rudimentary radar set stationed north of Pearl Harbor reported the large

---

* *Carl A. Spaatz and the Air War in Europe*, Richard G. Davis (Centre for Air Force History, Washington DC, 1993).

formation, but the Hawaiian base commander assumed the aircraft were the twelve B-17Ds of the 7th BG, four B-17Cs and two B-17Es of the 88th Reconnaissance Squadron, from Hamilton Field, which were en route to the island of Mindanao in the Philippines, and the radar operators were told to stand down. The B-17s arrived over Hawaii during the Japanese attack, and pilots put down wherever they could. The US Pacific Fleet was destroyed, and 4,575 personnel were either killed or wounded. At the time of the attack there were ten fighter squadrons, equipped with P-40 and P-36 aircraft, seven bomber squadrons, equipped with B-17s, one Troop Carrier squadron, with C-33 aircraft, and one reconnaissance squadron, equipped with O-47 and B-18 aircraft, stationed on the islands at three airfields: Wheeler Field, Hickham and Bellows. Of the 231 aircraft on Oahu, 97 planes, including 23 AAF bombers and 66 fighters, were destroyed and 88 damaged; 226 officers and EM were killed or later died of their wounds, and 396 were wounded.

Nine hours after the attack on Pearl Harbor, 54 Japanese bombers, escorted by 54 fighters, attacked US air and naval forces in the Philippines. Despite the earlier attack on Pearl Harbor, the US defences in the Philippines were ill prepared and could do little. At Clark Field, Luzon, just north-east of Manila, most of the P-40s of the 20th Pursuit Squadron and 18 of the 19 B-17s of the 28th and 30th Bomb Squadrons were destroyed. Nine B-17Ds of the 14th Bomb Squadron, 19th BG, which had arrived at Clark from Hawaii on 10 September, had already been transferred to Del Monte, a small satellite field on Mindanao, some 600 miles to the south of Clark, and the 93rd Bomb Squadron, which was on tactical manoeuvres at Del Carmen Field, escaped the attack. At the time of the attack, Gen. Lewis H. Brereton, the FEAF Commander, had ten squadrons, totalling 307 aircraft, in the Philippines. By the end of the day he had just 17 B-17s and 17 P-40s left.

On 10 December 1941 the first USAAF mission of the Second World War was flown, when five B-17s of the 93rd Squadron, 19th BG, led by Maj. Cecil Coombs, flying from Clark Field, attacked Japanese ships near Vigan in the Philippines. From then on, the surviving units in the Philippines fought with what they had left, until they were forced to retreat to Australia when the Philippines finally fell, on 24 December.

At the time of the Japanese attacks the USA had thirteen groups equipped with B-17s, but most were well below group strength of thirty-two aircraft. Some 150 B-17s, of all models, including twelve YB-17s, were well scattered throughout the Pacific seaboard, Alaska and Newfoundland. The 29 remaining B-17Es of the 7th BG, which left Salt Lake City, Utah, on 5 December for the Far East, were hurriedly diverted to Muroc to help defend California from possible Japanese attack. Only nineteen B-17Bs could be sent to Spokane, Washington State, to join the five B-17Cs of the 39th BG, while a paltry two B-17Bs were stationed in Alaska. Eight B-17Bs (and nineteen B-18s) of the 6th BG were stationed near the Canal Zone, and six B-17Bs (and one B-18) of the 41st Reconnaissance Squadron were based in Newfoundland. During the first week of December, eight new B-17Es were delivered to the 6th BG.

For six months after Pearl Harbor the USA and its allies were, for the most part, impotent as the Japanese invaded the East Indies, Guam and Wake. On

B-25C Mitchell 41-12633 and an A-20 on the line in very early war markings. Deliveries of the B-25C began in 1941. The B-25C had Bendix electric mid-upper and retractable underbelly turrets. The tail gun was deleted. (via Mike Bailey)

The B-25H first entered service in the Pacific in February 1944, armed with fourteen .50 in Browning machine-guns, a nose-firing 75 mm cannon and eight .5 in rockets for anti-shipping strikes and ground attack duties. It could also carry 3,000 lb of bombs. (USAF)

8 December 1941, 53 of the first 56 B-26A Marauders had taken off from Langley Field, Virginia, for Australia, where they formed the 22nd BG. In April 1942 they saw action for the first time, during attacks on New Guinea. B-25Bs of the 3rd BG were also first used against Japanese targets in April. Range and weight limitations resulted in all Marauders in the Pacific being replaced in February 1944 by the B-25H, which packed a nose-firing 75 mm cannon for anti-shipping strikes in the Pacific, where 'masthead' bombing strikes were the norm. The cannon proved unsuccessful, however, and the type was withdrawn in August 1944. The B-25J introduced four .5 in 'blister' guns, two on each side of the fuselage below the cockpit. The majority of USAAF B-25Js fought in the south-west Pacific.

Establishment dates of all the air forces in the Pacific and CBI theatres, February 1942–August 1945

5th (formerly FEAF)	5 February 1942
6th (formerly Panama Canal AF)	5 February 1942
7th (formerly Hawaiian AF)	5 February 1942
10th (India, Burma, Thailand, Bay of Bengal)	12 February 1942
11th (formerly Alaskan Air Force)	5 February 1942
13th (Solomons and Brunswick Archipelago)	13 January 1943
14th (South-east/Central China/Burma	10 March 1943
20th (India-Burma-Western Pacific)	4 April 1944

CBI theatre

On 12 February 1942 the 10th AF was activated for action in the China-Burma-India theatre. One LB-30 Liberator and four B-17s flew the first mission by this command on 2 April with an attack on the Andaman Islands. In March 1942 the 10th AF arrived in India with a motley collection of B-17s and B-24s. From here the 7th BG flew its first offensive mission north of the Yellow River on 21 October 1942, when a flight of B-24s of the 436th Bomb Squadron bombed the Lin-hsi mines, but with little success. By January 1943 the 7th BG was up to full strength and remained on the Indian side of the Himalayas (the 'Hump', as they were called), while the 308th BG, also equipped with Liberators, was sent to the Chinese side. The 308th BG was originally destined for the 8th AF in England, but in March 1943 it joined Gen. Claire L. Chennault's China Task Force (later the 14th AF). The Liberators of the 308th were unique among B-24 groups, for they had to double as transports, carrying their own supplies over the 'Hump' before flying their first mission in May 1943.

Pacific theatre

The US Navy was to bear much of the responsibility for regaining air superiority in the Pacific, but the part played by the AAFs cannot be overstated. The air war over the 64,000,000 square miles of the Pacific Ocean from Hawaii to the Philippines and Australia to the Japanese mainland was divided between three air forces: the 5th, 7th and 13th. A line of longitude placed the 5th AF on the south-west Pacific side and the 13th AF, activated in December 1942, on the south Pacific side.

B-24D of the 308th BG, 14th AF, at Kunming, China, takes off over the heads of Chinese wagons and parked C-46s and C-47s. (USAF)

The 5th AF (formerly the FEAF) fought in the Philippines at the outbreak of the Pacific war and covered the retreat south to Java, playing a small part in the Battle of the Coral Sea, 7–8 May 1942, but it really came to life late in 1942 when Gen. George C. Kenney assumed command. The 5th AF operated the A-20 at masthead height in the Pacific, and used the aircraft to excellent effect during the battle for Dutch New Guinea. B-17 Flying Fortresses operated in the Pacific until 1943, when the B-24 Liberator replaced them in the island-hopping campaign. Some of the most exciting offensive operations in the Pacific were carried out by B-24s of the 5th and 13th AFs, collectively known as the Far East Air Force, which in September 1944 began attacks on the Philippines and supported the island-hopping campaign across the Pacific.

In the Pacific, as in Europe, there was USAAF/RAF integration. In November 1943 South East Asia Command was activated under Admiral the Lord Louis Mountbatten. Maj.-Gen. George E. Stratemeyer was appointed Chief of Eastern Air Command, which effectively united the British and US air forces. (Plans had been made to transfer the 10th and 14th AFs to the Pacific to co-ordinate with the FEAF in the Philippines, but the war ended before the transfer could be made.)

In September 1944 the 5th AF, as part of the New Guinea campaign, began flying missions against the oil refineries at Balikpapan, in Borneo. This refinery was known as the 'Ploesti of the Pacific', and was second in production only to Palembang in Sumatra. The first raid on the Balikpapan

Fleet of C-109 'flying tankers' at a base in India. These converted B-24J/L Liberators had a capacity of 2,900 US gallons and were used very successfully to ferry fuel to advanced bases in China for B-29s. (B-24 Liberator Club)

oilfields had been made by B-24s of the 380th BG on 13 August 1943 in a seventeen-hour sortie from Darwin, Australia. Two further raids were made, and in September 1944 the airfield at Noemfoor in north-west New Guinea became available, reducing the flying time to fourteen hours and allowing the B-24s to carry a 2,500 lb bomb load.

From August 1944 until 19 February 1945 the 7th AF was engaged in strikes on Iwo Jima and surrounding islands. The Philippines fell on 16 February 1945, and by July 1945 all the Pacific air forces had begun moving northward for the final assault on Japan. The 5th AF, based at Okinawa, and the 13th AF, based at Clark Field in the Philippines, began attacking targets in Formosa and Indo-China. The 5th AF flew explosive and fire-bombing raids on Japan, but the honour of being the first group in the AAF to bomb Japan went to the 'Cobras' of the 494th BG, when its B-24s raided Omura airfield, on Kyushu. The armed forces of Japan were now being attacked from all sides, and the chief weapon was the B-29 Superfortress.

Four B-29 groups of the 58th Wing had moved to India in the spring of 1944, but before they could fly operational missions these groups had to fly over the 'Hump', moving in supplies and munitions to forward bases in China. The first B-29 mission took place on 5 June 1944, when landing fields in China were used as staging posts to refuel and re-arm 98 B-29s for the 2,000 mile round trip to bomb rail targets in Bangkok. Fourteen aircraft aborted and five crashed on landing and only eighteen bombs landed in the target area. On 15/16 June the first raid on the Japanese mainland was made when 47 B-29s made a night attack on the Imperial Iron and Steel Works at Yawata, on the island of Kyushu. Seven B-29s were lost.

B-24J-170-CO *King's X* of the 308th BG, 14th AF, leaving Japanese supply dumps at Henyang on the Siang River in south-east China. (USAF)

In June B-29s of XX Bomber Command, 20th AF, based in India, began bombing heavy industrial targets in Manchuria and Kyushu (Japan) from forward airfields near Chengtu in China. That month, the Marianas Islands, 1,200 miles from Tokyo, were captured, and once bases were established, they would allow B-29s of XXI Bomber Command, 20th AF, to mount an effective offensive against all Japan. During the summer months five B-29 bases were constructed in the newly captured Marianas, where it was decided to concentrate all B-29s of XX AF. It was from here, on 24 November 1944, that the first raid on Tokyo took place, when Brig.-Gen. O'Donnell's 73rd Wing (the second B-29 wing to be formed) bombed the Musashima aircraft factory. (The first airfield, on Saipan, was operational by the end of October 1944.) By January 1945 three B-29 Bomb Wings were based in the Marianas. XXI BC carried out a succession of daylight high-altitude bombing raids against Japanese aircraft factories in and around Tokyo, Yokohama, Kobe, Osaka and Nagoya, with 500 lb high explosive bombs. The first raid on Tokyo since the Doolittle raid of August 1942 took place on 24 November 1944, when 111 B-29s attacked. B-29s were also used in strategic bombing missions to support the invasion of Luzon, in the Philippines, in January 1945, and later that year the Ryukyu Islands, the largest of which is Okinawa. The 58th Wing continued to operate from their Chinese forward landing fields until March 1945. Among their missions was the longest of the war for a B-29 – a 3,950 mile flight from Ceylon to Palembang in Sumatra, in August 1944.

Throughout late 1944 and early 1945 the B-29s continued to conduct high-level daylight raids on Japanese targets, but without success. Losses were becoming prohibitive. In general, daylight precision bombing missions during January–March 1945 proved very disappointing, especially since the Japanese had by now largely dispersed their entire aircraft industry. Maj.-Gen. Curtis E. LeMay, who had arrived in the CBI theatre the previous August to command XX BC in India, decided to change tactics to those he had used successfully with the 8th AF in England. LeMay, who took over XXI BC on 19 January 1945 (and command of XX AF in July 1945), put the best and most experienced radar operators in XXI BC in lead planes, and used them as pathfinders designated to mark the targets. LeMay reasoned that as the B-29s could not hit their targets accurately, they must area-bomb from low level, using incendiaries to burn up large areas of Japanese towns and cities, which were largely constructed of wood.

On 4 February, 70 B-29s dropped over 60 tons of incendiaries on Kobe and completely burned up an area of ⅒ square mile. On 25 February, 172 B-29s dropped over 450 tons of incendiaries in a daylight raid on Tokyo. LeMay and his staff appreciated that, for accuracy, incendiary clusters would have to be released from 5,000–10,000 ft, and at night, for the Japanese had few night fighters, and generally, weather conditions were much improved during the hours of darkness.

In 1,595 sorties in eleven days, 9–20 March, XXI BC dropped over 9,000 tons of incendiary clusters on Japanese cities. The first B-29 low-level incendiary attack on Tokyo took place on the night of 9/10 March 1945, when over 300 B-29s followed pathfinder B-29s across Cape Noijima and north over Tokyo Bay and across Tokyo at altitudes ranging from 4,900 to 9,200 ft. Each B-29 carried 8 tons of M69 incendiaries to drop, following the pattern set by the fires started by the pathfinders. The M69s were set to burst at 2,000 ft, each in turn dividing into thirty-eight separate submunitions, covering a swath of Tokyo 500 ft by 2,500 ft with burning gasoline; 1,700 tons of incendiaries were dropped in less than three hours. Almost 16 square miles of the capital were razed to the ground as gusting winds whipped up the flames; 267,000 buildings were burned out, and 185,000 inhabitants were killed and injured. The firestorm consumed so much oxygen that those who did not die by the flames simply suffocated. Fourteen B-29s were lost, and forty-two were damaged.

LeMay scheduled a further five fire-bombing missions in ten days. On 11 March, 313 B-29s bombed Nagoya, dropping around 1,800 tons of incendiaries. On 13 March, 274 B-29s bombed Osaka. In spite of heavy cloud they dropped 1,644 tons of incendiaries, and the resulting fires destroyed 8 square miles of the city and 135,000 buildings, with 13,000 casualties. Only two B-29s were lost. On 16 March, 307 B-29s dropped 2,355 tons of combined oil and thermite clusters on Kobe; 242,000 people were made homeless, 2,669 were killed, 11,289 injured and 65,951 houses were destroyed for the loss of just three B-29s. The last fire raid, on 20 March, against Nagoya, destroyed 3 square miles of the city.

Fire raids on Japan were halted in April, and from 16 April to 11 May most of XXI BC's missions (2,104 B-29 sorties) were in support of the invasion of Okinawa. LeMay continued his fire-bombing offensive against Japanese cities once more. Nine million Japanese fled to the countryside around the cities, and war production plummeted. Despite the effective blockade and relentless bombing by an ever-increasing number of B-29s – by May 1945 LeMay had four wings and up to 500 Superfortresses under his command – Japan refused to surrender.

In July 1945 Gen. Carl A. Spaatz took over command of the new US Strategic Air Forces in the Pacific (5th, 7th, 13th and 20th Air Forces) while XXI BC was absorbed by the 20th AF and Maj.-Gen. LeMay became its new commander. On 16 July scientists test-exploded the first atomic device at Alamogordo, in the New Mexican desert. President Harry Truman authorized the use of the atomic bomb against Japan, and a mission directive was sent to Spaatz. The 393rd Bomb Squadron, the only squadron in the 509th Composite Group specifically formed for the mission, had fifteen specially modified B-29s in the 313th Wing, XXI Bomber Command, based on Tinian; they were ready to deliver the first atomic bomb, a uranium device code-named 'Little Boy', after 3 August 1945, as soon as weather would permit visual bombing.

A list of targets was issued to XXI BC: Hiroshima, Kokura, Niggata and Nagasaki. Hiroshima was selected, and the mission was scheduled for 6 August 1945. Lt.-Col. Paul Tibbets, Commander of the 509th Composite Group, flew the attacking B-29, *Enola Gay*. A reserve aircraft, three weather reconnaissance B-29s and two special observation aircraft also flew the mission. Capt. William 'Deke' Parsons, naval scientific observer, armed 'Little Boy'. At 0815 hours the 9,700 lb atomic bomb was released from a height of 31,600 ft. Tibbets pulled away sharply in a 155° turn to escape the glare and blast. The bomb detonated 1,900 ft above a hospital, causing destruction on an unprecedented scale: 176,000 people were made homeless, over 70,000 buildings were destroyed, 78,000 Japanese died immediately and 48,000 were severely injured (another 62,000 would die by the end of the year).

B-29 *Enola Gay*, named after the mother of Lt.-Col. Paul Tibbets, Command Pilot, 509th Composite Group, which dropped the first atomic bomb on Hiroshima on 6 August 1945. (USAF)

Maj. Charles W. Sweeney, Command Pilot of B-29 *Bock's Car*, used to deliver the second atomic bomb against Nagasaki on 9 August 1945. (USAF)

By 8 August President Truman had still not received any official reaction from the Japanese government, so a second atomic device was dropped on Japan. Kokura was selected as the primary target, with Nagasaki as the alternative. On 9 August the B-29 *Bock's Car*, named after its commander, Capt. Frederick C. Bock, but piloted on the mission by Maj. Charles W. Sweeney (whose own B-29, *The Great Artiste*, was still brim full with equipment following the Hiroshima mission), headed for Kokura. In the bomb bay was 'Fat Man', a plutonium device (which, because of its construction, was assembled and armed before take-off), and the only atomic device in existence at the time. Sweeney made three runs on Kokura, but the aiming point was obscured by smoke. After fifty minutes he headed for the secondary target, Nagasaki. He made 90 per cent of the run by radar. Only for the last few seconds was the target clear. 'Fat Man' was released, and it detonated at 1,650 ft above Nagasaki. An estimated 35,000 people died immediately in the conflagration, and a further 35,000 would die by the end of the year.

The Japanese government surrendered on 14 August, when a record 804 B-29s bombed targets in Japan. The official surrender ceremony took place aboard the USS *Missouri* in Tokyo Bay, on 2 September.

From 5 June 1944 to 15 August 1945, B-29s of XX Bomber Command and XXI Bomber Command, flew 27,611 bombing sorties, dropping 167,448 tons of bombs and mines.

CHAPTER THREE

Air Force Composition

A typical US Air Force consisted of four subdivisions: Air Service Command, Ground–Air Support Command, Fighter Command and Bomber Command. In general, air operations involved three tactical functions: air attack (medium, heavy, or very heavy bombardment), air fighting (fighter pursuit, fighter interceptor and fighter-bomber operations), and air reconnaissance and observation. In the case of the 9th AF, for example, troop carrier groups were also included in the overall structure.

Establishment dates of the US air forces that took part in the Second World War in Europe	
8th (deployed to ETO, 1942)	28 January 1942
9th (as Middle East AF, ETO from October 1943)	8 April 1942
12th (Italy)	20 August 1942
15th (Italy)	1 November 1943
US Strategic AFs in Europe	22 February 1944

It is impossible to describe here the intricacies of the formation and development of every US Air Force in the Second World War. However, the following summary of the inauguration, composition and development in England of the 8th AF, the largest of all US wartime air forces, is characteristic of the trials and tribulations involved in constructing a powerful air force in a foreign country during wartime.

At first, the US Air Forces operated largely independently of ground forces and the RAF. In the ETO, US daylight precision bombing and RAF Bomber Command area bombing at night were, in themselves, complementary to the overall air effort, especially when a target was bombed by both countries' air forces during the same time span. On 23 November 1942, at a meeting at Headquarters, 8th AF, Gen. Spaatz explained to his staff the general function of the new theatre air command. He saw its chief duty as strategic control, not operational or administrative control. It would be organized as follows: 8th AF, in command of all US Air Forces in the UK; 12th AF, in command of all US air forces in North Africa, and Iceland Air Forces.

At peak personnel strength, the 8th AF numbered more than 200,000 officers and men. At peak operating strength, it numbered 40½ heavy bomb groups, 15 fighter groups and 2 photo-reconnaissance groups operating from bases in the UK. At this strength, a typical mission consisted of 1,400 heavy bombers, escorted by 800 fighters, consuming 3½ million gallons of aviation gasoline, expending 250,000 rounds of .50 calibre ammunition, and dropping 3,300 tons of bombs on enemy targets. In 459 days when bombing operations were carried out, 46,456 men became casualties, maintenance and ground personnel repaired 59,644 battle-damaged aircraft, loaded the 732,231 tons of bombs expended, and linked and loaded the 99,256,341 rounds of ammunition.

8th Air Force: build-up, strategy and implementation

In January 1942 the War Department in Washington, DC, announced that US ground forces were to be sent to Northern Ireland. On 8 January the activation of US Forces in the British Isles (USAFBI) was announced. In addition, a bomber command was to be established in England. The 8th AF, which was activated at Savannah Army Air Force Base, Georgia, on 28 January 1942, under the command of Col. (later Brig.-Gen.) Asa M. Duncan, formed the nucleus for the build-up in the UK when its intended role as the air element of a task force which would invade north-west Africa was cancelled in order to meet the more pressing needs of the Pacific. Arnold instructed Brig.-Gen. Ira C. Eaker, who had spent a month in England in 1941 observing the RAF at close quarters, to assist in the formation of a headquarters for the US Air Forces in the UK. Eaker's brief included assisting in the preparation of both airfields and installations for the first Air Corps units sent to the UK, and he was to understudy the methods of RAF Bomber Command. Furthermore, his staff were to prepare training schedules for the first AAF units to reach the UK.

Eaker took up his duties as Commanding General of VIII Bomber Command and established his headquarters at RAF Bomber Command Headquarters at High Wycombe, where, on 22 February 1942, VIII Bomber Command was formally activated. However, Maj.-Gen. Chaney did not concur in the air plans of the War Department for the USAFBI. He said these plans were 'apparently intended for a virgin American theatre of operations', and were not appropriate in what was 'essentially a British Theatre'. Chaney reiterated these views when he wrote of the air defence of the US forces sent to Ireland under the MAGNET plan:

> All pursuit and anti-aircraft artillery organizations utilized for air defence in this theatre, which is geographically very small, must be controlled by the British Fighter Command. It is agreed that these units in Northern Ireland should be under the Commander, Northern Ireland Forces. However, the air defence of the British Isles is an undesirable entity, it is a single closely knit thing and the British Fighter Command of necessity must be responsible for the air defence of the British Isles.

Furthermore, Chaney added that if the bomber command were to be activated,

> officers rather senior in age and rank who have had experience in bombardment operations, should be selected for key positions in the bomber command headquarters . . . I have gone over personally the

backgrounds of the 19 staff officers supplied by Eaker and find that in general they have had only pursuit training. Moreover, a large number have come direct from civil life without military background of any kind. Three served with bombardment units some years ago and their bombing experience must therefore be regarded as virtually negligible.

Nearly six months were to elapse before the first all-US bombing mission over enemy territory, hence the staff of Brig.-Gen. Eaker had ample time to 'understudy' the bombing methods of the RAF.

Maintenance and maintenance depots

Chaney had been informed by the War Department on 28 December 1941 that the Lockheed Corporation had been asked to construct an aircraft maintenance depot at Langford Lodge, Northern Ireland. On 2 January 1942 Chaney reported briefly this plan for construction of this depot after negotiations with the British Air Ministry:

> British to provide facilities, buildings, utilities and housing for 1,200 man depot. Air Corps to furnish equipment and management and take over operation by contract with Lockheed or some other manufacturer. Equipment and facilities to provide for repair of British-operated Hudsons and Liberators in addition to American-operated planes.

On 20 April 1942 Maj.-Gen. Chaney reported that the 'technical area' of Langford Lodge would be completed by the Lockheed workers around 1 June 1942, and that the entire project would be finished on about 1 September of that year.

Originally, it was proposed that advance air depots for bomber aircraft modification and repair should be established for every three operational airfields. Gen. Spaatz planned for twenty small mobile air depots for VIII Bomber Command, but in August 1942, under the provisions of the Bradley Plan, it was decided to provide only three large advance depots, two for Bomber Command and one for Fighter Command, with additional depots if required. The Bradley Committee recommended that the Base Air Depots (Burtonwood, Warton, and Langford Lodge in Northern Ireland) would be called 1st, 2nd, and 3rd Base Air Depots. In January 1942 USAFBI Headquarters arranged with the Ministry of Aircraft Production for the construction of a signal and aircraft maintenance depot at Warton, a few miles from Liverpool. The plans envisaged the employment of 3,800 persons, of whom 3,000 were to be technical workers, while the balance represented the staff and casuals of the proposed Air Replacement Centre. The Ministry of Aircraft Production predicted that the project would be completed by 1 January 1943.

In view of the apparent need for an aircraft repair depot in England prior to the scheduled completion dates of the Langford Lodge and Warton installations, Col. Lyon recommended that the repair plant at Burtonwood, near Liverpool, be acquired by the US government. In April 1942 this plant was operated for the Ministry of Aircraft Production by a board consisting

A C-47 being completely overhauled by engineers at BAD 2, Warton. (Dave Mayor)

A P-51 Mustang undergoing refit at the 8th AF Repair and Replacement Centre at Warton, Lancashire. (Dave Mayor)

Aircraft like this B-17G
Fortress, *E-RAT-ICATOR*, of
the 452nd BG, 8th AF, were
often maintained in the field.
(USAF)

of officers of several British corporations. Lyon suggested that if the plant
were acquired, planes of both the RAF and USAAF should be repaired by
its personnel. Negotiations were initiated by USAFBI Headquarters for the
acquisition of Burtonwood. The completion of arrangements with the
Ministry of Aircraft Production for the transfer of the site to US command
was reported to Gen. Chaney on 23 May 1942. Burtonwood was probably
the largest military base in Europe during the Second World War,
processing over 11,500 aircraft between 1943 and 1945 alone, but beyond
that it was responsible for the support of the 8th, 9th, 12th and 15th Air
Forces. Over 35,000 men were under the direct control of Burtonwood,
with 18,500 on the base itself.* On a much smaller scale, Strategic Air
Depots were also used for the same purpose.

Strategic Air Depots
The transit depots were designated Strategic Air Depots. These were
organized, staffed and trained specifically to service Air Force Combat
Units. They were responsible for third- and fourth-echelon maintenance,

---

* *RAF Burtonwood: 50 Years in Photographs*, Aldon P. Ferguson (Airfield Publications, 1989).

plus all supply functions, and the salvage of crashed aircraft. On 1 August 1943 there were four SADs, at Honington (1st SAD), Little Staughton (2nd SAD), Watton (3rd SAD) and Wattisham (4th SAD). Because of the increasing needs and sizes of the SADs, they were relocated in 1944. Towards the end of the war a 5th SAD was located in France.

Airfield construction

In the UK, airfield construction was carried out on a massive scale. Of the 700 airfields in operation during 1939–45, almost 500 were built during the Second World War. Many of the bases used initially by VIII Bomber and Fighter Commands were pre-war, purpose-built RAF bases which were re-allocated to the 8th AF. In 1941 the members of the Special Observer Group in England had made many reconnaissance visits to areas regarded as potential sites for US Army installations. There were several tentative Air Corps sites prior to 8 January 1942, the most extensive ones being the proposed USAAF fields at Ayr, Scotland, and Warton, near Liverpool, the proposed site for a repair plant for US aircraft. Also considered were Polebrook, Grafton Underwood, Kimbolton, Little Staughton, Molesworth, Chelveston, Podington, Thurleigh, Desborough and Market Harborough. A more complete reconnaissance of the Huntingdon area, the proposed site of the bomber area, took place between 31 March and 3 April 1942.

On 13 June 1942, just one week before his departure from the theatre, Maj.-Gen. Chaney sent the War Department the outlines for a comprehensive plan which had been worked out with the British for the location of USAAF installations in the UK. The bulk of these were to be south of the line from the Wash to Leicester and north and north-east of London. This plan provided that the first US bomber units would be located near Cambridge, while those arriving later would be placed in East Anglia.

The USAAF originally had 75 airfields in the UK but the total finally reached 250. These cost £645 million, to which the Americans contributed £40 million. Each airfield, including buildings and services, cost on average £1 million. Eight miles of hedgerow and 1,500 trees had to be removed at each potential airfield site; 20 miles of drain, 10 miles of conduit, 6 miles of water main, 4 miles of sewer, 10 miles of road, 4.5 million bricks, 32,000 square miles of tarmac, 400,000 cubic yards of excavated soil and ½ million yards super area of concrete (175,000 cubic yards by volume) were used in its construction.★

The British Air Ministry made available 77 bases in 1942. One of the largest concentrations of airfields was in East Anglia, and these were used predominantly by bomber, fighter and transport aircraft of the 8th and 9th Air Forces. A standard bomber airfield (Class A) layout housed one group (with four squadrons of up to eighteen aircraft each) and consisted of three runways, the main one being 2,000 yd long and the other two at least 1,400 yd each. A 50 ft wide perimeter track or taxiway, with fifty hardstandings or dispersal points, normally encircled the flying field.

★ *Airfields of the 8th Then and Now*, Roger A. Freeman (After the Battle, 1978).

A B-17 comes into land past a black-and-white chequered runway control caravan. These were often obtained locally and highly improvised (note the domed observation canopy, a B-17 Plexiglas nose). (USAF)

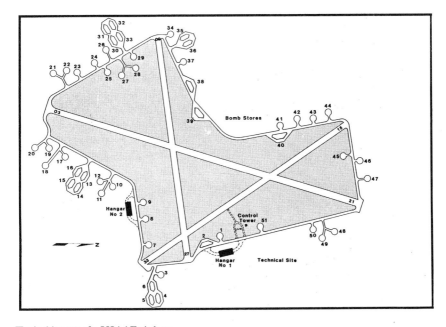

Typical layout of a USAAF air base.

Where grass airfields were used (normally by fighters and, early in the war, by medium bombers) pierced steel planking was laid. Pre-war RAF stations, like Bassingbourn and Horsham St Faith, for instance, were also made available to the USAAF. These had four brick-built C Type (hipped) hangars as standard. Where no hangars existed, two T2 rectangular, steel-framed structures were erected. The T2s spanned 115–120 ft, were 240 ft long and 39 ft high. Underground fuel storage contained 100,000 gallons of aviation fuel. About a dozen remote living sites and communal areas were situated in the surrounding area and linked to the main technical area and airfield proper by paved roads. In England the 8th AF eventually occupied 58 airfields.

Maintenance at airbases

Day-to-day maintenance of aircraft in all theatres of war was often an uncomfortable task, carried out in field conditions. The tempo of war called for immediate replacement of damaged or defective equipment, and professional-type shops were set up on each base to service and repair every major component, from armaments and instruments to propellers and sparking plugs. Field modifications were, as the name implies, performed on aircraft and aircraft armaments in the field at air bases. Also, it was not uncommon for complete engine changes to be carried out in the open, although specialized hangars were used for aero repair and engine repair. Out on the airfields and airstrips, ground crewmen made their remote locations and dispersal sites as convivial as possible with shacks often constructed from used ammunition boxes, and so on.

Build-up

The appointment of Maj.-Gen. Carl A. Spaatz as the Commanding General of the 8th AF was announced on 2 May 1942. His appointment was announced in the UK by General Order No. 4, Headquarters, 8th AF, of 18 June 1942. During June the vanguard of the vast US armada to come arrived in the UK. A portion of the VII BC, commanded by Capt. O'Dilliard Turner, reached Pinetree on 12 May, but of the aircraft there was still no sign. In April and May 1942 the War Department sent USAFBI Headquarters several telegrams containing predictions that the first planes for the 8th Bomber Command would reach the UK in May or June 1942.

Four B-17E/F groups – the 92nd, 97th, 301st and 303rd – and two B-24D Liberator groups – the 44th and 93rd – formed the nucleus of the 8th's heavy bombardment force in England. First to arrive in the UK was the ground echelon of the 97th BG, which disembarked on 9 June and entrained for its Polebrook base in Northamptonshire, from where, earlier, RAF Fortress Is had taken off on raids over Germany. The 1st Fighter Group, equipped with the P-38 Lightning, also arrived in England in June. The 14th Fighter Group also arrived in England that summer.

The delivery of aircraft for USAAF use began on 6 July 1942 with the arrival of a flight of C-47s. Two days earlier, on 4 July (Independence Day), six US crews of the 15th BG (Light), together with six RAF crews, were despatched from RAF Swanton Morley, Norfolk, in twelve RAF A-20s on a

B-17F *Lucky Strike* of the 303rd BG, 8th AF, at Molesworth being loaded with bombs by a Chevrolet M6 4 × 4 1½ ton bomb service truck. The 303rd flew its first mission on 17 November 1942. (USAF)

sweep against four German airfields in Holland. It was the first time US airmen had flown in US-built bombers against a German target, but although it was important historically, the raid was not an unqualified success, and two of the aircraft manned by Americans were shot down.

It took time to get the new groups ready for combat, and training was lacking in many areas. The first Fortress strike of the war went ahead on 17 August 1942, when the 97th BG attacked the marshalling yards at Rouen Sotteville in north-west France. When the news of the first bombing mission by VIII Bomber Command reached Washington, the Chief of Air Staff arranged for a memorandum prepared for Gen. 'Hap' Arnold's signature to be sent to Gen. George C. Marshall, Chief of Staff, for the attention of Admirals Ernest J. King and William D. Leahy.

Eaker's ability to wage a bombing offensive was hampered by the more pressing needs of Brig.-Gen. James H. Doolittle's 12th AF, which would have to be equipped and trained to support the TORCH invasion of North-west Africa in November 1942. The 8th AF was thus denied valuable replacement men and machines while new groups had to be trained for eventual transfer to the 12th. Worse, on 14 September both the 97th and 301st BGs were assigned to the new air force. In the meantime, Eaker sent all he had on missions to attack shipyards and airfields on the Continent.

Groundcrews and an RAF liaison officer at Snetterton Heath are pictured 'sweating out' a mission. This British crash truck was one of the benefits of reverse Lease-Lend which the 8th AF in the UK enjoyed during the early, formative days. (USAF)

Tactics

The offensive against U-boat bases and construction yards began in October 1942, and it remained the main focus of the 8th AF until June 1943. In the course of this campaign, 2,500 tons of bombs were dropped on enemy targets. Early raids by heavy bombers (mostly B-17s) from England in 1942 were flown at altitudes of around 20,000–25,000 ft. Even at these altitudes bombers were relatively easy targets for the flak crews and fighter attacks by the Luftwaffe. On almost every mission bombers were hitting the target, but not in large enough concentrations to cause serious damage. Experience proved that a single bomb, or even a few bombs, did not have enough destructive power on their own. Col. Curtis E. LeMay, CO of the 305th BG, was determined to achieve greater bombing accuracy by flying a straight course on the bomb run instead of zig-zagging every ten seconds – a tactic which had been designed to spoil the aim of the German flak batteries. His plan was to cross the target faster, and therefore reduce the amount of time available to the German flak batteries to fire on the formation.

As 1942 drew to a close, officers and men were still working on improving methods for bombing and aerial gunnery. The two problems were linked, and at Chelveston Col. LeMay worked hard to find the best method of combating fighter attacks without compromising bombing accuracy, and vice versa. LeMay was a great believer in 'close group formations': aircraft flying quite close together, changing the wingmen of all three squadrons up or down depending on the direction of attack by enemy fighters. LeMay wanted the group to fly as closely as possible without compromising safety,

The first US heavy bomber mission was flown by B-17s of the 97th BG from Grafton Underwood on 17 August 1942. The lead ship was flown by Maj. Paul Tibbets (back row, far left). Tibbets, Tom Ferebee, bombardier (3rd from left, back row), and Van Kirk, navigator (far right, back row), flew the same positions aboard *Enola Gay* on the first atomic bomb drop three years later. (Paul Tibbets)

and to be able to shift the formation to direct as much firepower at the enemy fighter as possible.

He began by shifting the formation with the sun as the focal point. When the formation turned away from or into the sun, the wingmen would change position, moving up or down in relation to the leader, and thereby always allowing the greatest firepower from the entire formation. To control stragglers and observe the formation, LeMay would ride in the upper gun-turret position, or designate one of his squadron commanders to do this. He was constantly on the radio, pointing out the weaknesses of any pilot and ordering improvements. Col. LeMay was also convinced that the aircraft should be flown steadily without manoeuvring while its guns were firing (at first, crews took evasive action, turns, up and down movements, whenever the enemy attacked). Providing a steady platform for the gunners was essential.

After trying 'stacked-up' formations of eighteen aircraft, LeMay finally decided upon staggered three-plane elements within squadrons and staggered squadrons within groups. This would result in a complicated bombing procedure if each aircraft tried manoeuvring to enable accurate aiming, so LeMay discarded individual bombing, which had been standard operating procedure from the outset. He replaced the technique with 'lead crews', whose

Col. Curtis E. LeMay at a DFC awards ceremony at the 384th BG base at Great Ashfield in 1943. (via Ian McLachlan)

bombardier signalled to the rest of the formation when to bomb, so that all bombs were released simultaneously no matter what formation the aircraft were flying. This simple but brilliant idea could lead to all the bombs missing the target, but if they all landed a short distance from the mean point of impact, then a target could be successfully destroyed instead of damaged. The very best bombardiers were selected for the task and put into lead crews. On 18 March 1943 the 305th BG, flying at 24,000 ft, placed 76 per cent of its bomb load within 1,000 ft of the MPI at Vegasack. It was on this mission that automatic flight control equipment was used in combat for the first time.

LeMay's tactics found support at Wing Headquarters, where first Brig.-Gen. Larry Kuter and later Brig.-Gen. Hayward 'Possum' Hansell lent encouragement, and gradually lead crews, comprising highly trained pilots, bombardiers and navigators, became standard operating procedure.

Strategy, 1943–4

Targets attacked in all theatres of war were divided mainly into *strategic* and *tactical*. The nature of the targets – oil campaign, interdiction campaign, transport campaign, and so on – was dictated by the policies agreed at the highest level. The primary object of the joint US/British bomber offensive was set out in the original directive issued by the Combined Chiefs of Staff

Fortresses enveloped by flak. Groups had to maintain their formation during the bombing run, so that if all the bombardiers dropped their bombs at the exact time they were supposed to, the bombs would fall as plotted. (USAF)

at their 65th meeting on 21 January 1943, at the Casablanca Conference: 'The progressive destruction and dislocation of the German military, industrial and economic system, and the undermining of the morale of the German people to a point where their capacity for armed resistance is fatally weakened.'

The intermediate objective was German fighter strength, but the primary objectives were German submarine yards and bases, the remainder of the German aircraft industry, ball-bearing factories and oil facilities (contingent upon attacks against Ploesti from the Mediterranean). The secondary objectives were synthetic rubber and tyre production facilities and military motor transport vehicles.

After Casablanca Gen. Eaker and his senior officers drew up more detailed plans for effecting the new bomber offensive approved by the conference. The POINTBLANK Directive which resulted was approved in principle by the Combined Chiefs of Staff at the Trident Conference on 18 May 1943 in Washington, DC. It set the pattern for the rest of the war, with the USAAF bombing by day and the RAF Bomber Command by night in a round-the-clock bomber offensive. (On 13 February 1944 POINTBLANK was modified to give first priority to the destruction of the 'German single-engine and twin-engine air frame and component production; and Axis-controlled ball-bearing production. Second priority was Installations supporting the German Air Force.')

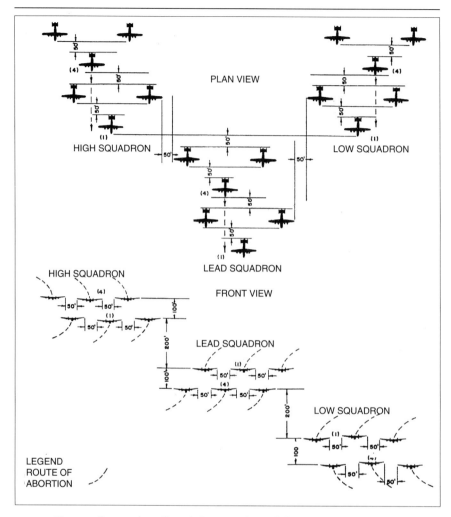

Group formation for eighteen aircraft in three squadrons.

Lockheed P-38J Lightnings of the 383rd Fighter Squadron, 364th Fighter Group, 8th AF, on a mission. (USAF)

Combat formations

Each group consisted of four squadrons of approximately twelve aircraft, based on one airfield. Squadrons were further divided, for purposes of flight control, into flights (six aircraft) and elements (three aircraft). On missions, 8th AF bomb groups took off and assembled into squadrons, then groups, then wings. 'Combat boxes' assembled in the vicinity of the airfield, 'combat wings' assembled at a place, time and altitude prescribed by the combat wing commander, normally with the leader at 2,500 ft, in a column of combat boxes, each combat box in staggered formation. The following combat boxes took position slightly above the lead combat box and flew in close formation in column. Each combat wing was assigned an area in which to form the combat boxes into combat wing formation. Each combat wing consisted of two or three combat boxes. When more than four combat boxes were employed, they would not normally attempt to close up into single formation, but would form two or more combat wings.

In April 1943 four new B-17F groups arrived in England. A fifth 'new' B-17 group was added to the force when the 92nd BG resumed bombing operations. Around this time the unit designations were changed from 'combat boxes' and 'combat groups' to 'groups' and 'wings'. The term 'combat wing' remained in use to describe the battle formation composed of two or three group boxes. A wing would normally assemble on a line about

Unarmed, war-weary, multi-coloured B-24 Liberators were used at the start of a mission by each group of the 2nd Air Division, 8th AF, as assembly ships to form units for the divisional assembly line. After forming, the assembly ship would return to base, leaving the group to continue to the target. This 'Judas Goat', as they were also called, is B-24D-30-CO, 42-40127, *First Sergeant* (93rd BG Ploesti veteran *Thar She Blows*) of the 458th BG at Horsham St Faith, which was destroyed in a flare accident in May 1944 and replaced by another similarly marked aircraft. (USAF)

30–40 miles long, with time and altitude prescribed for the lead combat wing at each end of the 'assembly line'. The assembly line was normally chosen at an angle to the first leg of the route, in order to permit the lead navigator to establish his ground speed and drift, to determine the strength and direction of the wind, while still over land, and to permit following combat wings to cut across in order to catch up, if they were late. Whenever possible, the ends of the wing assembly line were chosen to coincide with 'Splasher' radio beacon sites or MF/DF beacon sites, so that the radio compasses could be used to aid in assembly in overcast or broken overcast conditions when geographical landmarks might be obscured.

In June 1943 the 94th, 95th and 96th BGs formed a new 4th Bomb Wing in Essex and Suffolk under the command of Brig.-Gen. Fred L. Anderson. Following high losses, the 8th AF Marauder groups were transferred from the 3rd Bomb Wing to VIII Air Support Command for future medium-level bombing operations in a tactical role. This move would give the B-26s longer-range fighter cover. Their Essex bases were taken over by three B-17 groups in the 4th Wing, while the arrival of the 100th, 385th and 388th Groups, would increase the 4th Wing to six groups. The new 4th Wing CO, Col. Curtis E. LeMay, moved into the former 3rd Wing HQ at Elveden Hall, near Thetford. By September 1943 VIII Bomber Command totalled nine B-17 groups (1st Bomb Wing) and four B-24 groups (2nd Bomb Wing).

13 June 1943: Capt. Robert Morgan (in one-piece flight suit, A-2 jacket and RAF 1940-pattern boots), with the crew of the *Memphis Belle*, 324th Bomb Squadron, 91st BG, 8th AF, bidding farewell to Gen. Jacob Devers, Theatre Commander, and Ira C. Eaker, 8th AF Commander, before returning to the USA following completion of their tour. (USAF)

Men of an Engineer Aviation Fire Fighter platoon dousing the burning engine of a B-17. (USAF)

2nd AIR DIVISION

2ND COMBAT BOMB WING

389 Bomb Group (H)
(Hethel)
Hq 389 Bomb Gp (H)
564th Bomb Squadron [YO]
565th Bomb Squadron [EE]
566th Bomb Squadron [RR] — (C)
567th Bomb Squadron [HP]
327 Service Gp, Det A (atchd)
79 Service Gp (atchd)
463 Sub-Depot (atchd)
48 Sta Compl (atchd)
1215 QM Co (atchd)
1200 MP Co (atchd)
2032 Engineer Fire Fighter
Platoon (atchd)
209 Finance Co (atchd)
1750 Ord Co (atchd)
255 Med Disp (atchd)

445 Bomb Group (H)
(Tibenham)
Hq 445 Bomb Gp (H)
700th Bomb Squadron [IS]
701st Bomb Squadron [MK]
702nd Bomb Squadron [WV] — (F)
703rd Bomb Squadron [RN]
53 Sta Compl Squadron (atchd)
462 Sub-Depot (atchd)
1216 QM Serv Gp (atchd)
1200 MP Co, Det A (atchd)
210 Finance Section (atchd)
2043 Engineer Fire Fighter
Platoon (atchd)
858 Chem Co (atchd)
61 Army Postal Unit (atchd)
254 Med Disp (atchd)
830 Air Engineer Squadron
(atchd)
654 Air Mat Squadron (atchd)
1826 Ord Co (atchd)

453 Bomb Group (H)
(Old Buckenham)
Hq 453 Bomb Gp (H)
732nd Bomb Squadron [E3]
733rd Bomb Squadron [F8]
734th Bomb Squadron [E8] — (J)
735th Bomb Squadron [H6]
80 Sta Compl Squadron (atchd)
210 Finance Co, Det A (atchd)
256 Med Disp Avn (atchd)
467 Sub-Depot (atchd)
874 Chem Co, Det A (atchd)
1193 MP Co, Det A (atchd)
1231 QM Co (atchd)
1792 Ord Co (atchd)
2103 Engineer Fire Fighter
Platoon (atchd)

20TH COMBAT BOMB WING (H)

93 Bomb Group (H)
(Alconbury)
(Bungay)
(Hardwick)
Hq 93 Bomb Gp (H)
328th Bomb Squadron [GO]
329th Bomb Squadron [RE]
330th Bomb Squadron [AG] — (B)
409th Bomb Squadron [YM]
461 Sub-Depot (atchd)
885 Chem Co (atchd)
18 Wea Section (atchd)
1236 QM Co (atchd)
212 Finance Co (atchd)
1248 MP Co (atchd)
1675 Ord Co (atchd)
5 Sta Compl Squadron (atchd)
2031 Engineer Aviation Fire
Fighter Platoon (atchd)

446 Bomb Group (H)
(Flixton)
Hq 446 Bomb Gp (H)
704th Bomb Squadron [FL]
705th Bomb Squadron [HN]
706th Bomb Squadron [RT] — (H)
707th Bomb Squadron [JU]
25 Sta Compl Squadron (atchd)
460 Sub-Depot (atchd)
1248 MP Co, Det A (atchd)
558 Army Postal Unit (atchd)
2967 Finance Det (atchd)
212 Fin Section (atchd)
2035 Engineer Aviation Fire
Fighter Platoon (atchd)
1214 QM Co (atchd)
885 Chem Co, Det A (atchd)
1821 Ord Co (atchd)
260 Med Disp Avn (atchd)

448 Bomb Group (H)
(Seething)
Hq 448 Bomb Gp
712th Bomb Squadron [CT]
713th Bomb Squadron [IG]
714th Bomb Squadron [EI] — (I)
715th Bomb Squadron [IO]
2d AD & Relay Flt (Prov) (atchd)
862 Chem Co Air Ops (atchd)
1232 QM Co (atchd)
58 Sta Compl (atchd)
262 Med Disp Avn (atchd)
459 Sub-Depot (atchd)
2102 Engineer Aviation Fire Fighter
Platoon (atchd)
1193 MP Co (atchd)
1596 Ord Sup & Maint Co (atchd)

95TH COMBAT BOMB WING

489 Bomb Group (H)
(Halesworth)
Hq 489 Bomb Gp (H)
844th Bomb Squadron [4R]
845th Bomb Squadron [T4]
846th Bomb Squadron [8R] — (W)
847th Bomb Squadron [S4]
328 Sta Compl Squadron (atchd)
474 Sub-Depot (atchd)
1235 QM Co (atchd)
2982 Finance Det (atchd)
263 Med Disp (atchd)
867 Chem Co, Det A (atchd)
2106 Engineer Aviation Fire Fighter Platoon (atchd)
18 Wea Squadron, Det 365 (atchd)
B-24 MTU 27 (atchd)

14TH COMBAT BOMB WING (H)

44 Bomb Group (H)
(Shipham)
Hq 44 Bomb Gp (H)
66th Bomb Squadron [QK]
67th Bomb Squadron [NB]
68th Bomb Squadron [WQ]
506th Bomb Squadron [GJ]
317 Service Gp, (atchd)
340 Service Squadron (atchd)
1044 Ord Co (atchd)
646 Ord Co (Avn) (atchd)
1646 Ord Co (atchd)
876 Chem Co (atchd)
987 MP Det (atchd)
152 QM Det (atchd)
50 Sta Compl (atchd)
464 Sub-Depot (atchd)
1132 QM Co Service Gp (atchd)
806 Chem Co (atchd)
2983 Finance Det (atchd)
208 Finance Section (atchd)
2033 Engineer Fire Fighter Platoon (atchd)
265 Med Disp (atchd)
Weather Det (atchd)
1287 MP Det (atchd)

(A)

392 Bomb Group (H)
(Wandling)
Hq 392 Bomb Gp (H)
576th Bomb Squadron [CI]
577th Bomb Squadron [DC]
578th Bomb Squadron [EC]
579th Bomb Squadron [GC]
465 Sub-Depot (atchd)
10 Sta Compl Squadron (atchd)
1217 QM Co (atchd)
1287 MP Co, Det A (atchd)
1825 Ord Co (atchd)
2974 Finance Co (atchd)
2101 Engineer Avn Fire Fighter Platoon (atchd)
586 Army Postal Unit (atchd)

(D)

492 Bomb Group (H)
(North Pickenham)
Hq 492 Bomb Gp (H)
856th Bomb Squadron [5Z]
857th Bomb Squadron [9H]
858th Bomb Squadron [9A]
859th Bomb Squadron [X4]
326 Sta Compl Squadron (atchd)
Det A, 882 Chem Squadron (atchd)
1450 Ord Co (atchd)
1234 QM Co (atchd)
2967 Fin Det (atchd)
479 Sub-Depot (atchd)
2108 Engineer Avn Fire Fighter Platoon (atchd)
Det 143, 18 Wea Squadron (atchd)
1261 MP Co (atchd)

(U)

96TH COMBAT BOMB WING (H)

458 Bomb Group (H)
(Horsham St Faith)
Hq 458 Bomb Gp (H)
752nd Bomb Squadron [7V]
753rd Bomb Squadron [J4]
754th Bomb Squadron [Z5]
755th Bomb Squadron [J3]
60 Sta Compl Squadron (atchd)
469 Sub-Depot (atchd)
1105 QM Co (atchd)
258 Med Disp (atchd)
211 Finance Squadron Ava (atchd)
2983 Finance Det (atchd)
2016 Engineer Aviation Fire Fighter Platoon (atchd)
1119 MP Co (atchd)
130 Army Postal Unit (atchd)
858 Chem Co (atchd)

(K)

466 Bomb Group (H)
(Attlebridge)
Hq 466 Bomb Gp (H)
784th Bomb Squadron [T9]
785th Bomb Squadron [2U]
786th Bomb Squadron [U8]
787th Bomb Squadron [6L]
61 Sta Compl Squadron (atchd)
472 Sub-Depot (atchd)
1233 QM Co (atchd)
1452 Ord Co (atchd)
882 Chem Co (atchd)
1266 MP Co, Det A (atchd)
2014 Engineer Aviation Fire Fighter Platoon (atchd)
207 Finance Section (atchd)

(L)

467 Bomb Group (H)
(Rackheath)
Hq 467 Bomb Gp (H)
788th Bomb Squadron [X7]
789th Bomb Squadron [6A]
790th Bomb Squadron [Q2]
791st Bomb Squadron [4Z]
74 Sta Compl Squadron (atchd)
470 Sub-Depot (atchd)
1229 QM Co (atchd)
1286 MP Co (atchd)
1451 Ord Co (atchd)
862 Chem Co (atchd)
2015 Engineer Aviation Fire Fighter Platoon (atchd)
207 Finance Co (atchd)
259 Med Disp (atchd)

(P)

491 Bomb Group (H)
(Metfield)
(North Pickenham)
Hq 491 Bomb Gp (H)
852nd Bomb Squadron [3Q]
853rd Bomb Squadron [T8]
854th Bomb Squadron [6X]
855th Bomb Squadron [V2]
326 Sta Compl Squadron (atchd)
479 Sub-Depot (atchd)
1234 QM Svc Gp (atchd)
1450 Ord Co (atchd)
1261 MP Co (atchd)
2108 Engineer Aviation Fire Fighter Platoon (atchd)
266 Med Disp (atchd)
208 Finance Section (atchd)
882 Chem Co, Det A (atchd)

(Z)

Final command and combat wing assignments, 8th Air Force, England, 1 January 1945

8TH AIR FORCE
Lt.-Gen. James H. Doolittle
Maj.-Gen. W.E. Kepner (from 10 May 1945)

FIGHTER COMMAND

AIR SERVICE COMMAND

FIRST AIR DIVISION (B-17s)

1ST COMBAT WING
91stBG 301stBG 381stBG 398thBG

40TH COMBAT WING
92ndBG 303rdBG 305thBG 306thBG

41ST COMBAT WING
379thBG 384thBG

94TH COMBAT WING
351stBG 401stBG 457thBG

93RD COMBAT WING
34thBG

482ND BG
492ndBG CARPETBAGGERS

67TH FIGHTER WING
20thFG 352ndFG 356thFG
359thFG 364thFG - - - - - - - - -

BOMBER COMMAND

SECOND AIR DIVISION (B-24s)

2ND COMBAT WING
389thBG 453rdBG 445thBG

14TH COMBAT WING
44thBG 392ndBG 491stBG#

20TH COMBAT WING
93rdBG 446thBG 448thBG
#489thBG

95TH COMBAT WING
(DISBANDED 5 MAY 1944)

96TH COMBAT WING
458thBG 466thBG 467thBG

65TH FIGHTER WING
4thFG 56thFG 355thFG
361st (fr. 10 April 45)
479thFG

GROUND-AIR SUPPORT COMMAND

THIRD AIR DIVISION (B-17s)

4TH COMBAT WING
94thBG 385thBG* 447thBG
486thBG 487thBG

13TH COMBAT WING
95thBG 100thBG 390thBG

45TH COMBAT WING
96thBG 388thBG 452ndBG

93RD COMBAT WING
34thBG 490thBG 493rdBG

66TH FIGHTER WING
55th 78th 322nd 339th
353rd 357th 358th

* 385thBG to 93rd Wing 17 Feb 1945

Wing and group level

The organizational structure described above remained in existence until 13 September 1943, when VIII Bomber Command was officially divided into three bombardment divisions (and from 1 January 1945 into air divisions). The heavy bomb groups lost their provisional combat bombardment wings, which became simply combat bombardment wings. Each division controlled three to five combat bombardment wings, and each combat bombardment wing comprised, generally, three groups. (This was not true of all theatres. The 15th AF bomb groups, for example, were in four wings, each with three or four groups.) As will be seen from pages 54–5, each division in the 8th AF controlled several bombardment and fighter groups. The 2nd, for example, commanded fourteen bombardment groups flying B-24 Liberators, and five fighter groups (four P-51 Mustang and one P-47 group). Its maximum total strength was 8,870 officers and 43,884 enlisted personnel.

Sometimes all divisions would attack the same target or group of targets in a given area, but quite often the targets assigned on any one day differed according to the make-up of the division. The main reason for this was because the 3rd (until its change-over to an all-B-17 force) and 2nd Bomb Divisions operated Liberators, which were faster and had different power settings to the B-17s. Gen. James Doolittle did try to convert the 8th AF to an all-B-17 force, but not enough Fortresses were available.

CHAPTER FOUR

The Air Forces

1st Air Force, US ZOI

This Air Force was constituted as Northeast Air District on 19 October 1940, and was activated on 18 December 1940. Re-designated 1st Air Force early in 1941, it trained new organizations and, later, replacements for combat units. It also provided air defence for the eastern USA until August 1944.

Stations
Mitchel Field, New York, 18 December 1940–6

Commands
I Bomber, 1941–2: I Bomber was constituted as AAF Antisubmarine Command on 13 October 1942, and activated in the USA on 15 October 1942, assigned directly to the AAF. Re-designated I Bomber Command in August 1943, it was assigned to the 1st Air Force. It conducted antisubmarine operations from bases in the USA, the Caribbean, Newfoundland, north-west Africa and England until October 1943. Afterwards it trained bombardment organizations and personnel. It was later assigned to the 2nd Air Force and re-designated XX Bomber Command.

Wings:
25th Antisubmarine, 1942–3
26th Antisubmarine, 1942–3

I Fighter, 1941–6:
I Fighter was constituted as I Interceptor Command on 26 May 1941, and activated on 5 June 1941. It was re-designated I Fighter Command in May 1942.

Wings:
Boston Fighter, 1942–4
New York Fighter, 1942–4
Norfolk Fighter, 1942–4
Philadelphia Fighter, 1942–4
I Ground Air Support, 1941–2
I Bomber Command, 5 September 1941–15 October 1942 (inactivated and assigned to 2nd Air Force after re-activation on 1 May 1943)

1st AF commanders
Maj.-Gen. James E. Chaney, 18 December 1940
Maj.-Gen. Herbert A. Dargue, 24 June 1941
Brig.-Gen. Arnold N. Krogstad, 10 December 1941
Maj.-Gen. Follett Bradley, 5 March 1942
Maj.-Gen. James E. Chaney, 23 July 1942
Maj.-Gen. Ralph Royce, 18 April 1943
Maj.-Gen. Frank O. Hunter, 17 September 1943
Maj.-Gen. Robert W. Douglass Jr, 20 October 1945

2nd Air Force, US ZOI

This Air Force was constituted as Northwest Air
District on 19 October 1940, and activated on 18
December 1940. Re-designated 2nd Air Force early in
1941, it served as both an air defence and a training
organization during 1941. Afterwards it was engaged
chiefly in training units and replacements for heavy,
and later, very heavy bombing operations.

Stations
McChord Field, Washington State, 18 December 1940
Fort George Wright, Washington State, 9 January 1941
Colorado Springs, Colorado, June 1943–30 March 1946

Commands
II Air Support, 1941–3
II Bomber, September 1941–October 1943
II Fighter, 1941–2
IV Air Support, 1942–3
XX (formerly I) Bomber, 1 May 1943–1 October 1943 (XX Bomber
constituted 19 November 1943 and activated next day, moving to India in
1944, where it was assigned to the 20th AF)
XXI Bomber, 1 March 1944–late 1944 (moving to the Marianas and being
assigned to the 20th AF for VLR bombing operations until mid-July 1945)
XXII Bomber, August 1944–13 February 1945

2nd AF commanders
Maj.-Gen. John F. Curry, 18 December 1940
Maj.-Gen. Millard F. Harmon, 5 August 1941
Maj.-Gen. John B. Brooks, 19 December 1941
Maj.-Gen. Frederick L. Martin, 1 February 1942
Maj.-Gen. Robert Olds, 14 May 1942
Maj.-Gen. Davenport Johnson, 25 February 1943
Maj.-Gen. St Clair Streett, 9 September 1943
Maj.-Gen. Uzal G. Ent, 15 January 1944
Maj.-Gen. Robert B. Williams, 28 October 1944
Brig.-Gen. Julius K. Lacey, 21 November 1945

3rd Air Force, Antisubmarine, US ZOI

This Air Force was constituted as Southeast Air District on 19 October 1940, and activated on 18 December 1940. Re-designated 3rd Air Force early in 1941, it trained units, crews and individuals for bombardment, fighter and reconnaissance operations. It also had some air defence responsibilities during 1940–1, and engaged in anti-submarine activities from December 1941 to October 1942.

Stations
MacDill Field, Florida, 18 December 1940
Tampa, Florida, January 1941
Greenville AAB, South Carolina, 21 March–1 November 1946

Commands
II Air Support, 1943
III Air Support, September 1941–16 March 1942
III Bomber, September 1941–6
III Fighter (Interceptor, 26 May 1941–May 1942), 1941–6
III Reconnaissance (formerly I Ground Air Support), 1942–6
III Tactical Air, 1942–6

3rd AF commanders
Maj.-Gen. Barton K. Yount, 18 December 1940
Maj.-Gen. Lewis H. Brereton, 29 July 1941
Maj.-Gen. Walter H. Frank, 6 October 1941
Maj.-Gen. Caryle H. Wash, 25 June–26 November 1942
Maj.-Gen. St Clair Streett, 12 December 1942
Maj.-Gen. Westside T. Larson, 11 September 1943
Brig.-Gen. Edmund C. Lynch, 14 May 1945
Brig.-Gen. Thomas W. Blackburn, 26 May 1945
Lt.-Gen. Lewis H. Brereton, 1 July 1945

4th Air Force, US ZOI

This Air Force was constituted as Southwest Air District on 19 October 1940, and activated on 18 December 1940. Re-designated 4th Air Force early in 1941, it provided air defence for the western USA until 1943, and at the same time trained new organizations. Later, it was engaged primarily in training replacements for combat units.

Stations
March Field, California, 18 December 1940
Riverside, California, 16 January 1941

Hamilton Field, California, 7 December 1941
San Francisco, California, 5 January 1942–18 June 1946

Commands
IV Bomber, September 1941–31 March 1944
IV Fighter (Interceptor until May 1942), 1941–31 March 1944 (Wings: Los Angeles Fighter, 1942–4; Seattle Fighter, 1942–4; San Diego Fighter, 1942–4; San Francisco Fighter, 1942-4)
IV Ground Air Support: 1941–2

4th AF commanders
Maj.-Gen. Jacob E. Fickel, 18 December 1940
Maj.-Gen. George C. Kenney, 2 April 1942
Maj.-Gen. Barney M. Giles, 22 July 1942
Maj.-Gen. William E. Kepner, 18 March 1943
Maj.-Gen. William E. Lynd, 8 July 1943
Maj.-Gen. James E. Parker, 14 July 1943
Brig.-Gen. Edward M. Morris, 19 May 1945
Maj.-Gen. Willis H. Hale, 6 July 1945

5th Air Force

This Air Force operated in the Philippine Islands; East Indies; Air Offensive, Japan; China Defensive; Papua New Guinea; Northern Solomons; Bismarck Archipelago; western Pacific; Leyte; Luzon; southern Philippines, and the China Offensive.

It was constituted as the Philippine Department Air Force on 16 August 1941, and activated in the Philippines on 20 September 1941. Re-designated Far East Air Force in October 1941, and 5th Air Force in February 1942, it lost most of its men and equipment in the defence of the Philippines after 7 December 1941. Later that same month, its headquarters and some crews and aircraft moved to Australia, and in January 1942 they were sent to Java to help delay Japanese advances in the Dutch East Indies. The 5th did not function as an Air Force for some time after February 1942 (the AAF organizations in the south-west Pacific being under the control of US-British-Dutch-Australian Command, and later, Allied Air Forces). Its headquarters was re-manned in September 1942, and assumed control of AAF organizations in Australia and New Guinea. The 5th AF participated in operations that stopped the Japanese drive in Papua, recovered New Guinea, neutralized islands in the Bismarck Archipelago and the Dutch East Indies, and liberated the Philippines. When the war ended in August 1945, elements of the 5th AF were moving to the Ryukyus for the invasion of Japan.

Stations
Nichols Field, Luzon, Philippines, 20 September 1941
Darwin, Australia, December 1941
Java, January–February 1942
Brisbane, Australia, 3 September 1942
Nadzab, New Guinea, 15 June 1944
Owi, Schouten Islands, 10 August 1944
Leyte, Philippines *c.* 20 November 1944
Mindoro, Philippines, January 1945
Clark Field, Luzon, Philippines, April 1945
Okinawa, Japan, July 1945
Irumagawa, Japan, *c.* 25 September 1945

Commands
V Bomber, 28 October 1941–6
V Fighter, August 1942–6 (Groups: 3rd Air Commando, 1944–5; 8th Fighter, 1942–6; 35th Fighter, 1942–5; 38th Bombardment, 1945–6; 49th Fighter, 1942–5; 54th Fighter, 1941; 55th Fighter, 1941; 58th Fighter, 1943–5; 312th Bombardment, 1943–4; 348th Fighter, 1943–5; 475th Fighter, 1943–5)

5th AF commanders
Brig.-Gen. Henry B. Clagett, 20 September 1941
Maj.-Gen. Lewis H. Brereton, October 1941–February 1942
Lt.-Gen. George C. Kenney, 3 September 1942
Lt.-Gen. Ennis C. Whitehead, 15 June 1944
Maj.-Gen. Kenneth B. Wolfe, 4 October 1945

Bombardment and fighter group assignments, 5th Air Force, 1944–5

5th AIR FORCE

FIGHTER GROUPS	NIGHT FIGHTER GROUP	BOMB GROUPS	RECCE AND PHOTO GROUPS	TRANSPORT GROUPS
	(P-61s)	3rd BG		
35th FG	418th NFS	19th BG	6th RCN	374th TC
49th FG	421st NFS	43rd BG	71st RCN	317th TC
8th FG	547th NFS	38th BG	(Tactical)	375th TC
348th FG		22nd BG		433rd TC
475th FG		90th BG		2nd CC
		380th BG		
		345th BG		
		312th BG		
		417th BG		

6th Air Force, Antisubmarine, US ZOI

This Air Force was constituted as the Panama Canal Air Force on 19 October 1940, and activated in the Canal Zone on 20 November 1940. Re-designated Caribbean Air Force in August 1941, and 6th Air Force in February 1942, it served primarily in defence of the Panama Canal. It also engaged in antisubmarine operations.

Stations
Albrook Field, Canal Zone, 20 November 1940

Commands
VI Bomber, October 1941–6 (Groups: 6th, 1941–3; 9th, 1941–2; 25th, 1941–4; 40th, 1941–3)
VI Fighter, 1941–2
XXVI Fighter, 1942–6
XXXVI Fighter, 1942

6th AF commanders
Maj.-Gen. Frank M. Andrews, 6 December 1940
Maj.-Gen. Davenport Johnson, 19 September 1941
Maj.-Gen. Hubert R. Harmon, 23 November 1942
Brig.-Gen. Ralph H. Wooten, 8 November 1943
Brig.-Gen. Edgar P. Sorensen, 16 May 1944
Maj.-Gen. William O. Butler, 21 September 1944
Brig.-Gen. Earl H. De Ford, 24 July 1945–January 1946

7th Air Force

This Air Force operated in the central Pacific; Air Offensive, Japan; Eastern mandates; western Pacific; Ryukyus, and the China Offensive.

It was constituted as the Hawaiian Air Force on 19 October 1940, and activated in Hawaii on 1 November 1940. Re-designated 7th Air Force in February 1942, it provided air defence for the Hawaiian Islands and, after mid-1943, served in combat in the central and western Pacific areas. It was transferred back to Hawaii in January 1946.

Stations
Fort Shafter, Hawaii, 1 November 1940
Hickam Field, Hawaii, *c.* 12 July 1941
Saipan, 13 December 1944
Okinawa, Japan, 14 July–December 1945

B-24J of the 11th BG, 7th AF, over the swaying palms of Makin Island shortly before the arrival of the first group of fighter planes at new bases on the islands. (USAF)

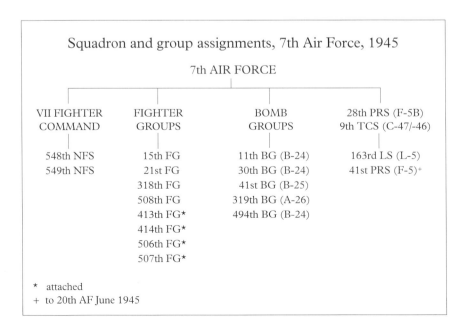

Squadron and group assignments, 7th Air Force, 1945

7th AIR FORCE

VII FIGHTER COMMAND	FIGHTER GROUPS	BOMB GROUPS	28th PRS (F-5B) 9th TCS (C-47/-46)
548th NFS	15th FG	11th BG (B-24)	163rd LS (L-5)
549th NFS	21st FG	30th BG (B-24)	41st PRS (F-5)+
	318th FG	41st BG (B-25)	
	508th FG	319th BG (A-26)	
	413th FG★	494th BG (B-24)	
	414th FG★		
	506th FG★		
	507th FG★		

★ attached
+ to 20th AF June 1945

Commands

VII Bomber, 23 January 1942–6 (Groups: 5th, 1942; 11th, 1942–5; 30th, 1943–5; 41st, 1943–5; 307th, 1942–3; 312th, 1945; 345th, 1945; 380th, 1945; 494th, 1944–5)

VII Fighter (Interceptor Command until May 1942), May 1942–5 (Groups: 15th, 1942–5; 18th, 1942–3; 21st, 1944–6; 318th, 1942–5)

7th AF commanders

Maj.-Gen. Frederick L. Martin, 2 November 1940
Maj.-Gen. Clarence L. Tinker, 18 December 1941
Brig.-Gen. Howard C. Davidson, 9 June 1942
Maj.-Gen. Willis H. Hale, 20 June 1942
Maj.-Gen. Robert W. Douglass Jr, 15 April 1944
Maj.-Gen. Thomas D. White, 23 June 1945–September 1946

8th Air Force (originally VIII Bomber Command)

This Air Force operated in the Air Offensive, Europe; Normandy; northern France; Rhineland; Ardennes–Alsace; central Europe, and the Asiatic-Pacific theatre.

It was constituted as VIII Bomber Command on 19 January 1942, and activated at Savannah AAB, Georgia, on 28 January 1942. An advanced detachment was established in England on 23 February, and units began arriving from the USA during the spring of 1942. The command conducted the heavy bombardment operations of the 8th Air Force from 17 August 1942 until early in 1944. Re-designated US Strategic Air Forces in Europe on 22 February 1944, afterwards it engaged primarily in bombardment of strategic targets in Europe. It was transferred, without personnel, equipment and combat elements, to Okinawa, Japan, on 16 July 1945. Although some personnel and combat units were assigned before VJ Day, the 8th AF did not participate in combat against Japan.

Stations

Langley Field, Virginia, 1 February 1942
Savannah AAB, Georgia, *c.* 10 February 1942
Daws Hill, England, 23 February 1942
High Wycombe, England, 15 May 1942–16 July 1945
Okinawa, Japan, 16 July 1945–June 1946

Commands

VIII Air Support Command: April 1942–July 1943
VIII Fighter Command (Interceptor Command until May 1942), February 1942–6 (Wings: 6th Fighter, 1942–3; 65th, 1943–5; 66th, 1943–5; 67th, 1943–5)

GROUP ASSIGNMENTS, 8th AIR FORCE ENGLAND
6 JUNE 1943

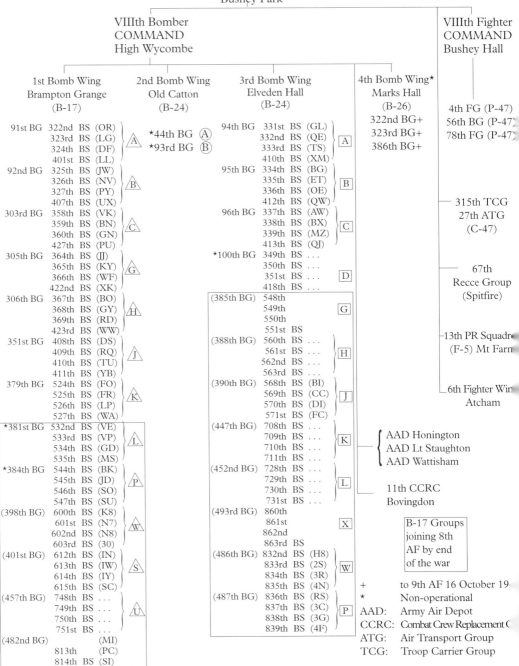

VIIIth AIR FORCE HQ
Bushey Park

VIIIth Bomber COMMAND
High Wycombe

VIIIth Fighter COMMAND
Bushey Hall

1st Bomb Wing
Brampton Grange
(B-17)

91st BG	322nd BS	(OR)
	323rd BS	(LG)
	324th BS	(DF)
	401st BS	(LL)
92nd BG	325th BS	(JW)
	326th BS	(NV)
	327th BS	(PY)
	407th BS	(UX)
303rd BG	358th BS	(VK)
	359th BS	(BN)
	360th BS	(GN)
	427th BS	(PU)
305th BG	364th BS	(JJ)
	365th BS	(KY)
	366th BS	(WF)
	422nd BS	(XK)
306th BG	367th BS	(BO)
	368th BS	(GY)
	369th BS	(RD)
	423rd BS	(WW)
351st BG	408th BS	(DS)
	409th BS	(RQ)
	410th BS	(TU)
	411th BS	(YB)
379th BG	524th BS	(FO)
	525th BS	(FR)
	526th BS	(LP)
	527th BS	(WA)
*381st BG	532nd BS	(VE)
	533rd BS	(VP)
	534th BS	(GD)
	535th BS	(MS)
*384th BG	544th BS	(BK)
	545th BS	(JD)
	546th BS	(SO)
	547th BS	(SU)
(398th BG)	600th BS	(K8)
	601st BS	(N7)
	602nd BS	(N8)
	603rd BS	(30)
(401st BG)	612th BS	(IN)
	613th BS	(IW)
	614th BS	(IY)
	615th BS	(SC)
(457th BG)	748th BS	…
	749th BS	…
	750th BS	…
	751st BS	…
(482nd BG)		(MI)
	813th	(PC)
	814th BS	(SI)

(△A) (△B) (△C) (△G) (△H) (△J) (△K) (△L) (△P) (△W) (△S) (△U)

2nd Bomb Wing
Old Catton
(B-24)

*44th BG Ⓐ
*93rd BG Ⓑ

3rd Bomb Wing
Elveden Hall
(B-24)

94th BG	331st BS	(GL)
	332nd BS	(QE)
	333rd BS	(TS)
	410th BS	(XM)
95th BG	334th BS	(BG)
	335th BS	(ET)
	336th BS	(OE)
	412th BS	(QW)
96th BG	337th BS	(AW)
	338th BS	(BX)
	339th BS	(MZ)
	413th BS	(QJ)
*100th BG	349th BS	…
	350th BS	…
	351st BS	…
	418th BS	…
(385th BG)	548th	
	549th	
	550th	
	551st BS	
(388th BG)	560th BS	…
	561st BS	…
	562nd BS	…
	563rd BS	…
(390th BG)	568th BS	(BI)
	569th BS	(CC)
	570th BS	(DI)
	571st BS	(FC)
(447th BG)	708th BS	…
	709th BS	…
	710th BS	…
	711th BS	…
(452nd BG)	728th BS	…
	729th BS	…
	730th BS	…
	731st BS	…
(493rd BG)	860th	
	861st	
	862nd	
	863rd BS	
(486th BG)	832nd BS	(H8)
	833rd BS	(2S)
	834th BS	(3R)
	835th BS	(4N)
(487th BG)	836th BS	(RS)
	837th BS	(3C)
	838th BS	(3G)
	839th BS	(4F)

□A □B □C □D □G □H □J □K □L □X □W □P

4th Bomb Wing★
Marks Hall
(B-26)

322nd BG+
323rd BG+
386th BG+

AAD Honington
AAD Lt Staughton
AAD Wattisham

11th CCRC
Bovingdon

B-17 Groups joining 8th AF by end of the war

VIIIth Fighter COMMAND
Bushey Hall

4th FG (P-47)
56th BG (P-47)
78th FG (P-47)

315th TCG
27th ATG
(C-47)

67th Recce Group
(Spitfire)

13th PR Squadron
(F-5) Mt Farm

6th Fighter Wing
Atcham

+   to 9th AF 16 October 19..
★   Non-operational
AAD: Army Air Depot
CCRC: Combat Crew Replacement C..
ATG: Air Transport Group
TCG: Troop Carrier Group

Group identification letters were displayed on aircraft tail and wings;
1st BW were indicated by △; 2nd BW by O; and 3rd BW by □.

Bomber Command components:
1st Bombardment Wing, 1942–3
2nd Bombardment Wing, 1942–3
3rd Bombardment Wing, 1942–3
4th Bombardment Wing, 1942–3
12th Bombardment Wing, 1942–4
1st Air Division, 1943–5
2nd Air Division, 1943–5
3rd Air Division, 1943–5

8th AF commanders
Maj.-Gen. Ira C. Eaker, 23 February 1942
Brig.-Gen. Newton Longfellow, 2 December 1942
Maj.-Gen. Frederick L. Anderson, 1 July 1943
Lt.-Gen. James H. Doolittle, 6 January 1944
Maj.-Gen. William E. Kepner, 10 May 1945
Maj.-Gen. Westside T. Larson, 21 June 1945
Lt.-Gen. James H. Doolittle, 19 July 1945
Maj.-Gen. Earle E. Patridge, 12 September 1945
Brig.-Gen. Patrick W. Timberlake, 30 November 1945

9th Air Force

This Air Force served in the US ZOI; air combat, EAME theatre; Egypt–Libya; Air Offensive, Europe; Tunisia; Sicily; Naples–Foggia; Normandy; northern France; Rhineland; Ardennes–Alsace, and central Europe.

It was constituted as V Air Support Command on 21 August 1941, and activated on 1 September 1941. Re-designated 9th Air Force in April 1942, it moved to Egypt and began operations on 12 November 1942, participating in the Allied drive across Egypt and Libya, the campaign in Tunisia, and the invasions of Sicily and Italy. It moved to England in October 1943 to become the tactical Air Force for the invasion of the Continent. It helped prepare for the assault on Normandy, supported operations on the beachhead in June 1944, and took part in the drive that carried the Allies across France and culminated in victory over Germany in May 1945. It was inactivated in Germany on 2 December 1945.

Stations
Bowman Field, Kentucky, 1 September 1941
New Orleans AAB, Louisiana, 24 January 1942
Bolling Field, DC, 22 July–October 1942
Egypt, 12 November 1942–October 1943
England, 16 October 1943–September 1944

A mix of solid-nosed and Plexiglas-nosed A-20Gs of the 668th Squadron, 416th BG, 9th AF. (USAF)

France, 15 September 1944
Germany, 6 June–2 December 1945

Commands
9th Air Division (formerly IX Bomber Command), 1942–5
IX Air Defence Command (71st Fighter Wing), 19 June 1944–6
IX Fighter Command, 1942–5 (Wings: 8th Fighter, 1942–3; 9th, 1942–3; 70th, 1943–4; 71st, 1943–4; 84th, 1944–5; 100th, 1943–4; 303rd, 1944–5)
IX Tactical Air Command, December 1943–October 1945 (Wings: 70th Fighter, 1944–5; 71st, 1944; 84th, 1944; 100th, 1944)
IX Troop Carrier Command, 16 October 1943–5 (Wings: 50th, 1943–5; 52nd, 1944–5; 53rd, 1944–5)
XIX Tactical Air Command, 4 January 1944–5 (Wings: 100th Fighter, 1944–5; 303rd Fighter, 1944)
XXIX Tactical Air Command, 1945

9th AF commanders

Brig.-Gen. Julius W. Jones, September 1941
Col. Rosenham Beam, 1942
Lt.-Gen. Lewis H. Brereton, 12 November 1942
Lt.-Gen. Hoyt S. Vandenburg, 8 August 1944
Maj.-Gen. Otto P. Weyland, 23 May 1945
Maj.-Gen. William E. Kepner, 4 August–2 December 1945

10th Air Force

This Air Force operated in Burma, 1942; India–Burma; the China Defensive; central Burma, and the China Offensive.

It was constituted as the 10th Air Force on 4 February 1942, and activated on 12 February. It moved to India during March–May 1942. It served in India, Burma and China until March 1943, when the 14th Air Force was activated in China. Then the 10th AF operated in India and Burma until it moved to China late in July 1945. It returned to the USA during December 1945–January 1946.

Groups
3rd Combat Cargo, 1944–5
7th Bombardment, 1942–5
12th Bombardment, 1944–5
33rd Fighter, 1944–5
80th Fighter, 1943–5
311th Fighter, 1943–4
341st Bombardment, 1942–4
443rd Troop Carrier, 1944–5

Stations
Patterson Field, Ohio, 12 February–8 March 1942
New Delhi, India, 16 May 1942
Myitkyina, Burma, 2 November 1944
Piardoba, India, 15 May 1945
Kunming, China, 1 August 1945
Liuchow, China, 9 August–15 December 1945
Fort Lawton, Washington State, 5–6 January 1946

10th AF commanders
Col. Harry A. Halverson, 17 February 1942
Maj.-Gen. Lewis H. Brereton, 5 March 1942
Brig.-Gen. Earl L. Naiden, 26 June 1942
Maj.-Gen. Clayton L. Bissell, 18 August 1942
Maj.-Gen. Howard C. Davidson, 19 August 1943
Maj.-Gen. Albert F. Hegenberger, 1 August 1945

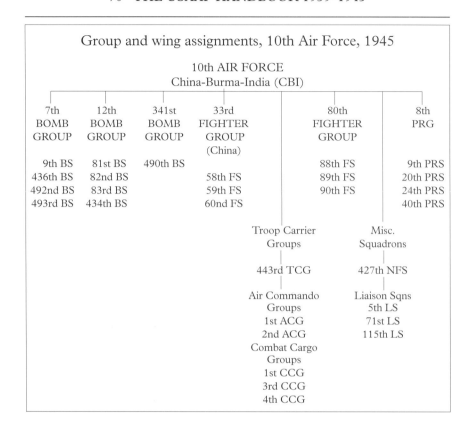

Group and wing assignments, 10th Air Force, 1945

10th AIR FORCE
China-Burma-India (CBI)

7th BOMB GROUP	12th BOMB GROUP	341st BOMB GROUP	33rd FIGHTER GROUP (China)		80th FIGHTER GROUP	8th PRG
9th BS	81st BS	490th BS			88th FS	9th PRS
436th BS	82nd BS		58th FS		89th FS	20th PRS
492nd BS	83rd BS		59th FS		90th FS	24th PRS
493rd BS	434th BS		60nd FS			40th PRS

Troop Carrier Groups
443rd TCG

Air Commando Groups
1st ACG
2nd ACG
Combat Cargo Groups
1st CCG
3rd CCG
4th CCG

Misc. Squadrons
427th NFS

Liaison Sqns
5th LS
71st LS
115th LS

7th BG B-24 Liberator passes over Bilin, Burma, after an attack on 13 November 1944. The 7th BG was the only US Liberator group in Burma, and served with the Strategic Air Force. (USAF)

11th Air Force

This Air Force operated in the Air Offensive, Japan, and the Aleutian Islands.

It was constituted as the Alaskan Air Force on 28 December 1941, and activated in Alaska on 15 January 1942. Re-designated 11th Air Force in February 1942, it participated in the offensive that drove the Japanese from the Aleutians, attacked the enemy in the Kurile Islands and, both during and after the war, served as part of the defence force for Alaska. It was re-designated Alaskan Air Command in December 1945.

Stations
Elmendorf Field, Alaska, 15 January 1942
Adak, Alaska, 10 August 1943–September 1946

Commands
XI Bomber, March 1943–March 1944 (Groups: 28th Composite, 1943–4)
XI Fighter (Interceptor Command until May 1942), March 1942–March 1944 (Groups: 343rd 1942–4)

11th AF commanders
Lt.-Col. Everett S. Davis, 15 January 1942
Col. Lionel H. Dunlap, 17 February 1942
Maj.-Gen. William O. Butler, 8 March 1942
Maj.-Gen. Davenport Johnson, 13 September 1943
Brig.-Gen. Isaiah Davies, 4 May 1945
Maj.-Gen. John B. Brooks, 22 June 1945
Brig.-Gen. Edmund C. Lynch, 21 December 1945–September 1946

12th Air Force

This Air Force operated in air combat, EAME theatre; Algeria–French Morocco; Tunisia; Sicily; Naples–Foggia; Anzio; Rome–Arno; southern France; north Appennines, and the Po Valley.

It was constituted as the 12th Air Force on 20 August 1942, and activated the same day. It moved to England during August–September 1942, and then on to North Africa for the invasion of Algeria and French Morocco (Operation TORCH) in November 1942. It operated in the Mediterranean theatre until the end of the war, serving with the Northwest African Air Forces from February to December 1943, and afterwards with the Mediterranean Allied Air Forces. It was inactivated in Italy on 31 August 1945.

Stations

Bolling Field, DC, 20–28 August 1942
England, 12 September–22 October 1942
Algeria, 9 November 1942
Tunisia, 10 August 1943
Italy, 5 December 1943–31 August 1945

Commands

XII Bomber, March 1942–June 1944 (Wings: 5th, 1943; 42nd, 1943–4; 47th, formerly 7th Fighter, 1943; 57th, 1944)
XII Tactical Air, 1942–4 (Wings: 5th Bombardment, 1942; 7th Fighter, 1942; 42nd Bombardment, 1945; 57th Bombardment, 1943–4; 63rd Fighter, 1945; 64th Fighter, formerly 3rd Air Defence, 1943–5; 70th Fighter, 1945; 71st Fighter, 1945; 87th Fighter, 1944)
XXII Tactical Air (formerly XII Fighter), 1942–5

12th AF commanders

Lt.-Col. Roger J. Browne, 26 August 1942
Lt.-Col. Harold L. Neely, 28 August 1942
Maj.-Gen. James H. Doolittle, 23 September 1942
Lt.-Gen. Carl A. Spaatz, 1 March 1943
Lt.-Gen. John K. Cannon, 21 December 1943
Maj.-Gen. Benjamin W. Chidlaw, 2 April 1945
Brig.-Gen. Charles T. Myers, 26 May–31 August 1945

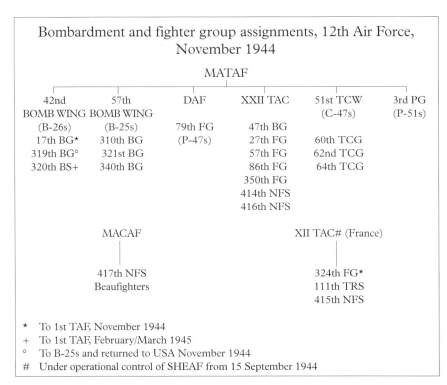

Bombardment and fighter group assignments, 12th Air Force, November 1944

MATAF

42nd BOMB WING (B-26s)	57th BOMB WING (B-25s)	DAF	XXII TAC	51st TCW (C-47s)	3rd PG (P-51s)
17th BG★	310th BG	79th FG (P-47s)	47th BG		
319th BG°	321st BG		27th FG	60th TCG	
320th BS+	340th BG		57th FG	62nd TCG	
			86th FG	64th TCG	
			350th FG		
			414th NFS		
			416th NFS		

MACAF

417th NFS
Beaufighters

XII TAC# (France)

324th FG★
111th TRS
415th NFS

★   To 1st TAF, November 1944
+   To 1st TAF, February/March 1945
°   To B-25s and returned to USA November 1944
Under operational control of SHEAF from 15 September 1944

13th Air Force

This Air Force operated in the China Defensive; Guadalcanal, Solomon Islands; New Guinea; northern Solomons; Eastern mandates; Bismarck Archipelago; western Pacific; Leyte, Philippines; Luzon, Philippines; southern Philippines, and the China Offensive.

It was constituted as the 13th Air Force on 14 December 1942, and activated in New Caledonia on 13 January 1943. It served in the south Pacific and, later, south-west Pacific, participating in the Allied drive north and west from the Solomons to the Philippines. It remained in the Philippines, as part of the Far East Air Forces, after the war.

Stations

New Caledonia, 13 January 1943
Espiritu Santo, Mexico, 21 January 1943
Guadalcanal, Solomon Islands, 13 January 1944
Los Negros, 15 June 1944
Hollandia, New Guinea, 13 September 1944
Noemfoor, 23 September 1944
Morotai, Indonesia, 29 October 1944
Leyte, Philippines, 1 March 1945

Group and wing assignments, 13th Air Force, 1943

13th AIR FORCE

11th BOMB GROUP* (B-17s)	5th BOMB GROUP+ (B-17s)	307th BOMB GROUP (B-24s)	42nd BOMB GROUP (B-25s)	347th FIGHTER GROUP (P-39 to P-38)	18th FIGHTER GROUP (P-39 to P-38)
26th BS	23rd BS	370th BS	69th BS	67th FS	6th FS#
42nd BS	31st BS	371st BS	70th BS	68th FS	12th FS
98th BS	72nd BS	372nd BS	75th BS	70th FS	44th FS
431st BS	394th BS	424th BS	390th BS	339th FS	70th FS
					40th PRS
					419th FS°

403rd
TROOP CARRIER
GROUP
(C-47)
13th TCS
63rd TCS

4th
PHOTO GROUP
(F-5/B-25)
17th PRS
18th PMS/CMS

*   to 7th AF 1943
+   to B-24s in 1944
°   419th NFS (P-38 to P-61) from late 1943
Det 'B' 6th NFS to 7th Air Force September 1943

Commands

XIII Bomber, 13 January 1943–6 (Groups: 5th, 1943–6; 11th, 1943; 42nd, 1943–5; 307th, 1943–5)

XIII Fighter, 13 January 1943–6 (Groups: 18th, 1943–6, 347th, 1943–5)

13th AF commanders

Maj.-Gen. Nathan F. Twining, 13 January 1943

Brig.-Gen. Ray L. Owens, 27 July 1943

Maj.-Gen. Hubert R. Harmon, 7 January 1944

Maj.-Gen. St Clair Streett, 15 June 1944

Maj.-Gen. Paul B. Wurtsmith, 19 February 1945–June 1946

14th Air Force

This Air Force operated in India–Burma; the China Defensive, and the China Offensive.

It was constituted as the 14th Air Force on 5 March 1943, and activated in China on 10 March. It served in combat against the Japanese, operating primarily in China, until the end of the war.

Wings

68th Composite, 1943–5

69th Composite, 1943–5

312th Fighter, 1944–5

Stations

Kunming, China, 10 March 1943

Peishiyi, China, 7 August–15 December 1945

14th AF commanders

Maj.-Gen. Claire L. Chennault, 10 March 1943

Maj.-Gen. Charles B. Stone III, 10 August 1945–31 December 1945

Final bombardment and fighter group assignments, 14th Air Force, Pacific, 1945					
14TH AIR FORCE					
308th BOMB GROUP (B-24s)	341st BOMB GROUP (B-25s)	23rd FIGHTER GROUP (P-51s)	51st FIGHTER GROUP (P-51s)	81st FIGHTER GROUP (P-47s)	311th FIGHTER GROUP (P-51s)
373rd BS	11th BS	74th FS	16th FS	91st FS	528th FS
374th BS	22nd BS	75th BS	25th FS	92nd FS	529th FS
375th BS	491st BS	76th BS	26th FS	93rd FS	530th FS
425th BS		118th TRS	449th FS★		
426th NFS (P-61s)		322nd TCS (C-47s)		21st PRS (F-5s)	27th TCS (C-47s)
★ P-38 Lightnings					

15th Air Force

This Air Force operated in air combat, EAME theatre; Air Offensive, Europe; Naples–Foggia; Anzio; Rome–Arno; Normandy; northern France; southern France; north Appennines; Rhineland; central Europe, and the Po Valley.

It was constituted as the 15th Air Force on 30 October 1943, and activated in the Mediterranean theatre on 1 November 1943. It began operations on 2 November, and engaged primarily in strategic bombing of targets in Italy, France, Germany, Poland, Czechoslovakia, Austria, Hungary and the Balkans until the end of the war. It was inactivated in Italy on 15 September 1945.

Wings

5th Bombardment, 1943–5
42nd Bombardment, 1943
47th Bombardment, 1944–5
49th Bombardment, 1944–5
55th Bombardment, 1944–5
304th Bombardment, 1943–5
305th Bombardment, 1943–5
306th Fighter, 1944–5
307th Bombardment, 1944

B-17Gs of the 463rd BG, 15th AF, accompanied by a P-38 Lightning with its starboard engine feathered. (USAF)

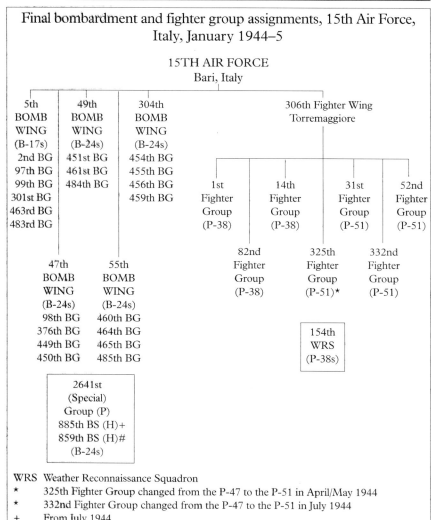

Final bombardment and fighter group assignments, 15th Air Force, Italy, January 1944–5

WRS Weather Reconnaissance Squadron
★   325th Fighter Group changed from the P-47 to the P-51 in April/May 1944
★   332nd Fighter Group changed from the P-47 to the P-51 in July 1944
+   From July 1944
#   From January 1945 (when 2641st (Special) Group (Provisional) was activated)

Stations
Tunis, Tunisia, 1 November 1943
Bari, Italy, 1 December 1943–15 September 1945

15th AF commanders
Maj.-Gen. James H. Doolittle, 1 November 1943
Maj.-Gen. Nathan F. Twining, 3 January 1944
Brig.-Gen. James A. Mollison, 26 May 1945

20th Air Force

This Air Force operated in the US ZOI; India–Burma; Air Offensive, Japan; China Defensive; Eastern mandates; western Pacific, and central Burma.

It was constituted as the 20th Air Force on 4 April 1944, and activated the same day. In the summer of 1944 some combat elements moved from the USA to India, where they carried out very heavy bombardment operations against targets in Japan, Formosa, Thailand and Burma. Late in 1944 other combat elements began moving from the USA to the Marianas, being joined there early in 1945 by the elements that had been in India. Its headquarters, which had remained in the USA, transferred to Guam in July 1945. From the Marianas, the 20th AF conducted a strategic air offensive that climaxed in the dropping of two atomic bombs on Japan in August 1945.

Stations
Washington, DC, 4 April 1944
Harmon Field, Guam, 16 July 1945

Commands
VII Fighter, 1945
XX Bomber, early 1944–March 1945 (Wings: 58th, 1943–5; 73rd, 1943–4)
XXI Bomber, late 1944–16 July 1945 (Wings: 58th, 1945; 73rd, 1944–5; 313th, 1944–5; 314th, 1944–5; 315th, 1945)

20th AF commanders
General of the Army Henry H. Arnold, 6 April 1944
Maj.-Gen. Curtis E. LeMay, 16 July 1945
Lt.-Gen. Nathan F. Twining, 2 August 1945

US Strategic Air Forces in Europe

These forces operated in air combat, EAME theatre; Air Offensive, Europe; Normandy; northern France; Rhineland; Ardennes–Alsace, and central Europe.

On 4 January 1944 heavy bombers of the 8th Air Force flew their last mission under the command of the 8th AF. The 8th and the 15th AFs were merged into a new headquarters called US Strategic Air Forces, Europe (the overall USAAF command organization in Europe) at Bushey Hall, Teddington, Middlesex, previously HQ of the 8th AF. Gen. Carl 'Tooey' Spaatz returned to England to command the new organization, which was re-designated USSTAFE on 22 February 1944, while Maj.-Gen. Jimmy Doolittle took command of the 8th AF, its HQ moving to High Wycombe. Lt.-Gen. Ira C. Eaker was transferred to the Mediterranean theatre to take command of the new Mediterranean Allied Air Forces. USSTAFE co-ordinated AAF activities in the EAME theatre, exercising some operational control over both the 8th AF (originally VIII Bomber Command) and the 15th, and some administrative control over the 8th and 9th AFs. It served with the occupation forces in Europe after the Second World War. It was re-designated United States Air Force in Europe in August 1945.

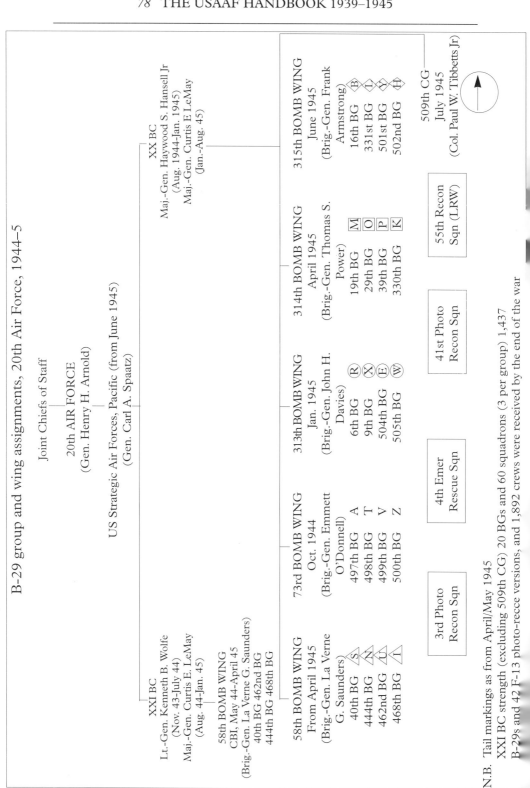

B-29 group and wing assignments, 20th Air Force, 1944–5

Joint Chiefs of Staff

20th AIR FORCE
(Gen. Henry H. Arnold)

US Strategic Air Forces, Pacific (from June 1945)
(Gen. Carl A. Spaatz)

XX BC
Maj.-Gen. Haywood S. Hansell Jr
(Aug. 1944-Jan. 1945)
Maj.-Gen. Curtis E LeMay
(Jan.-Aug. 45)

XXI BC
Lt.-Gen. Kenneth B. Wolfe
(Nov. 43-July 44)
Maj.-Gen. Curtis E. LeMay
(Aug. 44-Jan. 45)

58th BOMB WING
CBI, May 44-April 45
(Brig.-Gen. La Verne G. Saunders)
40th BG 462nd BG
444th BG 468th BG

58th BOMB WING
From April 1945
(Brig.-Gen. La Verne
G. Saunders)

40th BG	S
444th BG	N
462nd BG	U
468th BG	I

73rd BOMB WING
Oct. 1944
(Brig.-Gen. Emmett
O'Donnell)

497th BG	A
498th BG	T
499th BG	V
500th BG	Z

313th BOMB WING
Jan. 1945
(Brig.-Gen. John H.
Davies)

6th BG	R
9th BG	X
504th BG	E
505th BG	W

314th BOMB WING
April 1945
(Brig.-Gen. Thomas S.
Power)

19th BG	M
29th BG	O
39th BG	P
330th BG	K

315th BOMB WING
June 1945
(Brig.-Gen. Frank
Armstrong)

16th BG	B
331st BG	I
501st BG	Y
502nd BG	H

509th CG
July 1945
(Col. Paul W. Tibbetts Jr)

3rd Photo
Recon Sqn

4th Emer
Rescue Sqn

41st Photo
Recon Sqn

55th Recon
Sqn (LRW)

N.B. Tail markings as from April/May 1945
XXI BC strength (excluding 509th CG) 20 BGs and 60 squadrons (3 per group) 1,437
B-29s and 42 F-13 photo-recce versions, and 1,892 crews were received by the end of the war

Stations
Bushey Hall, London, January 1944
St. Germain-en-Laye, France, 26 September 1944
Wiesbaden, Germany, *c.* 28 September 1945

Commands
VIII Air Support, 1942–3
VIII Bomber, 1942–4
VIII Fighter, 1942–4

USSTAFE commanders
Gen. Carl A. Spaatz, 6 January 1944
Lt.-Gen. John K. Cannon, 3 June 1945
Gen. Carl A. Spaatz, 13 June 1945
Lt.-Gen. John K. Cannon, 4 July 1945

Far East Air Forces

These forces were constituted as a provisional command on 31 July 1944, and reconstituted as a regular unit and activated on 3 August 1944 to control the operations of the 5th and 13th Air Forces.

Stations
Brisbane, Australia, 5 August 1944
Hollandia, New Guinea, 16 September 1944
Fort McKinley, Philippines, 20 March 1945

FEAF commanders
Lt.-Gen. George C. Kenney, 31 July 1944–1945

Continental Air Forces

These forces were constituted on 13 December 1944, and activated on 15 December as an element to control the activities of all numbered Air Forces that remained in the USA during the war.

Stations
Washington DC, 13 December 1944–1945

Commands
1st Air Force, 13 December 1944–1945
2nd Air Force, 13 December 1944–1945
3rd Air Force, 13 December 1944–1945
4th Air Force, 13 December 1944–1945

Continental air forces commanders
Brig.-Gen. E.H. Beene, 15 December 1944
Maj.-Gen. St Clair Streett, 1 March 1945
General of the Army Henry H. Arnold, 1 July 1945

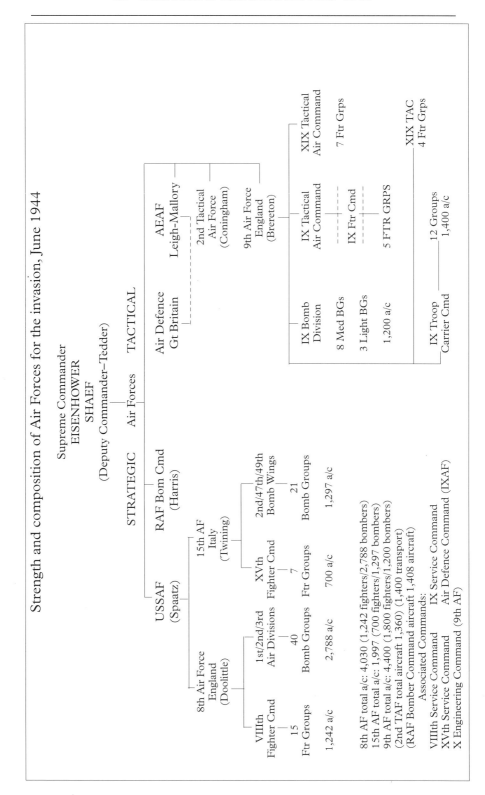

Strength and composition of Air Forces for the invasion, June 1944

Supreme Commander
EISENHOWER
SHAEF
(Deputy Commander–Tedder)

Air Forces

STRATEGIC   TACTICAL

USSAF
(Spaatz)

RAF Bom Cmd
(Harris)

Air Defence
Gt Britain

AEAF
Leigh-Mallory

2nd Tactical
Air Force
(Coningham)

9th Air Force
England
(Brereton)

8th Air Force
England
(Doolittle)

15th AF
Italy
(Twining)

VIIIth
Fighter Cmd

1st/2nd/3rd
Air Divisions

XVth
Fighter Cmd

2nd/47th/49th
Bomb Wings

15
Ftr Groups

40
Bomb Groups

7
Ftr Groups

21
Bomb Groups

1,242 a/c

2,788 a/c

700 a/c

1,297 a/c

IX Bomb
Division

IX Tactical
Air Command

XIX Tactical
Air Command

8 Med BGs

IX Ftr Cmd

3 Light BGs

5 FTR GRPS

7 Ftr Grps

1,200 a/c

IX Troop
Carrier Cmd

XIX TAC

12 Groups
1,400 a/c

4 Ftr Grps

8th AF total a/c: 4,030 (1,242 fighters/2,788 bombers)
15th AF total a/c: 1,997 (700 fighters/1,297 bombers)
9th AF total a/c: 4,400 (1,800 fighters/1,200 bombers)
(2nd TAF total aircraft 1,360) (1,400 transport)
(RAF Bomber Command aircraft 1,408 aircraft)
    Associated Commands:
VIIIth Service Command   IX Service Command
XVth Service Command   Air Defence Command (IXAF)
X Engineering Command (9th AF)

CHAPTER FIVE

US Flight Training

In the AAFs more than 500 separate skills were reckoned to contribute to the success of a routine bombing mission. Therefore, training, in the little time available during wartime, was crucial. By early 1942 the bulk of the training programme had been unified under two new commands: the Technical Training Command and the Flying Training Command. (As of 7 July 1943 the Flying Training Command and the Technical Training Command were reorganized and combined into the AAF Training Command. The functions of the new command were essentially those of the two it supplanted.) In June 1943 the War Department announced the creation of twelve Flying Training wings, to subdivide further the constantly mounting supervisory duties of officials in charge of the nation's programme for training pilots, bombardiers, navigators and gunners. Four wings were activated within each of the three training centres which made up the coast-to-coast span of Flying Training Command.

In 1942 Technical Training Command leased 68 civilian mechanics schools and increased the number of its own schools from 3 to 33. Within two years, 600,000 graduates were turned out. All personnel assigned to the AAF for aviation cadet training were given a five-week basic military course which included exhaustive physical, psychological and mental tests to determine their fitness for the flying programme and to ascertain the speciality for which they were best suited. After basic training, each man was ready to begin training in his speciality. The individual training schedule was divided into two major categories: Flying Training and Technical, Administrative and Service Training.

Flying Training Command had to construct sufficient airfields to train pilots, bombardiers and navigators. In 1939 plans were laid for training 1,200 pilots a year by 1941 (raised to 7,000 a year in 1940, and to 30,000 in 1941). The AAF itself could not accomplish this, and in the spring of 1939 Gen. Arnold, Chief of Staff, Army Air Corps, called in eight operators of civilian flying schools to Washington, DC. His plan was that the primary training phase of flight instruction should be placed with civilian-operated schools, where all services and facilities, except the aircraft, were furnished by the operator, but with AAF control of the methods and manner of the instruction. Arnold suggested to all of them that they become contractors with the Army to provide primary pilot training for 12,000 pilots per year. Like most businessmen in the USA at the time, they had been badly hit by the Depression, and the offer of government contracts met with unanimous approval.

The plan was successful, with as many as forty of these schools scattered across the southern United States, from California to Georgia. An average of 600 potential pilots attended each school for the required nine weeks of instruction,

300 in each of the upper and lower classes of four-and-a-half weeks each. The early contracts provided that the Air Corps would pay $1,170 for each graduate of primary school, and pay $18 per hour of flight time for each eliminated cadet. This was to cover all costs that the contractor incurred in operating the school.

The flying training programme that Arnold recommended would take up to 36 weeks to complete, with 12 weeks each for *primary, basic,* and *advanced* pilot training (ultimately, these training sessions would be conducted in ten-week periods to save time). By 1944 the standard Air Corps programme for the minimum number of hours required to produce a qualified pilot was: Primary, 60 hours; Basic 70 hours; Advanced 75 hours – a total of 205 hours. Primary training was to consist of 225 hours of ground school instruction and 65 hours of flight training, to produce cadets who could fly single-engined, elementary aircraft. Most had never even driven a car before, let alone flown an aircraft, but they were expected to fly solo after six hours' tuition.

Potential pilots who reached the primary stage arrived via Classification and Pre-Flight Training. (College Training Detachments were established by the AAF early in 1943, and everyone entering the Aviation Cadet Programme from then until the end of the war was assigned to one of these detachments for a period of one to five months, depending on the scores achieved on a battery of tests administered at both Basic Training and at the College Training Detachment.) The AAF had four Classification and Pre-Flight Centres, at Nashville, Tennessee, Maxwell Field, Alabama, San Antonio, Texas, and Santa Ana, California. Classification consisted of general education tests, fifty questions per test, multiple-choice, physio-motor tests (to test co-ordination), and a 64 physical examination. Those who did not 'wash out' awaited cadet classification for pilot, navigator or bombardier pre-flight training.

Pre-flight training normally lasted between seven and ten weeks, depending on the various stages of the war, during which cadets daily attended academic classes, marched in formation, took part in PT and drill, pistol shooting, and aquatic training to learn ditching procedures. Cadet pilots studied armaments and gunnery, 30 hours were spent on sea and air recognition, 48 hours on codes, 24 hours on physics, 20 hours on mathematics and 18 hours on maps and charts.

Navigator and bombardier trainees attended the same pre-flight school, and they took 48 hours of codes, 28 hours of mathematics, 24 hours of maps and charts, 30 hours of aircraft recognition, 12 hours of naval recognition, 12 hours of principles of flight, 20 hours of aero-physics and 9 hours of altitude equipment training. All who were successful moved on to the next stage of flight training. Potential pilots were now given the chance to learn to fly.

Primary flying training

An average of 600 potential pilots attended each primary training school. They spent 60 hours in 125–225 hp PT-13/17 or PT-21/22 open-cockpit biplanes, or PT-19/23/26 low-wing monoplanes, 94 hours were devoted to academic work in ground school and 54 hours to military training. The standard primary school flight training was divided into four phases:

Pre-solo phase – general operation of a light aircraft, proficiency in landing techniques, and recovery from stalls and spins;

Second phase – pre-solo work review, and development of precision control by flying patterns such as elementary 8s, lazy 8s, pylon 8s and chandeles;

Third phase – developing high proficiency in landing approaches and landing;

Fourth Phase – aerobatics.

Of the total flight time, there was to be a maximum of 50 per cent dual time and a minimum of 40 per cent solo time. Each cadet had to make at least 175 landings.

Ground school

There were five major topics to be covered, for a total of 96 hours:

Aircraft and equipment – understanding the aircraft and how everything worked; this included engines and theory;

Navigation – preparation for cross-country flights;

Aircraft recognition – 'friendly' and hostile;

Principles of flight;

Radio codes and radio communication for pilots.

A link trainer was also available for the use of rated pilots, if they wished, and to allow cadets to begin learning about instrument flying.

There were no standard designs for primary schools, the aim being to get them started as soon as possible. The AAC representatives on base were to maintain constant supervision and inspections, to observe all phases of the cadets' training, and to pass judgement on the proficiency of the cadets. Every primary school contractor had to furnish all facilities – except for the aircraft and associated flying equipment, which the Air Corps furnished.

Those who soloed went on to basic flying training school. This was a ten-week course: 70 hours in a 450 hp BT-13/15 basic trainer (regarded by many as too easy to fly, and replaced by the AT-6 during the latter period of the war), 94 hours in ground school and 47 hours of military training. By the end of basic school, trainees would have learned to fly an aircraft competently. Further training taught them to fly a warplane the AAF way. Before the end of basic training, trainees were classified – on the basis of choice and instructors' reports – for single-engine training (fighter pilots) or twin-engine training (bomber, transport or twin-engined fighter pilots).

There were two final stages: advanced flying training and transition flying training.

Advanced flying training

This was a ten-week course (single-engine and twin engine), involving 70 hours flying; 60 hours ground school and 19 hours military training. Single-engine trainees flew 600 hp AT-6s and took a course in fixed gunnery. Twin-engine trainees flew AT-24s, AT-17s, AT-9s or AT-10s (later, AT-25

B-24D Liberators on a training flight early in the war. (USAF)

Mitchells were also used). Based on performance and choice, they were then earmarked for heavy or medium bombardment, transports, troop-carriers or twin-engined fighters.

At the end of advanced training, the graduates, single- and twin-engine, were awarded the silver pilot's wings of the AAF and appointed flight officers or commissioned as 2nd lieutenants.

Transition flying training

Before they began to train in units, pilots learned to fly the type of aircraft they would handle in combat. For example, those earmarked for B-26 assignment took a ten-week transition course, of which 105 hours were spent flying B-26s, and the rest in ground school. B-17 and B-24 pilots also received 105 hours of four-engine training and additional ground school training in a ten-week postgraduate transition course. Fighter pilots received a five-week transition course; single-engine pilots flew ten hours in P-40s; P-38 pilots received ten hours' training in P-322s (modified P-38s). Gunnery was part of fighter transition training.

At the conclusion of transition training, pilots reported to unit training groups, where they were welded into fighting teams.

Navigator and bombardier training

Because every bomber crew member had to be an expert gunner, navigator and bombardier, trainees were sent to a flexible gunnery school after pre-flight school.

Gunnery school

This was a six-week course in weapons, ballistics, turret operation and maintenance; gun repairs; air, sea and land recognition; shooting from a moving base and from a turret; firing from the air at ground objects, at towed targets, and at other aircraft with a gun camera.

After gunnery school, bombardier and navigator trainees separated, and each took a specialized advanced course.

Bombardier school

This was a twenty-week course. Following gunnery school, bombardier trainees spent 120 hours in AT-11 training aircraft in practice-bombing runs, and 718 hours in ground school. The latter consisted of navigation, 96 hours; bombing theory, 388 hours; and navigation, bombing and related training (codes, meteorology, air and sea recognition), 254 hours.

At the conclusion of the course, trainees were awarded bombardier's silver wings, appointed flight officers or commissioned as 2nd lieutenants, and sent on to unit training.

Navigator school

This was a twenty-week course. Following gunnery school, navigator trainees spent 104 hours in the air on practical navigation problems, and 782 hours in ground school. The latter included pilotage, 8 hours; instruments, 83 hours; dead reckoning, 54 hours; radio, 8 hours; celestial navigation, 53 hours; meteorology, 47 hours, and codes and recognition, 9 hours each.

Upon completing the course, trainees were awarded navigator's silver wings, appointed flight officers or commissioned as 2nd lieutenants, and sent on to unit training.

Bombardier-navigator school

This was a twelve-week course. Each month, a specified number of graduate navigators (180 per month on 1 March 1944) received full bombardier's training, excluding navigation, in which they were already proficient.

Bombardier-navigator training provided the dual-role officers needed for B-29s and for lead planes in medium-bomber missions.

Aircrew, enlisted men

All enlisted men in an aircrew were aerial gunners. At the end of the basic training period, men chosen to train as career gunners were eligible to enter the six-week gunnery school. Aeroplane armourer-gunner trainees took a twenty-week course in the operation and maintenance of aircraft armaments. Aircraft mechanic-gunner trainees took twenty-seven weeks training in aircraft inspection and maintenance. Radio operator mechanic gunner trainees received twenty weeks of combat crew radio operation and repair training.

At the conclusion of their technical training, specialist-gunner trainees were eligible to go to gunnery school.

Graduates

A total of 193,440 pilots graduated from AAF advanced flying training schools from 1 July 1939 to 31 August 1945.* The peak was in December 1943, when over 740,000 students were at various stages of individual pilot training. In 1941, 7,244 pilot, 601 navigator and 310 bombardier graduates were turned out by AAF schools. By 1943, 65,797 pilots, 15,928 navigators, 16,057 bombardiers, 91,595 gunners and 544,374 technicians had graduated from AAF schools. From 1939 to VJ Day, more than 124,000 students 'washed out' of pilot training (most were reassigned as navigators, bombardiers, etc.). By VJ Day more than 50,000 students had graduated from the specialized navigation schools. During 1941–5, 45,000 bombardiers graduated. In the same period, 297,000 officers and EM graduated from gunnery schools, and 7,600 radar observers and 7,800 flight engineers graduated; 2,000 reconnaissance crews were trained from 1943 until VJ Day. In the period December 1942–August 1945, 27,000 heavy bombardment crews (slightly more than half were B-24 crews), 6,000 medium bomber crews and 1,600 light bombardment crews were trained; 35,000 day-fighter crews, and 485 night-fighter crews, were trained from December 1942 to August 1945.

Unit and crew training

All fighter, bombardment, transport, reconnaissance and troop carrier units were supplied by the operational training unit programme (originally, medium, heavy and very heavy bombardment training took ninety days, with units being formed by breaking off 'cadres' or 'skeleton groups' from within the four domestic air forces). Simultaneously, a replacement unit training programme (ninety-day course) within the four domestic air forces provided replacements for overseas aircrew who had been lost in combat or rotated home for reassignment. By mid-1944 all air unit and crew training was RTU, except for B-29 groups (four months' training).

By late 1944 the policy of training for specific theatres of war was made standard. Certain Combat Crew Training Stations in the 3rd AF, for example, trained crews for operations against Japan. From late 1943 to 1945, 2,350 B-29 crews were trained by 2nd AF and AAF HQ (until late 1944, when B-29 crew training was transferred to Training Command). Pilot recruits for B-29 units had to have at least 300 hours (from 1944, 1,000 hours) four-engine flying experience at B-17 or B-24 transition schools or with four-engine combat groups. Co-pilots were new graduates of four-engine transition schools. Other members of the B-29 aircrew were two bombardier-navigators, an aerial engineering officer, a radio operator-mechanic and gunners.

---

* From May 1941 to the end of 1945, 21,302 airmen from 31 foreign nations graduated from flying and technical schools in the USA: 12,561 were British, 2,238 were Chinese, 4,113 French and 532 Dutch.

By mid-1944 single-seater pilots had to gain 120 hours (previously 60 hours) of flying experience in fighter and fighter-bomber RTU training. For reconnaissance, pilots with at least forty hours flying time in a P-38 took an eight-week course (Tactical Reconnaissance, sixty hours experience/six-week course). Complete F-7 (B-24) crews also received eight weeks training, learning photo-mapping. Night-fighter crews took a four-month OTU course. The ground complement joined the unit half-way through the course and trained with it for the final two months. Night-fighter RTUs – aircrew only – trained for five months.

Troop carrier training

By mid-1944 this was almost entirely conducted by RTUs. Pilots had to be graduates of advanced twin-engine schools. After thirty days transition training on C-47s, they were sent to train in a troop carrier unit. At the end of two months they were joined by their crew members: a co-pilot, engineer, radio operator, and in some cases, a navigator. Air transport units were classified into five categories, depending on the type of aircraft:

1. small, single-engined trainers;
2. twin-engined advanced trainers and small, twin-engined cargo planes;
3. heavy, twin-engined cargo planes;
4. twin-engined fighters and medium bombers;
5. heavy bombers and four-engined cargo aircraft.

Upon attaining the rating of Class 5 pilot, the ATC pilot could then fly any aircraft in the AAF. During December 1942–August 1945, I Troop Carrier Command produced more than 45,000 ATC crews (normally a pilot, co-pilot, navigator, radio operator and aerial engineer) and 5,000 glider pilots.

Technical, administrative and service training (officers and officer trainees)

Graduates of courses in maintenance for the AAF in 1938–9 numbered less than 900. Between July 1939 and August 1945, the number of graduates of courses in maintenance organized by or on behalf of the AAF was more than 700,000 (including some who had graduated from more than one course).

AAF Administrative Officers Candidate School (Miami Beach, Florida)

This was a sixteen-week course, divided into two eight-week periods. The first period covered the requisites for administration, the second period (which included ten days field training) offered specialized training in the type of administration for which they were best qualified: adjutant, personnel, intelligence, mess management, physical training, statistical, supply or training.

Upon graduation, all candidates were commissioned as 2nd lieutenants.

Aviation Cadets (Ground)

This was a twelve-week special basic training course, followed by a specialized technical course, after which they were commissioned as 2nd lieutenants. Cadets attended one of the following schools:
Photographic Laboratory Commanders School (16 weeks);
Communications Officers School (18 weeks);
Armament Officers School (19 weeks);
Engineering Officers School (20 weeks);
Weather Officers School (33 weeks);
Radar Officers School (three types – 38, 42 and 48 weeks).

Resident Graduate Programme

Medical officers who entered the service directly from their final year at medical school or from internship, worked for the first six months under the supervision of experienced medical officers in an AAF hospital. This half-year's training supplied the practical experience necessary to fulfil the duties of medical officers.

Nurses Training Programme

This was a thirty-day course, after which they reported for duty at AAF hospitals.

AAF Engineering School

This was a three-month course. At Wright Field, Ohio, the Materiel Command conducted a course in aeronautical engineering for pilots with degrees. The curriculum was designed to make students more valuable for Materiel Command duties.

Technical, administrative and service training (enlisted men)

The preparation of enlisted men for ground duty was the AAFs largest single training job; 34 separate skills were taught in 80 different types of courses as follows:
Communications (radio, telegraph, telephone, radar) – 26 courses, ranging from 4 to 44 weeks;
Aircraft repair and maintenance – 15, ranging from 5 to 29 weeks;
Armament and equipment – 5 courses, ranging from 8 to 23 weeks;
Weather – two courses, of 11 and 33 weeks each;
Photography – five courses, ranging from 2 to 16 weeks;
Aviation engineers – 8 courses, ranging from 4 to 12 weeks;
Motor transport – 4 courses, ranging from 5 to 10 weeks;
Link trainer – 4 courses, ranging from 8 to 12 weeks;
Miscellaneous – 7 courses, ranging from 3 to 9 weeks.

Ground unit training for technical school graduates

This was usually a two-phase process, covering thirty-three types of unit, including: airborne engineering aviation; chemical; engineering; medical; ordnance; quartermaster; service; and signal and station complement. Courses ranged from 6 to 16 weeks combined training.

Further training

The School of Aviation Medicine at Randolph Field, Texas, operated a nine-week aviation medicine examiners' course whereby, after a year's experience and fifty hours flying time, trainees could become flight surgeons.

From June 1943 the School of Air Evacuation at Bowman Field, Kentucky, taught flight surgeons, nurses and enlisted men methods of transporting patients by air to hospitals far behind the lines. The course lasted two months.

The AAC Engineering School at Wright Field, Dayton, Ohio, was established in 1919, and since then has been the centre of developments in aeronautical engineering.

The AAC Technical School has also been in operation since 1919, and for many years had its headquarters at Chanute Field, Illinois. Subsequent expansion resulted in branches at Lowry Field, Colorado; Morrison Field, at West Palm Beach, Florida, and in many civilian schools of aeronautics.

The first AAC Navigation School was established at Langley Field, Virginia, with additional schools at Rockwell Field, California; Kelly Field, Texas; Mather Field, California, and Miami, Florida.

Other special training programmes included Emergency Rescue, Convalescent, Rehabilitation, Instructors and Foreign Student Training. Two civilian training programmes, the High School Victory Corps and the Civil Air Patrol prepared men and women cadets for future duty in the AAF.

As overseas operations expanded, a need arose for skilled young officers to assume staff duties in higher echelons – wing and above. The AAF Staff Course provided this. In July 1943 an eight-week AAF Staff Course for captains, majors and, in some cases, colonels between the ages of 25 and 35 was established. It involved three phases: a two-week course at the AAF Tactical Centre; two weeks tour of stations, and finally, four weeks at AAF Headquarters.

Overseas, AAF personnel entering a combat theatre for the first time attended theatre indoctrination schools. In the UK, every new aircrew attended a combat crew replacement centre prior to joining a combat group.

AAF School of Applied Tactics, Orlando, Florida

This was established on 9 October 1942 for the purpose of training selected officers under simulated combat conditions. The total number of graduates from November 1942 to VJ Day was almost 54,000 (two-thirds of them AAF personnel). A system of twelve airfields – ranging from a vacant field to large bomber bases with 10,000 ft runways dotted around in a 'war theatre' of 8,000 square miles – was created to allow the mounting of war

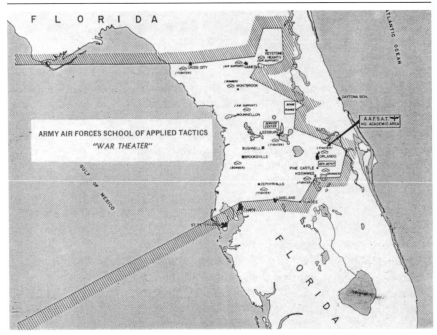

Unique in military training history, the huge AAFSAT war theatre involved widely separated fighter, bomber and air support commands.

games with 'enemy' bombers and fighters. The mission of AAFSAT was:
1. to train Air Force cadres – the personnel framework around which all new combat groups were formed;
2. to test and develop new techniques;
3. to accelerate the spread of new developments and methods to the theatres of combat.

Preparation for overseas movement

Six months were usually required after the formation of a cadre to complete the organization and training of a new group. Continental Air Forces and I Troop Carrier Command were principally responsible for training ground echelons of combat groups. Ground echelons were usually ordered overseas about six weeks in advance of the air echelons. By 1943 preparations to move an air unit overseas took more than four months. It normally took almost 120 days and seventeen separate actions by HQ officers to move the unit to its port of embarkation.

From July 1942 to 5 December 1942 the AAF used the Foreign Service Concentration Command to deal with the special problems of overseas movement, but in December this function was restored to the four Continental Air Forces. This action was accompanied by instructions that all units destined for overseas duty should be carefully checked in accordance with a new inspection system, called Preparation for Overseas Movement, which was under the supervision of the Air Inspector.

CHAPTER SIX

Fighter Development and Tactics

In the First World War, US aviation's only free-ranging 'pursuit' activity had been to 'scout' for the Army. Between the wars subordination of the Air Corps to the senior service dictated that bombers and pursuits (a designation adopted in 1925) continue that support for the infantry and cavalry, coastal and field artillery. During the 1920s each of the six US field armies had an attack group, two pursuit groups and an observation group, or a total force of 4 attack, 8 pursuit and 16 observation squadrons per army. The US Navy was responsible for providing a long-range striking force, preferably with aircraft that could accompany the fleet at sea, while the primary role of the Air Service (from 1926, the Air Corps) was the coastal defence of the continental USA – in effect, 'bomber destroyers'. In a portent of things to come, on the morning of Sunday 7 February 1932, 152 biplanes from two large carriers completely surprised the Pearl Harbor naval base in a simulated strike.

Curtiss C-46 Commando and a Curtiss P-40E of the 26th Fighter Squadron, 51st FG, 14th AF, in China. (USAF)

15th AF P-51 Mustangs with wing drop tanks. HL-A belongs to the 308th Fighter Squadron, 31st Fighter Group; WD-Q is a 4th Fighter Squadron, 52nd Fighter Group; machine no. 7 comes from the 332nd Fighter Group; and OO is a 325th Fighter Group P-51. (USAF)

Monoplane types began to replace biplanes and more powerful radial and in-line engines increased their top speeds to improve their ability to catch or evade an enemy. Tactically, he who has the height has the advantage. However, there was no need to develop pursuits as tactical fighters or as long-range escorts for heavy bombers because these, being heavily armed, were expected to be able to defend themselves on daylight missions over enemy territory. Where pursuits were concerned, speed, if they were to intercept high-flying bombers, was everything, and much effort, often at the expense of everything else, was made to enable them to reach altitudes and speeds hitherto undreamt of.

Since the power produced by a piston engine is directly related to the amount of air passing through it in a given time, the greater the mass of air that can be 'rammed' into the cylinders, the greater the high-altitude performance would be. For this purpose a supercharger, or 'blower', driven by the crankshaft of the engine, was developed by Dr Sanford Moss of General Electric, and it was first used in flight tests in 1920. Another development was the turbosupercharger, which was driven by the exhaust gases of the engine. Early supercharged engines, besides being complex and prone to failure, increased overall weight dramatically. (A turbosupercharger housed in the rear fuselage of the P-47 for example, needed 60 ft of air

Each FG totalled 48 aircraft in three squadrons. Here, 15 P-51B, D and K Mustangs of the 359th FG, 67th Fighter Wing, 1st BD, 8th AF, fly in flights of three and four in 1944. By the spring of 1944 one fighter group was normally assigned to protect each combat bomb wing box. After being relieved of escort duties, and if fuel reserves were adequate, fighter leaders were allowed to take their formations down to strafe airfields in the target area.

A Luftwaffe pilot bales out of his doomed Bf 109G after a losing battle with a US fighter. Chuck Yeager wrote: 'Tactics? Keep the sun at your back and as much altitude advantage as possible; bounce the enemy out of the sun . . . You fought wide open, full-throttle. With experience, you knew before a kill when you were going to score. Once you zeroed in, began to outmanoeuvre your opponent while closing in, you became a cat with a mouse. You set him up, and there was no way out; both of you knew he was finished.' (USAF)

ducting alone). More weight was incurred when the rifle-calibre guns of First World War vintage were discarded in favour of .30 in, .50 in, and even larger calibre machine-guns. As a result of all this, pursuit fighters developed in the late 1930s were big, powerful and on the whole, lightly armed.

In June 1937, responding to an Air Corps design competition for a high-altitude interceptor capable of speeds up to 360 mph, Lockheed Aircraft Corporation designer Kelly Johnson and chief engineer Hall Hibbard, had offered the winning Model 22, which became the XP-38, forerunner of the famous P-38 Lightning. The XP-38 flew for the first time on 27 January 1939, powered by two turbosupercharged Allison C-type V1710 engines. Locating the superchargers and the radiators in the twin-booms, directly behind the engines, dictated the XP-38's distinctive layout and removed the need for lengthy air ducting. While XP-38 and XP-39 high-altitude 'pursuit interceptors', designed to operate at 15,000 ft and using cannon armament, were encouraged, the AAC first wanted a mass-produced, *medium*-altitude pursuit with two .30 in calibre machine-guns, which could operate comfortably at 10,000 ft. Contenders in this class included Seversky pursuits powered by air-cooled Pratt & Whitney R-1830 radial engines, but the XP-40 with its liquid-cooled V1710–19 in-line V-12 was faster and less expensive. In September 1938 the V1710-19 powerplant with a geared supercharger favoured by P-40 chief designer, Don Berlin, was duly delivered and it powered the XP-40 on its first flight on 14 October.

In May 1929 Norman Gilman and his team began to sketch the V1710 in-line engine that in the Second World War would power many thousands of American pursuits such as the P-38, P-39, P-40 and the first P-51 Mustangs. (From P-51B onwards, Mustangs were powered by Rolls-Royce Merlin engines produced under licence by Packard.) In 1938 the 28-litre V1710-19 was selected to power the Curtiss XP-40 which was to take part in the AAC Pursuit competition scheduled for November. The competition was postponed until May 1939, when the XP-40 relegated the Seversky radial-engined pursuits to also-rans. An order received for 524 P-40s (later reduced to 200) was the largest yet placed for an American fighter. By the outbreak of war the P-40 was available in large numbers with highly trained pilots to fly them. An export model was ordered by France but none were delivered before France capitulated in 1940 so these were taken over for the RAF.

While the P-40 operated extensively in most theatres in the Second World War, its undoubted claim to fame is due to the achievements of less than 100 aircraft of Gen. Claire Chennault's American Volunteer Group in China. More popularly known as the 'Flying Tigers', the AVG was formed in 1941 with three pursuit squadrons trained in Burma. When they went into combat on 20 December 1941, two weeks after Pearl Harbor, they shot down six Mitsubishi bombers. Operating in a hostile environment using equipment inferior to the enemy's, the P-40s, each with their red and white shark teeth emblems on the nose, created one of the most memorable of all P-40 legends. Before being disbanded in 1942, the AVG had shot down 286 Japanese aircraft for the loss of just twelve pilots.

Lt David H. Rust, a P-40 pilot who joined the 23rd Fighter Group's 75th

Fighter Squadron in China early in 1944, recalls: 'The P-40, P-39 and the early Allison-powered P-51 were not more appreciated in the European Theatre, where most combats took place at higher altitudes. I never understood why the Allisons were not retro-fitted with two-stage blowers, or perhaps turbo-superchargers as was done with the P-38, but I suppose it turned out for the best. Airspeed alone was not the deciding element that it has often been pictured to be. It was hardly ever that absolute top speed was a deciding factor in fighter combat in China. You couldn't outrun those bullets. By the time you outran an enemy plane, assuming you could do it, he could be shooting you down several times over. In fact, we never challenged the Japanese to speed contests if we could help it, even in P-51s.'

It was not long since 'experts' had believed high-performance fighters would consign 'dog-fighting' to the history books but the old adage, 'It isn't the size of the dog in the fight that counts; it's the size of the fight in the dog', was as true as it ever was. One sizable dog, a real heavyweight exception among the sleek, high-performance pack during the pre-war period, was the P-47, which first flew in prototype form on 6 May 1941. Powered by a 2,000 hp Pratt & Whitney R-2800 series radial, the Thunderbolt had flirted briefly with the Allison when in 1940 attempts had been made to develop the XP-47A lightweight interceptor armed with just two .5 in machine-guns using the liquid-cooled V-1710-39. The P-47 finally weighed in at just over 12,000 lb. Even so, it developed into a very effective strategic escort for deep penetration missions by B-17s and B-24s over Europe, the P-51s flying all the way to Berlin and back.

P-47 and P-51 pilots added ground-strafing of fighter airfields to their close escort and dog-fighting skills. Space does not permit a complete dissertation here on pursuit tactics in the many combat theatres around the globe, but fighter pilots were nearly always singled out for their dog-fighting prowess, although they also performed bombing, ground-attack and strafing using rocketry, machine-guns, cannon and bombs. When AI radar replaced the Mk 1 eyeball, more diverse operations flown in all weathers and at night became effective for the first time, and soon specialized aircraft types like the P-61 Black Widow arrived. In effect, the pursuit became a multi-role combat aircraft.

Lt David H. Rust participated in dog-fighting, bomber escort, ground-attack and strafing in the P-40 and the P-51. 'We went out to parafrag bombs to a town called Sienning. The weather was good enough that we had no trouble finding the town, which was located on an identifiable stream. I found the parafrags easy to drop accurately. As they said, you just "scraped 'em off on the roofs". We dropped three at a time, one cluster from each wing. Each bomb only weighed 20 lbs, but broke up into about 1,500 fragments. One parafrag would actually flatten rice for a radius of 20 or 30 yards. I would guess that I carried and dropped parafrags on a good three-quarters of my missions.

'Strafing was also a bit eye-opening. We shot up compounds and stirred up a few likely looking haystacks. We even found a few barges on the river, but nothing blew up, nothing burned. We carried six .50 calibre M2 Browning machine-guns on the P-40s I flew in combat. This had become all but universal on US fighters of the Second World War. Their sustained firing rate was 800 rounds per minute, and the P-40 would hold about 260 rounds per gun.

'My first air-to-air combat, in a P-40N, was on 5 August 1944. Eight of us took to the air. Red Flight was led by one of our less aggressive flight leaders. I was leading Blue. I was absolutely tigerish in my eagerness and the mood was intensified all the way. About 30 miles north of Hengyang I saw them. It was the usual gaggle, some thirty Oscars with no particular formation pattern, heading our way. I called them out. We all dropped our belly tanks and put on max. continuous power, but the Japs were already higher than we were and gaining. Red Flight kept climbing southward, still in much too close formation for a combat situation. I put my flight into wide formation, waiting for Red to attack; but they never did. Finally, I decided to take the initiative myself. The Japs were getting close to firing range behind Red flight. I called the break to the left, and the ball opened.

'The lead Jap broke into me and down before I got a shot at him. I took a snap shot at one of the others, then had to break down myself when three or four of them turned in on me. I eluded them, and then saw a Zero chasing a P-40 down below me, but out of range. He was too close to my buddy for comfort, so I pulled my sight way out in front of him and snapped of a quick burst. We were still using tracers at that point. As I had hoped, the Jap broke off his attack when he saw my tracers. He flipped into my attack and started pulling streamers "a yard wide", as we were prone to say.

'We were told not to turn with the Zeroes, but I had the bit in my teeth this time, and I wasn't going to miss a chance. I split-essed with everything to the wall, and with every muscle rocktight I was able to pull my pipper out ahead of the Jap. He was straight below me, a full 90° deflection shot, but I kept gaining on him in the turn. I knew I would not be able to lead him visually enough to hit him, because the long nose of my P-40 blocked my view. But I pulled straight through his flight path until he disappeared below my nose, then kept pulling until I thought he had enough lead. I started firing, for what seemed like minutes but was probably less than a second.

'For one fleeting instant I thought I had overdone it and was about to ram him, but at that precise time, there he was! He was 50 yards ahead of me, still at 90° to my line of flight, the red meatballs on his wings looking big as sunrise. He was still pulling streamers, and I could see the pilot's face turned up looking at me. I hit his prop wash like flying through a bomb blast, and only then heeded the voice of prudence and continued my dive. I looked back for him, but couldn't see him, so started a high-speed climb back toward the fight. I had better sense than to spend time and attention looking for my victim with Zeroes around, but the temptation was strong. I was positive that I had hit him, and longed to see a blazing wreck or parachute.

'Soon I picked up a couple of other Japs and went after them hammer and tongs, using War Emergency power once more. Each time I rammed that throttle through the gate, it was an awesome experience. The big Allison would bellow and press you back in the seat, the engine cowling actually seemed to swell with power, and the black smoke rolled. One of the Oscars broke away, but I stayed with the other one and even followed him through some violent manoeuvring. This, plus the essential glances over my own tail, occupied my total attention. Though I didn't realize it at that moment, I actually lost track of where the ground was. I was closing in on my Jap, and had just begun firing at a relatively favourable range and angle-off, when to my astonishment and alarm, the horizon hove into view – upside down! I had committed one of the major no-no's in letting this Jap lead me into a loop. But I stayed on my target as long as I could, getting a number of visible hits on his fuselage.

'Slowed down as we were, he was able to pull a tighter loop than I could, so I had to break off. Knowing I was vulnerable at that point, I went right into the Chennault manoeuvre, stick and rudder full right and forward. The airplane threw me against the seat belt, going around an outside barrel roll straight down. I stayed in it for a few seconds, but couldn't see anybody behind me and pulled out, bringing the throttle back to max. continuous and starting another high-speed climb with my eyes scanning the sky with increasing urgency. I saw two fires burning below; but no planes at all. I flew north for a while, calling for positions of Japs, but apparently the fight was over. Finally, I gave it up and went down to use up the rest of my ammo strafing. I put in claims for one Oscar probably destroyed, the one I almost rammed, and another damaged.'

Escorts for the bombers and the far more frequent job of top-covering each other on fighter sweeps required a high degree of formation discipline. T/Sgt Jack Kings, a B-17 waist gunner in the 388th BG in England, which on 31 December 1943 went to Paris, says, 'Our fighter cover made sure no enemy aircraft would bother us. We really had deep respect for those fighter pilots.' On 11 January 1944 Maj. James H. Howard, an ex-'Flying Tigers' pilot, now CO 356th Squadron, 354th FG, displayed 'conspicuous gallantry and intrepidity above and beyond the call of duty in action with the enemy near Oscheresleben, Germany', when he went to the rescue of some 8th AF Fortresses. Howard dived his P-51 single-handedly into the formation of more than thirty German fighters and for 30 minutes pressed home a series of determined attacks. He shot down three fighters and probably destroyed and damaged others. Toward the end of his action, Howard continued to fight on with his one remaining machine-gun and his fuel supply dangerously low. Maj. Howard's brave single action undoubtedly saved the formation. He was awarded the Medal of Honor.

The first fighter escorts in the ETO had been P-38s. By mid-1942, when heavy losses in the bomber groups in England made it obvious that long-range escort fighters would after all be required, the P-38F began to be deployed in large numbers. Although slightly slower and less manoeuvrable than most single-engined fighters then in service, the Lightning's greater range made it an excellent escort fighter. Beginning in November 1942 P-38s also saw large-scale service in North Africa and the Mediterranean theatre.

Despite its drawbacks the P-38's devastating firepower and excellent rate of climb earned the respect of its German adversaries who referred to it as the 'Fork-Tailed Devil'. The Japanese, too, learned to hate the Lightning. The P-38 destroyed more Japanese aircraft than any other American aircraft and the two leading American aces, Major Richard Bong and Major Tom McGuire (40 and 38 kills respectively), both flew P-38s in the Pacific Theatre.

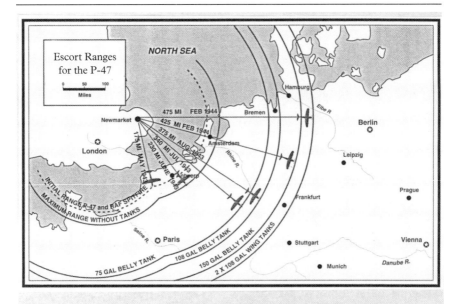

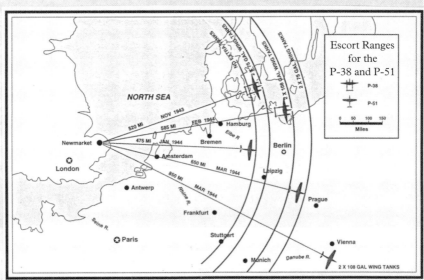

Source: *Carl A. Spaatz and the Air War in Europe*, Richard G. Davis (Centre for Air Force History, Washington DC, 1993).

By February 1943 both the 56th and 78th Fighter Groups of the 8th Air Force in England were operational on the P-47C and P-47D, flying their inaugural mission on 4 May when the 56th accompanied B-17s to Antwerp. After early teething troubles the P-47's value as a long-range escort was proved when two 150-gallon drop tanks were fitted below the wings to enable the P-47 to fly all the way to the target. On 28 July 1943, during 'Blitz Week', Thunderbolts of the 56th and 78th Fighter Groups carried un-pressurized 200-gallon ferry tanks below the centre fuselage for the first time. On 30 July they escorted 186 Fortresses almost to Kassel and back again. Maj. Eugene Roberts, pilot of 78th FG P-47, *Spokane Chief*, made the first 'hat-trick' of kills, becoming the first US pilot to score a triple victory in Europe. He wrote: 'Looking up, I observed six E/A flying parallel to the bombers and about 1,000 ft directly above me. They failed to see us and did not take any action, so after they passed I made a climbing turn to the left to come up to their level and behind them. At this point I missed my second element and found myself alone with my wingman. In our pull up we missed the original six E/A but sighted a single E/A ahead on same level at about 1,500 yards. I dived slightly below, opened full throttle, and closed to about 400 yards. I pulled up directly behind the E/A and opened fire. Several strikes were observed on E/A, his wheels dropped and he spun down trailing a large volume of dark smoke and flame.

'I continued parallel to the bombers and sighted two more E/A about 2,000 yards ahead. I used the same tactics, closing to 400 yards astern, pulled up and opened fire on the port aircraft. Observed strike reports and E/A billowed smoke and flame, rolled over and went down. I was closing so fast that I had to pull up to avoid hitting him. I observed my wingman, F/O Koontz, firing at the second aircraft but did not see the results. Both of these aircraft were FW 190s.

'After this second engagement, we were about 2 miles ahead of the bombers and still well out to their starboard side. About this time I observed one E/A, an Me 109, peeling to starboard to attack the bombers head-on, and I followed, closing to 500 yards before opening fire. Two bursts were behind but the third burst caught him and he spun down, trailing smoke and flame, some 1,500 yards ahead of the bombers.'

Planners in the AAF saw the Mustang as a tactical fighter so the first deliveries of Packard-Merlin-engined P-51Bs to England in November 1943 were assigned to three groups of the tactical 9th AF at the expense of VIIIth Fighter Command. The need for the long-range escort fighter, which could fly as far on its internal fuel as the P-47 could with drop tanks, was critical. On 1 December P-51Bs of the 354th FG, 9th AF, flew their first mission, a sweep over Belgium. The first Mustang fighter escort mission for the bombers was not flown until 5 December. In a record flight on 13 December, when 649 bombers bombed Bremen, Hamburg and Kiel, P-51s escorting the heavies reached the limit of their escort range for the first time. A compromise was later reached between the 8th and 9th Air Forces, and the first 8th AF unit to receive the P-51B was the 357th FG, stationed at Raydon, Essex. They flew their first escort mission on 11 February 1944.

Fighter Sorties Flown against Germany
January 1943 to May 1945

	European Theater of Operations					Mediterranean Theater of Operations				
	Escort	Bombing, Strafing	Recon	Other*	Total	Escort	Bombing, Strafing	Recon	Other*	Total
1943										
Jan	-	-	-	429	429	1,352	286	186	876	2,700
Feb	-	-	-	450	450	1,093	350	312	266	2,021
Mar	-	-	-	608	608	2,238	505	68	1,698	4,509
Apr	8	-	8	524	540	3,433	2,063	388	3,089	8,973
May	384	-	-	1,836	2,220	2,889	2,393	204	2,803	8,289
Jun	169	-	-	1,828	1,997	3,769	1,770	94	2,894	8,527
Jul	607	-	-	1,679	2,286	6,232	3,916	353	5,843	16,344
Aug	1,578	-	-	686	2,264	4,486	4,011	521	5,653	14,671
Sep	2,167	-	-	1,257	3,424	2,493	4,491	210	5,127	12,321
Oct	2,890	-	-	506	3,396	2,241	3,951	151	2,517	8,860
Nov	2,638	105	2	1,160	3,905	3,036	4,161	334	3,182	10,713
Dec	5,095	89	57	500	5,741	3,713	6,157	291	4,104	14,265
Total	15,536	194	67	11,463	27,260	36,975	34,054	3,112	38,052	112,193
1944										
Jan	6,080	201	-	886	7,167	4,526	6,359	-	8,454	19,339
Feb	10,295	83	-	301	10,679	2,628	4,014	-	5,880	12,522
Mar	14,659	887	-	715	16,261	4,487	4,037	-	6,137	14,661
Apr	14,072	3,803	-	3,679	21,554	6,050	6,844	-	3,416	16,310
May	26,091	6,405	-	3,714	36,210	6,746	11,759	-	2,574	21,079
Jun	27,970	11,320	-	16,170	55,460	5,862	8,232	-	2,672	16,766
Jul	20,577	9,098	-	13,278	42,953	8,235	5,223	-	2,592	16,050
Aug	23,793	4,524	-	17,510	45,827	7,887	6,461	-	4,624	18,972
Sep	13,531	11,056	-	9,098	33,685	4,513	4,164	-	2,624	11,301
Oct	15,659	11,731	-	2,491	29,881	4,003	4,583	-	977	9,563
Nov	19,082	7,542	-	3,496	30,120	4,270	6,822	-	893	11,985
Dec	15,723	12,940	-	6,824	35,487	6,141	7,988	-	851	14,980
Total	207,532	79,590	-	78,162	365,284	65,348	76,486	-	41,694	183,528
1945										
Jan	10,898	9,878	4,473	1,169	26,418	2,311	7,402	1	251	9,965
Feb	13,261	13,906	8,410	649	36,226	6,658	6,868	-	380	13,906
Mar	19,853	37,311	452	5,226	62,842	-	15,062	4	432	15,498
Apr	16,654	25,420	4,452	1,530	48,056	5,340	11,749	1,400	408	18,897
May	168	729	362	1,752	3,011	-	332	176	37	545
Total	60,834	87,244	18,149	10,326	176,553	14,309	41,413	1,581	1,508	58,811
Grand Total	283,902	167,028	18,216	99,951	569,097	116,632	151,953	4,693	81,254	354,532

*Includes patrol, interception, sweep, and sea-search sorties.

Source: *Carl A. Spaatz and the Air War in Europe*, Richard G. Davis (Centre for Air Force History, Washington DC, 1993).

In March 1944 P-51Bs of the 8th AF flew to Berlin and back for the first time. From thenceforth the Mustang saw widespread use as an escort fighter on long-penetration raids deep into Germany. The Mustang's range of 2,080 miles, achieved by the use of wing drop tanks, was far in excess of that available in other fighters of the day. By the end of the war the P-51 equipped all but one of the 8th AF fighter groups. The 56th was unique in the 8th, choosing to retain its P-47s until the end of hostilities. The P-51D appeared in Europe in 1944, having been flown for the first time on 17 November 1943. Without the Rolls-Royce Merlin the Mustang's contribution to victory would have been muted and development stunted. By far the greatest contribution made by the Mustang and Thunderbolt was in Europe where they were the saviours of the B-17 and B-24 bomber crews of the 8th AF, who were severely demoralized after the battles of Schweinfurt and the like. Even the arrival of German jet aircraft failed to test the two American escort fighters to any noticeable degree. The *Jagdverbande* had made a few concerted attempts at turning back the bombers late in 1944 but on each occasion they had been beaten off with heavy losses by escorting P-51s and P-47s of the 8th AF. On 2 November 1944 defending Mustangs routed their German attackers and the 352nd FG established a record thirty-eight kills on that occasion. On 14 January 1945 the 352nd FG shot down no less than 60½ enemy aircraft; a record for any 8th AF fighter group, and unsurpassed by the end of the war.

The Mustang also served on escort duty in the Pacific. Lt. David Rust's 92nd mission was in the P-51 and the one where he finally tasted victory in the air. 'I was leading a flight of four Mustangs to escort two flights of P-40s. We were to swing by Hengyang to check for activity there. As usual, the mission observed radio silence. We aimed for the Siang Valley road and railway routes a bit north of Hengyang, but I swung wide with my four to look over the airbase. I was at about 12,000 ft. Suddenly I saw a flight of four bogies off to the left, about level with us. They were in finger-four formation, so I guessed they were probably Chinese Air Force P-40s. I had never known Japs to fly that kind of formation. We crossed over the bogies 2–3,000 ft above. As we came closer the blunt noses and meat-balls hit like an electric shock. I already had my gun switches on. I broke into a left split-ess to the attack. They were Oscars, in unpainted aluminium like our '51s. I levelled down on the lead Oscar, expecting him to flip as I came into range. He did, just as I started firing, but I was able to stay right with him and continued firing on target as he split-essed. My converging fire centred him right at the break. To my utter and complete jubilation a ball of clear, smokeless flame rolled out of him. I think I must have killed the pilot, because from then on his plane seemed out of control. It was diving vertically, spiralling slowly to the left, still burning with a small gasoline flame. I quit firing . . . watched him go in.

'I had tasted blood and I wanted some more. The fight was swirling all around; three more Oscars had joined in, and I took a snap shot at one. The other two got on my tail. Without even thinking about being in a much faster airplane, I went into the Chennault escape manoeuvre. I looked behind, not hurrying too much, and found that the Zeroes had lost me.

'I went after a Zero. He turned inside me for the first couple of passes. But he wasn't able to get his guns on me, so I kept after him. We had been losing altitude during these exchanges, and now he tried what should have been his last mistake. He led me over the ground guns at Hengyang, flying straight and level at a thousand feet. I was gaining on him by 150 mph now.

I took dead aim from line astern, the first time I had ever had a point-blank shot like that but when I pulled the trigger, the airplane slewed to the left. The right-hand guns had jammed. [This was a chronic problem with the P-51Bs and Cs. They had wings so thin that the guns had to be slanted at about 75° angle in order to fit. This meant that the ammo was feeding uphill, and whenever the guns were fired while pulling significant g force, some of them were sure to jam.]

'I was overhauling the Zero rapidly. I tried my best to hold rudder against the kick of the left-wing guns. Some of my bullets went into him, but quite soon I had to break off to avoid ramming him. I put my plane into a diving, jinking escape to throw the ground gunners off. When I looked back, I couldn't find my Zero and there was another fire burning off to the north . . . When I got back I gave vent to a long-cherished vanity and pulled a low victory roll right over the 75th alert shack.'

The Thunderbolt also distinguished itself during its exclusive service with Air Command, SE Asia, against the Japanese from September 1944. The final Thunderbolt models were the P-47M, of which 130 were built by 1945, and the P-47N, built solely for the Pacific Theatre. Near the end of the war P-47Ns flew escort for the B-29s bombing targets in Japan.

In February 1945 P-51Ds flying from Iwo Jima escorted B-29s to attack Japan. On 7 April P-51Ds penetrated Tokyo airspace for the first time. A few P-51H models reached the Pacific before the end of the war and served operationally. This was the fastest of all Mustangs, having a top speed of 487 mph. By August 1945 P-47s had flown on every front, destroying over 7,000 enemy aircraft on the ground and in the air.

Without the P-40, P-38, P-47 and the P-51, the Strategic Air Forces could not have achieved the measure of air superiority that they did, both in Europe and the Pacific. Just ask a B-17, B-24 or B-29 bomber crewman.

CHAPTER SEVEN

Formation and Bombing Procedures

In Chapter Three various combat formations in the 8th Air Force were discussed. Many resulted from initiatives by individual group commanders and staffs, while some came about at the instigation of in-theatre Tactical Advisory Boards. Many of the theoretical procedures contained later became SOP throughout the air forces. This chapter describes bomber formation flying procedures, as taught in the 2nd Air Force in late 1944 (as a result of experience in combat in the war theatres), and bombing doctrine, contained in the Tactical Advisory Board recommendations, 1st Bomb Wing, England, April–May 1943.

RESTRICTED: SECTION IV – FORMATION

A. Position of Aircraft
1. Principles:
a. The basic principle for a combat formation is to have the aircraft grouped into units of sufficient size to deliver maximum supporting fire yet deployed so that maximum manoeuvrability is maintained. Combat experience has resulted in the development of several types of formation to meet the above criteria. These include the Stagger, Combat Box, and Combat Box Stagger that are being used in various theatres of operation. The formation which will be used in the Second Air Force and outlined herein incorporates qualities of all the above listed types of formation. Therefore, if crews are properly instructed and experienced in flying this formation, they will find little difficulty, if any, in flying any of the types of formations used in the various theatres.
b. This formation will be referred to as the Combat Training Formation. It has enough aircraft, properly disposed, to cover all areas of attack by enemy fighter aircraft. It is fairly compact with a high degree of manoeuvrability. It offers crews experience in large compact formations and yet incorporates a maximum of safety for relatively inexperienced combat training crews by demanding a greater vertical clearance between elements and squadrons than is normally used in combat.
2. A simple description of how this formation is built is as follows:
a. The Element – Three aircraft in a 'V' with wingmen flying wing tip to wing tip, nose to tail on the leader with safe clearance (minimum of 50 ft) laterally or horizontally in case of mechanical difficulties on the part of

any aircraft; each crew commander must constantly remember that his failure to fly properly his proper position in any one element will disrupt and make penetrable the entire formation in which he is flying, regardless of its size. An element wingman who fails to hold his proper position in any element in the lead of a formation disrupts the entire formation to his rear. The lesson taught a straggling wingman from a rear element of a formation is too well known to recite here. The most desired position of a wingman in an element which is staggered up is on a level plain with the leader or slightly up. If his element leader is staggered down, a wingman should fly on a level plain or slightly down.

b. The Squadron – Two elements with the second element echeloned right or left with 100 ft vertical clearance. The second element leader will normally assume a position to the rear on a line extended between the lead aircraft and outside wingman of the lead element echeloned away from the centre of the formation.

c. The Group Formation – Three squadrons with a lead squadron, high squadron and low squadron. The high squadron is above and on the right and the low squadron is below and to the left. The second element of the lead squadron is below and to the right. The second element of the high squadron is above and to the right. The second element of the low squadron is below and to the left. A rule of thumb for second element leaders and wingmen may be stated here. If your squadron is echeloned up from the group leader, your element is echeloned up. If your squadron is echeloned down, your element is echeloned down. If your squadron is echeloned to the right of the group leader, your element will be echeloned right. If your squadron is on the left, your element is echeloned left. The leaders of all elements should be competent, experienced personnel and particularly the leader of the second element of the high squadron for this is considered the most difficult position to fly in the formation. Squadrons do slide over or under on turns, but normally retain their relative position. Squadrons in a Group Formation will maintain 200 ft of vertical clearance. This group formation is the basic unit and must be practised at every possible opportunity. It is from a group formation that the bombing on precision targets is usually done. However, if enemy opposition decreases, it is expected that the bombing will be done from six-ship formations diverging at the initial point and converging on the target, assembling back into an 18-ship group stagger formation at the rally point. If 21 aircraft are used, the additional element of three flies stacked up on the high squadron.

d. The Combat Wing – Three groups with a lead group, high group, and low group. The high group is usually on the flank away from the sun and the low group is on the flank into the sun. The combat wing formation is for protection against fighters, and is usually used for bombing. It divides at the Initial Point (IP), putting the bombing responsibility on the individual group leaders. Assembly and climb will be accomplished with groups in echelon up. At bombing altitude, the proper defensive formation will be effected.

3. Flight Leaders:

a. Each group formation will have three experienced lead ships with a superior bombing team in each. The deputy group leader will be on the lead ship's right wing and will take the lead upon signal from the group leader that he is going to abort. The signal for any aircraft which is going to abort will be lowering of landing gear.

b. When the deputy group leader moves into the lead, his vacancy is filled by the right ship of the second element. This airplane has in it the third superior bombing team and replaces the deputy leader if he must return to base.

4. Formation Control Officer:

a. A Formation Control Officer will fly in the tail gun position of the lead aircraft of each group. In addition to his gunnery duties, he will pay particular attention to the group and combat wing formation, enemy tactics, bomb bursts, etc., and report his observations constantly to his Airplane Commander. Any tendency of the formation to spread must be passed to the leader so that immediate steps may be taken to remedy this situation.

b. Upon this man's judgement may rest the difference between a successful and unsuccessful mission. It is necessary to choose a very high calibre, responsible officer who can be relied upon to act as the rearward eyes of the group leader.

B. Take-off and Landing Procedure

1. General:

a. Preparation is 75% of the mission. Commanders, service agencies and individuals must assure themselves that preparation of a mission is complete in every respect. Airplane Commanders must check their ship and crew before every mission. This should be a thorough and unhurried inspection with all members of the crew present. Air discipline begins with punctuality, getting out to the airplane in plenty of time, taxiing out on time, and taking off on time. Minutes spent in checking equipment, crew men, and aircraft may mean the difference between life and death, or success and failure on the mission.

b. It is very important that the taxi route be well worked out to avoid confusion and enable all aircraft to get off on time. Plenty of time should be allowed for safe, unhurried taxiing to the take-off point. Great care must be exercised in taxiing, especially when the ships are heavily loaded. Fast taxiing and quick braked turns may twist or weaken the landing gear to such an extent that it may easily fail on some future landing. Cletracs should be held in readiness to aid any ships that have experienced trouble while taxiing and may block the perimeter strip.

c. Because of the short distance between airdromes, and the low visibility that is generally prevalent within theatres of operations, traffic patterns must be confined to the immediate vicinity of the home airdromes. Long approaches and large patterns should be avoided.

2. Taxi:

a. Crews will get to their airplanes in time to make complete final inspection and be at their stations with equipment adjusted not less than 15 minutes before taxi time.

b. Group Flying Control Officers will brief crews on the taxi route.

c. Operations will check to see that Flying Control has cleared the perimeter strips to be used.

3. Take-Off:

a. take-off interval – 30 seconds.

b. Climb – approximately 400ft/min/150 mph for B-17 and 155 mph for B-24, with overload 200ft/min/150 mph for B-17 and 155 mph for B-24, but in all cases Briefing Officers must brief on definite speeds and climb to be used consistent with type of aircraft and load.

c. Altitude – level off at 1,500 ft, minimum, above the airdrome.

d. The time that the squadron leader will fly straight ahead from beginning of take-off roll until beginning of turn is determined by the following formula:

Time until turn = 1 min + (30 sec, multiplied by number of aircraft)

e. This will give the last airplane 500 ft altitude before beginning turn, which, for training purposes, is considered to be the minimum safe altitude.

f. The assembly should be in 6-plane squadron units and then assemble squadrons into groups. This method is considered the most desired for B-17 and B-24 type of aircraft. However, the greatest failure in this type of assembly is that squadron leaders frequently fail to assemble their squadrons rapidly and hold proper pattern in reference to group leader. To avoid this failure, squadron leaders must train their individual crew commanders to join rapidly, but at the same time, the squadron leader must be flying the *proper* pattern so that his squadron will intercept the group leader at the proper time.

g. When the squadron leaders have flown the proper number of minutes for the size of their formations, they will then start one-half needle width turn to the left, completing to 180° and taking up a course parallel to the reciprocal heading of the runway. The lead squadron will level off at assembly altitude (1,500 ft minimum above airdrome) and cruise at 150 mph indicated air speed for B-17 or 160 mph for B-24. He will fly this course for a time equal to twice the time interval of roll to first turn. This will place him downwind from the field. He will then execute a half-needle width turn to the left for 180° and fly a heading parallel to the runway. The other squadrons should have joined the formation shortly after the lead squadron completed the second 180° turn.

h. A group formation leader will, under no circumstances, leave the vicinity of the airdrome until all aircraft are in their proper positions in the formation.

i. Successive airplanes of the elements or squadrons will gauge their turns after take-off so they will be able to pick up their proper position in the formation as soon as possible. This will ordinarily be about ten seconds after the plane ahead of them starts to turn.

j. An individual airplane, when joining in a squadron assembly, will intercept slightly below his element leader and will pull up into his proper position when squared away on the downwind heading of the squadron leader. This applies to both the first and second element of any squadron. Also on squadron assembly, the high and low squadron should perform the assembly in exactly the same manner as the lead squadron. That is, with the second element stacked down and to the right. In the case of the high squadron, a subsequent manoeuvre must necessarily be performed at some point on the downwind leg in order to put the second element higher than the lead element. This is done by the second element leader pulling his element out to avoid prop wash and then up into his proper high position before his squadron joins the lead squadron in group assembly. In the case of the low squadron, it is necessary only for the second element leader to slide his element over to the left at some point before his squadron joins the lead squadron in the group assembly.

4 Landing:

a. The group will approach the airdrome in a normal formation except the leader of the second element of the low squadron will move his element to the right assuming a position on a line extended, between the lead aircraft and No. 2 aircraft of the lead element of his squadron. This will place the low squadron in a formation identical to that of the lead squadron.

b. After receiving landing instructions, the formation will fly an upwind course parallel to the landing strip at a minimum altitude of 1,500 ft, above the airdrome. As the low squadron approaches the end of the runway, the No. 3 man of the first element of the low squadron will break away for the landing. The lead plane of the first element of the low squadron will continue on course for ten seconds before breaking away to follow No. 3. The No. 2 man will then continue on course for ten seconds before breaking away to follow the leader. Second element will use same procedure following at ten second intervals. The remainder of the formation will make a 360° left turn starting the turn upon breakaway of first aircraft of low squadron with the lead squadron landing next. The high squadron will make a second 360° left turn landing last. The same breakaway will be used in each squadron as they come over the airdrome after completing their 360° turn. (Caution: It is imperative for reasons of safety that each peel off be level until a minimum of 90° turn has been accomplished.) Each airplane, upon landing, will continue to the end of the runway in order to get the entire flight down with minimum of delay.

c. It is important that the approach be short and the original pattern be close in.

d. Landing priority should be given to ships in trouble. Pilots suspecting any mechanical difficulties should not attempt to land in their regular order, but take time to thoroughly check their ships before landing, and if they expect trouble in the landing, and if gas permits, they should land last.

e. Short and relatively high approaches should be stressed and practised. Long approaches in poor visibility will result in airplanes becoming improperly aligned with landing strip. An airplane failing to fly in on the proper course will mislead following airplanes with the result that they will be forced to go around. Proper spacing must be acquired before turning on base leg to retain proper pattern as the base leg must remain the same for all aircraft.

f. In periods of low visibility, both on landing and take-off, all aircraft will burn Aldis lamps in tail or top turret position, and the operator will make sure that the lamp is aimed at the aircraft immediately behind. The use of the Aldis lamp should be continued until the assembly of landing is completed.

g. Caution. All supervisory personnel must never fail to take into realization that any type of formation flying involves a greater risk to safety than flying individual aircraft. The larger the formation, the greater the danger. With this fact in mind, no organization, in the training programme, should ever neglect to completely brief each crew before each formation flight regardless of experience of crews or number of times the crews have been briefed and flown formation on past missions. The following points will be covered and clearly explained at each formation briefing:

(1)   Exact position of each aircraft stressing minimum distance both vertically and horizontally.
(2)   How each aircraft should join formation, stressing joining wingmen to element leaders from <u>below</u> and slightly to the rear at all times.
(3)   The proper method and direction for each aircraft to abort when necessary. Stress that if pilots fail to abort properly or know exact position of all aircraft in the formation before they attempt to abort they may endanger safety because some other aircraft may not be flying in its proper position.
(4)   The proper position of each element must be clearly briefed.
(5)   The proper method of landing, stressing order of breakaway for each aircraft must be covered at each briefing.

C. Combat Wing Assembly
1. Assembly:
a. To assemble a large number of units quickly and without confusion, it is necessary to have one unit well formed before the main assembly and that designated altitude, times, and places are rigidly adhered to.
b. Lead units should be at the base altitude ordered so as to facilitate recognition and assembly by other units. Assembly procedures assuming overcast conditions must be practised frequently.
2. Under Combat Conditions:
a. Groups or sections will form as a unit over their own airdrome, as

described in Section VI (Take-off and Landing Procedures), before proceeding to the Combat Wing Assembly line.

(1)   Splasher beacons, MF/DF beacons, and G Ships will be utilised in locating the assembly points under conditions of poor visibility.

b. Combat Wings will assemble along a line approximately 35 miles long, with time and altitude prescribed for the lead group at each end of the Assembly Line. The Assembly Line will be at an angle of 45 degrees to the first 'leg' of the route, necessitating a right turn by the formation. Groups will be stepped up in 1,000 ft intervals and assemble in a Combat Wing Formation.

3. Over an Overcast:

a. Groups will use the standard take-off and assembly procedure as given in Section V, and proceed to the wing assembly point as designated by the Wing Operations. This will normally be over a splasher beacon. Groups will stack up in 1,000 ft intervals with the lead group at base altitude to facilitate recognition and assembly.

b. It is extremely important that all pilots determine the assembling altitudes from a setting of 29.92 so that altitude will be relatively correct.

c. Suggested Assembly Speed: (1) B-17 – 150 mph; (2) B-24 – 160 mph.

4. Assembly on Air Division Assembly Line:

a. Assembly of the Air Division will be accomplished along the Air Division Assembly Line. Succeeding Combat Wings will endeavour to join the lead Combat Wing as near the first point of the Air Division Assembly Line as possible, but may gain or lose time along this line as necessary to complete assembly by the time the second point is reached by the lead Combat Wing. The second Combat Wing will fly approximately two miles behind, and echeloned slightly to one side of the lead Combat Wing, or fly in close support behind and at sufficient altitude to clear the prop wash of the leading Combat Wing (see TACTICAL DOCTRINE III C, Air Division).

b. Assembly Altitude:

Assembly altitude will be given for the lead Combat Wing and will be held constant along the Air Division Assembly Line.

D. Enroute and Return Target

1. Enroute:

a. The Combat Wing formation is retained from the assembly to the initial point because of its high fire power and manoeuvrability.

2. Initial Point (IP):

a. The manoeuvre at the IP depends on the target to be bombed, the AA, and fighter opposition. However, this is decided before take-off and is understood by all pilots. If any change is made in flight, the new IP is designated by flare, Aldis lamps, or open bomb bay doors.

(1)   if the bombing is to be done from the combat wing formation the combat boxes or groups keep their positions.

(2)   However, if the combat box or groups are going to bomb individually, the following procedure is used:

(a)   The lead group turns toward the target.
(b)   The low group continues on for 20 seconds, and turns to behind and below the lead group.
(c)   The high group continues 20 seconds further and turns to behind and above both the lead and low groups.
(d)   Each group goes from their altitude at the IP, at approximately 170 mph to their bombing altitude as designated. It is on this run that evasive action is taken.

3. Rally Point:
a. The rally point is designated in the Field Order. Normally the point will be on the opposite side of the target from the IP and so located so the lead group or wing will have to make a 45°–90° turn to take up a course for the route back.

(1)   The lead group or wing will proceed to the Rally Point at normal cruise, S-ing if necessary for the following formations to join it. The Rally Point is normally 1,000 ft below bombing altitude.
(2)   Descent from altitude will be as specified in Field Order and will not be started until the Groups are back in a defensive Combat Wing Formation.

4. Battle Tactics: The aim of fighters attacking from head-on may be effectively spoiled by slight weaving of the squadron under attack. This weaving takes place as the E/A initiate their attack, and results in:
a. Forcing E/A to keep changing deflection which is extremely difficult at high closing speeds.
Bombing Procedure: The Initial Point (IP) is the place at which the units of the wing begin the manoeuvre for the bombing attack. Although it is designated in orders as a geographical locality, its final selection is on signal from the combat leader of the lead combat box. The location of the IP varies with the method of bombing, the nature of the AA defences, the position of the sun, and the size of the target. If the lead combat box does not or cannot use the designated IP, succeeding combat boxes have to base their manoeuvre on that of the lead combat box. The lead combat box of each Combat Wing has to designate the IP by firing a red pyrotechnic flare, signalling 'IP' on the Aldis Lamp and lowering bomb bay doors.

Aldis Lamp Signal Code

Initial Point Signal	Letters 'IP'
Increase Speed	Letters 'IM'
Decrease Speed	Letters 'DS'

Close Formation	Letter 'X'
Lead Aircraft unable to bomb	Continuous 'Dots'
Aircraft in Distress	Continuous 'Dots'
Aircraft in Overcast	Climb 'OC'
Aircraft Overcast	Descend 'OD'

Fighter Support Signal: An aircraft in distress will fire a series of green flares which is a signal for friendly fighters to give close support.

Wing Formation Bombing: If the Wing is to bomb in column or slight echelon of Combat Wings, the IP is, if possible, chosen at about four minutes run from the target. Under average wind conditions at 25,000 ft this is about 20 miles for a down-wind bombing run and about 12–15 miles for an up-wind bombing run.

Combat Wing Formation Bombing: If the Wing is to split into two or more units, bombing at different altitudes and on different axes of approach, then the IP has to be further from the target in order to permit the units to take up this disposition.

Manoeuvre at the Initial Point: On the approach to the IP Combat Wings normally are in column or echeloned away from the turn. The axis of attack is as determined by the lead combat box. The lead combat box of the first Combat Wing begins the turn over the IP. The 2nd combat box (low) proceeds straight ahead after the lead combat box has started its turn and turns towards the target as soon as the lead combat box uncovers. The 3rd combat box (high) proceeds straight ahead until the 2nd combat box uncovers and turns toward the target. Turns of lead combat boxes are normally at ½ needle width rate.

The combat boxes of a Combat Wing attack in the following order: lead combat box, 2nd combat box (low), 3rd combat box (high). Successive Combat Wings uncover by proceeding successively farther beyond the IP.

Bombing Run: If the Group maintains its integrity of formation during the bombing run, and if all the bombardiers drop their bombs at the exact time they are supposed to, the bombs will fall as plotted. The lead bombardier releases his bombs so that the last bomb in his train hits the target instead of the centre of his train hitting the target. By doing this the mean point of impact (MPI) of all the bombs of the Group is moved closer to the Aiming Point than would otherwise be the case. This is done by the bombardier displacing his horizontal cross hair short of the target by the proper amount just before his indices meet. The lead bombardier could, theoretically, place the centre of impact of all bombs of the Group where he wants them. [The leader of each Combat Wing formation was to then send a brief message in bomber code to the Wing Ground Station as soon as the English coast was approached on the return flight indicating whether 'primary', 'secondary' or 'no target' was attacked].

Manoeuvre after Bombing: The Lead Combat Box proceeds to the Rally

Point* at 155 IAS, making S-turns if necessary for succeeding combat boxes to close the interval. Succeeding combat boxes fly so as to close on lead combat boxes as quickly as possible.

Descent from Bombing Altitude: The lead combat box crosses the Rally Point at bombing altitude less 1,000 ft. Succeeding combat boxes descend to bombing altitude less 1,000 ft. Further descent only to be begun after the Combat Wing has reformed into defensive formation. Rate of descent, 500 ft per minute at 170 IAS.

---

* Normally the point on the opposite side of the target from the IP located so that the lead combat box has to make a 45° to 90° turn at the Rally Point to take up course for the route back.

CHAPTER EIGHT

The Combat Aircraft, 1939–45

Type designations

A	–	Attack	O	–	Observation
AT	–	Advanced Trainer	OA	–	Observation-amphibian
B	–	Bomber	P	–	Pursuit (fighter)
BT	–	Basic Trainer	PT	–	Primary Trainer
C	–	Cargo/Transport	R	–	Rotary wing (helicopter)
CG	–	Cargo/Transport Glider	TG	–	Glider Trainer
F	–	Reconnaissance ('foto')	UC	–	Utility
L	–	Liaison			

Aircraft

Airspeed Oxford

About 132 of these British-built six-seat, twin-engined training aircraft were obtained by the 8th AF in England in 1942 for communications duties.

Beech C-43 Traveler

The first aircraft produced by the Beech Corporation of Wichita, Kansas, after its foundation in 1932, the C-43 was powered by a 450 hp R-985-AN-1 engine, and it could carry three passengers in addition to the pilot. It was very popular among private and commercial owners before the AAC took an interest in 1939 when it needed a small utility and communications aircraft.

Shortly after the USA entered the Second World War, the Beech 17, as it was known, was commandeered in large numbers for military use. An earlier YC-43 served at the US Air Attache in London, and in 1944, thirty were supplied to the UK under Lend-Lease.

Beech C-45, AT-7, AT-11, F-2

Contracts were awarded to Beech in 1940 for variants of the Model B-18S commercial light transport. More than 4,000 of these twin-engined examples were built over the next five years. In 1941 the AT-7 was specially equipped as the first USAAC navigation trainer, and a total of 1,141 AT-7A, AN-1 and AT-7C Navigators were delivered; 1,582 AT-11 Kansan bombing

Beechcraft YC-43 39-139 of the US Embassy, London, one of three examples of the pre-war commercial D-17S used by the AAC. (Beech)

and gunnery trainers (including 36 modified as AT-11As for navigation training) were also built. The 24 AT-11s ordered by the Netherlands were repossessed for service in the AAC; 14 B-18s and 13 UC-45A/Bs were modified to F-2 models for specialized photographic reconnaissance; 42 F-2B (UC-45F) versions with a trimetrogen camera system were also built.

In the later stages of the Second World War, UC-45Fs were used as directors for radio-controlled targets, under the designation CQ-3.

Bell P-39 Airacobra

When the AAC contracted the Bell Aircraft Corporation of Buffalo, New York, to build a single XP-39 prototype on 7 October 1937, it was the first tricycle, single-engined fighter to be ordered by that body. The design was drawn around the nose-mounted 37 mm T-9 gun built by the American Armament Corporation. The gun mounting dictated the engine position, buried in the fuselage section aft of the cockpit. This in turn dictated the tricycle undercarriage arrangement, the engine being the centre of gravity. The XP-39 prototype flew on 6 April 1939, and twelve YP-39s and one YP-39A (all with the turbosupercharger deleted because of cost) were ordered for evaluation. The P-39 went into full production in August 1939, but by deleting the turbosupercharger the AAC jeopardized any potential success the aircraft might have had at high altitude.

In December 1941 the USAAF had five P-39 groups. The first saw combat, operating from Australia, on 30 April 1942. Airacobras were also operated in Alaska (until December 1942), in the Pacific (until August 1944) and in North Africa and the Mediterranean.

Of the 9,558 P-39s built, 4,846 were sent to the USSR, where it became the most numerous of all US aircraft supplied to the Soviet Air Force.

Boeing B-17G *Outhouse Mouse* of the 323rd BS, 91st BG, 8th AF, based at Bassington, England, in 1944. (© Mike Bailey)

B-17s of the 91st BG at Bassingbourn. Two visiting P-47 Thunderbolts of the 78th FG and a Mustang can also be seen. (USAF)

Bell P-63 Kingcobra

Developed as a more powerful variant of the P-39 Airacobra (three XP-39Es were built during 1941 using P-39D fuselages), P-63 production began in September 1942; 3,303 were built, but only a handful actually reached USAAC units during the Second World War (as operational trainers), 2,421 models going to the USSR.

Boeing B-17 Flying Fortress

Results of European combat experience were incorporated into the extensively improved B-17E, which was ordered on 30 August 1940, and first flew on 5 September 1941. Power-operated gun turrets and a tail gun position were installed, and the .30 in guns were replaced with .50 in guns. The most distinctive recognition feature of the B-17E was the greatly enlarged tail surfaces to give better control and stability for high-altitude bombing. About 100 B-17Es had been delivered to the AAC by 7 December 1941. A handful of B-17 bomb groups fought the Japanese in the Philippines and Java, and the survivors retreated to India. (The B-17 continued to operate in the Pacific theatre until 1943.)

A total of 512 B-17Es were built, the first B-17Es of the 97th BG flying the first US Flying Fortress mission in the ETO on 17 August 1942. Large-scale production really began with the B-17F, which could be distinguished from the B-17E by its moulded Plexiglas nose. Boeing built 2,300 B-17Es, Douglas built 600 and Lockheed-Vega built 500.

The B-17G had an added two-gun, power-operated 'chin' turret under its nose for defence against direct frontal attack. Boeing built 4,035 B-17Gs, Douglas built 2,395 and Lockheed built 2,250. Altogether, 12,677 B-17s were accepted by the USAAF.

Boeing B-29, XB-29
In 1938 initial studies were carried out at the Boeing Aircraft Company for an improved B-17 bomber with a pressurized cabin. The Boeing Model 345 design featured a high-aspect wing, engine nacelles designed to minimize drag, and a tricycle undercarriage fitted with dual wheels. The Wright R-3350 engines, with two superchargers, developing 2,200 hp at sea-level, were the most powerful installed in an aircraft at that time. The fuselage was divided into three pressurized compartments, two of which were connected by a tunnel over the tandem bomb bays. The forward pressurized area contained the pilots, navigator, bombardier, flight engineer and radio operator, while the aft section housed three gunners and a radar operator. The tail gunner had his own separate pressurized compartment. The B-29 was far ahead of its contemporaries, with its ten-gun defensive armament in four remote-controlled power turrets and a single directly-controlled tail turret.

Following the Japanese attack on Pearl Harbor on 7 December 1941, US military strategists realized the importance of the long-range bomber to strike at targets in the Pacific. The Boeing Wichita plant was expanded, and a new factory at Renton was given over entirely to B-29 production. (The designation B-29A was assigned to Renton-built aircraft, which featured a different type of centre wing construction.) Further production lines were started by Bell at Marietta, Georgia, and by Martin at Omaha.

The first XB-29 was flown at Seattle by Edward Allen on 21 September 1942, and the second on 28 December 1942. There followed a spate of engine failures and fires, and in February 1943 an engine fire caused the second XB-29 to crash, killing Allen, his crew and nineteen civilian workers. Faults were rectified, and the Sperry remote-controlled gun turrets fitted to the second XB-29 were replaced by General Electric turrets in the third, which first flew in June 1943.

On 1 June 1943 the 58th Very Heavy Bombardment Wing was activated. The first XX BC B-29 mission took place on 5 June 1944, when landing fields in China were used as staging posts to refuel and re-arm 98 B-29s whose targets were railways in Bangkok: 14 aborted the 2,000 mile round

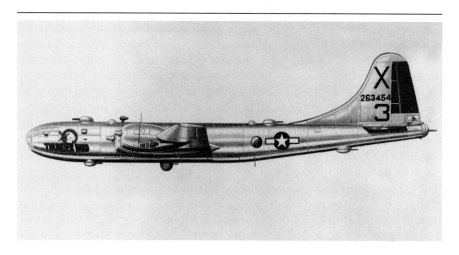

Boeing B-29 Superfortress *Thunderbird* of the 462nd BG, 20th AF, based in the Marianas in 1944–5. (© Mike Bailey)

B-29s of the 500th BG (Very Heavy), 73rd Bomb Wing, commanded by Brig.-Gen. Emmett O'Donnell, dropping bombs on Japan. (USAF)

trip, and 5 crashed on landing. Only eighteen bombs landed in the target area. Ten days later, the first raid on the Japanese mainland took place, when 47 B-29s made a night attack on the Imperial Iron and Steel Works at Yawata, on Kyushu. During the summer five B-29 bases were constructed in the Marianas, where it was decided to concentrate all the B-29s of the 20th AF. It was from here, on 24 November 1944, that the first raid on Tokyo took place, when Brig.-Gen. O'Donnell's 73rd Wing bombed the Musashima aircraft factory. Throughout late 1944 and early 1945, B-29s made high-level daylight raids on Japanese targets without success and at high cost. In March 1945 Maj.-Gen. LeMay switched his B-29s to area bombing from low level at night, using incendiaries to raze Japanese cities to the ground. Throughout early 1945, B-29s based on Saipan, Tinian and Guam continued the bombing of Japanese targets. B-29s finally brought the Pacific War to an end with the dropping of atomic bombs on Hiroshima on 6 August, and Nagasaki on 9 August.

Altogether, 3,970 B-29s were built (2,766 by Boeing at Seattle and Renton, Washington State, and Wichita, Kansas; 668 by Bell Aircraft Corporation, Atlanta, Georgia; and 536 by Glenn L. Martin Co., Baltimore, Maryland).

Bristol Beaufighter
In the 12th Air Force, a shortage of 'Black Widows' resulted in this heavily armed, British-built ground attack and night-fighter being used from June 1943 until the end of the war by the 414th, 415th, 416th and 417th Night Fighter Squadrons.

Cessna AT-8, AT-17, UC-78 Bobcat
This twin-engined, five-seat, light T-50 transport, originally built in 1939, was used as a light personnel transport by the AAC. Thirty-three Lycoming-powered AT-8 models were followed by Jacobs-powered AT-17 models, and 223 AT-17As with metal propellers followed. Some 466 AT-17B and AT-17C models were also built. Of the total number built, 550 went to Canada as the Crane 1A. The AAC ordered 1,287 C-78 (later UC-78) Bobcat light personnel transports, and 17 commercial T-50 examples (UC-78A) were also commandeered for service; 1,806 UC-78B and 327 UC-78C models with two-bladed, fixed-pitch, wooden propellers were also built by Cessna.

Consolidated B-24 Liberator
The first significant version to see service with the USAAF was the B-24D. The first US B-24s to see action were those in Java, where, on 16 January 1942, five bombed Japanese airfields and shipping during the enemy advance in the Dutch East Indies. Experience of head-on attacks by fighters on the glass-nosed B-24Ds in Europe led to the B-24G/H/J series, with a nose turret containing two .50 in machine-guns.

The B-24G, fitted with the Emerson nose turret, served only with the 15th AF in Italy. Variants similar to the B-24G were built by Convair at Fort Worth, and by Douglas and Ford, as the B-24H. Convair built 738 B-24Js with hydraulically

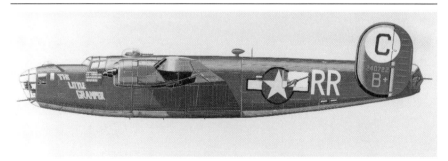

Consolidated B-24D Liberator *The Little Gramper* of the 566th BS, 389th BG, 8th AF, based at Hethel, England, in 1944. (© Mike Bailey)

These 9th AF B-24D Liberators heading low over the Adriatic to their target in 1943 are painted 'Desert Pink' (more familiarly known as 'Titty Pink' by crews). (USAF)

operated Consolidated nose turrets, while Douglas built 582 with electrically operated Emerson turrets. Two other types of nose turret – the Consolidated, with staggered guns, and the hydraulically operated Motor Products turret (an improved version of the Consolidated turret) – were also used.

Ford built 1,780 B-24Hs, which were also fitted with Emerson nose turrets. A further 1,587 B-24Js, similar in appearance to the B-24H, had a Motor Products nose turret, and later, an autopilot and bomb sight. Altogether, 6,678 B-24Js were built by all five Liberator plants, the greatest number of all Liberator variants. Consolidated and Motor Products turrets were also used in the tail.

The B-24L differed from previous models primarily in the installation of a Convair-designed tail station, containing two hand-held .50 in machine-guns.

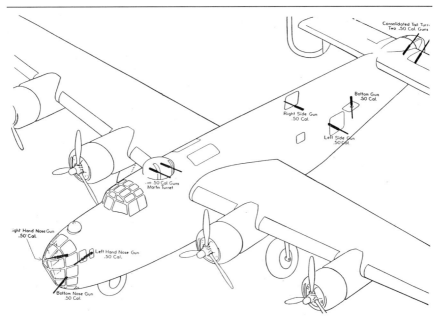

B-24 turrets and gun locations.

Altogether, 18,188 Liberators were built by Consolidated-Vultee at San Diego, California (B-24D/J/L/M); Convair at Fort Worth, Texas (B-24D/H/J/L/M); Douglas at Tulsa, Oklahoma (B-24D/E/H/J); Ford Motor Company at Willow Run, Dearborn, Michigan (B-24H/J/L/M), and North American at Dallas, Texas (B-24G/J), the highest production of any US aircraft of the period. In September 1944, 6,043 B-24s (24 per cent more than the peak B-17 force) were in operation with the USAAF, equipping 45½ groups world-wide.

Convair B-32 Dominator
Developed as a parallel project to the B-29 as a safeguard against delays in production, prototypes were ordered in September 1940, ostensibly as replacements for the B-17 and B-24. The first of three XB-32s were flown on 7 September 1942, and the second on 2 July 1943. The third prototype, which was changed from twin- to single-tail, was flown on 9 November 1943.

Technical troubles delayed the B-32's introduction into service until 1945, when only fifteen saw limited action in the western Pacific before the end of the war. Forty TB-32s were completed as trainers, and another 1,588 B-32s were cancelled.

Curtiss C-46 Commando
The design originated in 1937 as a 36-seat commercial transport, but by the end of the Second World War the C-46 had been widely used as a troop and freight carrier for the AAFs. It was the largest and heaviest twin-engined transport aircraft to see operational service with the USAAF. It was

successfully introduced into ATC and TCG in 1942, providing much-needed airlift capability. The C-46A was fitted with a large cargo loading door in the rear fuselage, a cargo floor, and folding seats along the cabin walls for forty fully-equipped troops. Altogether, 1,491 C-46s were built.

The C-46 operated primarily in the Pacific, because of its greater load-carrying capability and better performance at high altitude than the C-47's. Its most famous theatre of operations was the supply of war material to China from India over the 'Hump' (Himalayas). The C-46D had a revised nose and double loading doors. Further variants similar in appearance to the C-46D followed, and many remained in service after the war.

Curtiss P-40 Warhawk

After evaluation trials in May 1939 in competition with other pursuit prototypes, the XP-40 was declared the most acceptable, and an order for 524 P-40s was placed. Production continued with the P-40B, similar to the British Tomahawk II. The P-40B introduced armour protection for the pilot and doubled the wing firepower from two to four .30 in guns, in addition to two .50 in guns mounted on the engine cowling. Curtiss built 131 P-40Bs in 1941 before going over to P-40C production with improved self-sealing fuel tanks.

On 7 December 1941 a few P-40s managed to get into the air during the Japanese attack on Pearl Harbor and scored the first US fighter 'kills' on Japanese aircraft. Although short on performance when compared with other US fighters in service at the outbreak of war, P-40s were available in large numbers, with highly trained pilots to fly them.

The P-40 earned fame through the activities of less than 100 aircraft flying in China with the American Volunteer Group (better known as the 'Flying Tigers'), commanded by Gen. Claire Chennault. Operating in a hostile environment, using equipment inferior to the enemy's, the P-40s, with their red-and-white shark teeth emblems on the nose, went into combat two weeks after Pearl Harbor. Before being disbanded in 1942, they shot down 286 Japanese aircraft for the loss of only twelve pilots.

Curtiss P-63 Hawk

Development of the Model 75 monoplane by the Curtiss Airplane Division of the Curtiss-Wright Corporation, Buffalo, New York, began in November 1934. The AAC held a series of design competitions in 1935–6 between the Seversky P-35 and the Model 75. These were the first single-seat monoplane pursuits to feature a retractable undercarriage, enclosed cockpit and other modern features. In July 1936 production orders were placed for the Seversky pursuit and just three Y1P-36 service test models. However, on 7 July 1937, 210 P-36 production models were ordered. The first of 178 P-36A and 31 P-36C models were delivered to the USAAC in April 1938 (the other aircraft became the XP-40, which led to the P-40 series).

On 7 December 1941 four P-36As of the Hawaii-based 46th Pursuit Squadron shot down two Japanese bombers during the second phase of the attack on Pearl Harbor.

Four-engined bomber specifications

	B-17C/D	B-17F	B-17G	B-24D	B-24H/J	B-29B
			Max Bomb Loads (Long Range Mission)			
Crew:	10	10	10	10	10	10
Power Plant:	Four 1,200 hp R-1820-65 Cyclone	Four 1,200 hp R-1820-97 Cyclone	Four 1,200 hp R-1820-97 Cyclone	Four 1,200 hp R-1830-65 Twin-Wasp	Four 1,200 hp R-1830-65 Twin-wasp	Four 2,200 hp Wright R-3350 radials
Dimensions:						
Span	103 ft 9 in	103 ft 9 in	103 ft 9 in	110 ft 0 in	100 ft 0 in	141 ft 33 in
Length	68 ft 4 in	74 ft 8 in	74 ft 3 in*	66 ft 4 in	67 ft 2 in	99 ft 0 in
Height	18 ft 4 in	19 ft 2 in	19 ft 2 in	17 ft 11 in	18 ft 0 in	29 ft 7 in
Wing area	1,420 sq. ft	1,420 sq. ft	1,420 sq. ft	1,048 sq. ft	1,048 sq. ft	1,736 sq. ft
Weights:						
Empty	27,650 lb	35,728 lb	36,134 lb	32,605 lb	36,500 lb	69,000 lb
Gross	46,650 lb	40,260 lb	40,260 lb	60,000 lb	64,500 lb	137,500 lb
Performance:						
Max speed	291 mph/25,000 ft	325 mph/25,000 ft	302 mph/25,000 ft	303 mph/25,000 ft	290 mph/25,000 ft	364 mph/25,000 ft
Cruise Speed	217 mph	160 mph	160 mph	200 mph	215 mph	228 mph
Range	2,400 miles	2,420 miles	3,750 miles	2,850 miles	2,100 miles	4,200 miles
Service Ceiling	36,000 ft	38,500 ft	35,600 ft	32,000 ft	28,000 ft	32,000 ft
Bomb Load:	4,800 lb (8 × 600 lb or 14 × 300 lb or 4 × 1,000 lb or 2 × 2,000 lb)	4-6,000 lb (26 × 100 lb or 16 × 300 lb or 12 × 500 lb or 2 × 2,000 lb)	4-6,000 lb (26 × 100 lb or 16 × 300 lb or 12 × 500 lb or 2 × 2,000 lb)	5-8,800 lb (20 × 100 lb or 12 × 300 lb or 8 × 1,000 lb or 4 × 2,000 lb)	5-8,800 lb (20 × 100 lb or 12 × 300 lb or 8 × 1,000 lb or 4 × 2,000 lb)	20,000 lb (4 × 4,000 lb or 8 × 2,000 lb or 12 × 1,600 lb or 40 × 500 lb)
Armament:	6 × .50 in 1 × .30 in Brownings One .30 in	8/11 × .50 in 1 × .30 in Brownings	11/13 .50 in 1 × .30 in Brownings	10 × .50 in calibre Brownings	10 × .50 in calibre Brownings	2.50 in guns in each of 4 remotely controlled turrets + 2.50s in tail turret.

* Cheyenne tail

de Havilland F-8 Mosquito

This famous British aircraft was much coveted in the Second World War, but British and Canadian production could not keep pace with US demands, and only about 200 models were operated by the USAAF. In USAAF service the Mosquito PR Mk XVI was used in the light weather-reconnaissance, radar reconnaissance and 'Joan-Eleanor' spy communication roles in England. Deliveries of the P-61A were slow, so in the 12th AF the 416th Night Fighter Squadron operated the Mosquito and in the 9th AF in England, the 425th Night Fighter Squadron used some Mosquito NF-XIIIs.

Douglas A-20, P-70 Nighthawk, F-3 Havoc

Originally designed in 1938 as an attack bomber, that year the Model 7B was entered for the July 1938 attack bomber design competition, and the prototype flew on 26 October 1938. France and the UK operated the DB-7 in combat, the RAF using the aircraft for the duration of the war.

Early in 1939 the AAC ordered 143 A-20As, and these were delivered to light bombardment groups in the USA and Hawaii. On 2 October the AAF ordered 999 A-20B models, which benefited from recent combat experience in Europe. The A-20B was fitted with self-sealing fuel tanks, armour plate, increased fuel capacity and .50 in guns in place of all but one of the earlier .30s. Deliveries to the AAF commenced in December 1941.

In England, on 4 July 1942, six crews from the 15th Bomb Squadron and six RAF crews, all flying DB-7Bs, carried out the first raid in which Americans participated, on German airfields in Holland.

In November 1942 the Boston entered service in North Africa. The 9th AF used the A-20 in tactical missions against German defences prior to the Normandy landings.

Douglas A-20B Havocs of the 97th Squadron, 47th BG, in North Africa. The 47th BG, 12th AF, together with A-20Bs of the 68th Observation Group and those of the 15th Squadron, operated in North Africa from 1942. (USAF)

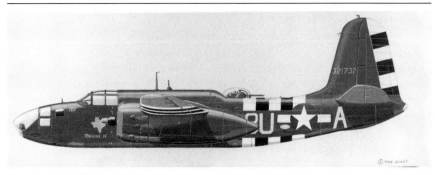

Douglas A-20J Havoc *Maxine IV* of the 646th BS, 410th BG, 9th AF, based at Gosfield, England, in 1944. (© Mike Bailey)

A-20G and A-20J Havocs were attack bombers with a solid 'gun nose' containing 20 mm cannon and .50 in machine-guns. The 5th AF operated the A-20 at masthead height in the Pacific, and used the aircraft to excellent effect during the Battle for Dutch New Guinea, while the 47th BG of the 12th AF used it during the Italian campaign. A few P-70 Nighthawk models fitted with AI radar were operated by night-fighter squadrons including the 6th, 418th and 421st NFS over Guadalcanal and New Guinea. Three A-20s were converted to F-3 photo-reconnaissance aircraft, and were followed by 46 similarly converted A-20J/K aircraft, which were re-designated F-3A and used by the 155th Photographic Squadron (Night) in the 9th AF in Europe in 1944–5.

When production of the A-20 ended in September 1944, 7,098 had been built by Douglas and 380 by Boeing.

Douglas A-24
At the time of the Japanese attack in December 1941, 52 of these single-engined dive-bombers, similar to the Navy SBD attack bomber, were en route by sea to the 27th BG (Light) in the Philippines and were diverted to Australia.

In February 1942 they were used for the first time by the 91st Bomb Squadron in the Dutch East Indies, but with little success.

Douglas A-26 Invader
As early as 1942 it was planned to replace all other medium bombers with the A-26 Invader, but production delays, caused by a shortage of machine tools, meant that only twenty-one aeroplanes had been accepted into service by March 1944.

A-26s arrived in the ETO in September 1944 for assignment with the 9th AF, first seeing action on 6 September, when a force of 545 bombers, including 18 Invaders attached to the 386th BG, attacked Brest.

On 17 November the Invader made its group debut when A-26Bs of the 416th BG, led by A-20J/K Havocs, bombed the stores depot at Hagenau. Weather conditions were bad, and the 416th BG was the only group out of the six dispatched that managed to bomb the target. Two days later, 41

A-26B-DL Invader 41-39456 with six .50 in machine-guns in the nose and remote-controlled dorsal and ventral turrets. Eight more guns could be added – two each side of the nose and four under the wings. (USAF)

A-26Bs and three groups of B-26 Marauders, led by 8 A-20K Havocs, bombed an ordnance depot at Merzig in front of advancing US troops.

Glass-nosed A-26Cs satisfied the requirement for a light bomber operating at medium altitude, and the A-26 overcame a period of uncertainty in 1944, replacing the A-20 in combat units. The A-26C medium bomber variant had only six machine-guns: two in the nose and two in each turret. A co-pilot-bombardier was added as a fourth crew member.

The Invader flew its final mission in Europe on 3 May 1945, when 130 A-26s of the 386th, 391st, 409th and 418th BGs, 9th AF, led by 8 PFF Marauders of the 1st Pathfinder Squadron, bombed the Stod Ammon Plant in Czechoslovakia. Only six A-26 groups were in service overseas by August 1945. In the Pacific they were operated by the 3rd BG in the 5th AF and the 319th BG in the 7th AF until 12 August 1945.

Invader production ceased at the war's end, and all outstanding contracts were cancelled. Only 2,450 A-26s had been delivered. It was the last propeller-driven, twin-engined bomber to be built for the US Air Force.

Douglas B-18 Bolo, B-23, UC-67 Dragon

The DB-1 (B-18) twin-engined medium bomber was built to meet a 1934 requirement to replace the Martin B-10 as the standard US bomber. A production order for 133 B-18 models was placed in January 1936, followed by two more, in June 1937 and mid-1938, for 217 B-18A versions. By 1940 the B-18 was standard equipment in the USSAC, and it was still in front-line service in Hawaii and Alaska at the time of the Japanese attack on Pearl Harbor. Most of the 33 B-18As of the 5th and 11th BGs in Hawaii were destroyed.

In 1942 the B-18 was replaced by the B-17, and 76 B-18Bs were converted for magnetic airborne detection and used on antisubmarine patrol in the Caribbean. The B-23 Dragon development of the Bolo was notable for being the first US bomber to carry a tail gun position. The B-23 first flew on 27 July 1939 and 38 were built.

Douglas C-32, C-33, C-34, C-39 series
The C-32 was the military version of the Douglas Commercial DC-2, and first entered service with the AAC in 1934. Two YC-34s, which were similar, were ordered in 1936, followed by 18 C-33 models with a larger tail. They were supplemented in 1939 by the first of 35 C-39 versions.

Late in 1941 the 16-seat C-39s ferried supplies to Newfoundland, and in December they evacuated survivors from the Philippines to Australia. The single C-41 and single C-42 versions were fitted with 'Twin-Wasp' and Wright 'Cyclone' engines respectively. In 1942 commercial DC-2s commandeered for military service were re-designated C-32A.

Douglas C-47 Skytrain, C-48, C-49, C-53 Skytrooper
The most widely used aircraft in the history of the US Air Forces served in every theatre in the Second World War. It was also produced in greater numbers than any other Army transport. Affectionately called the 'Gooney Bird', the C-47 was developed from the DC-3 Commercial airliner, from

Douglas C-47A-DK *Iron Ass* 42-92099 of the 75th Squadron, 435th Troop Carrier Group, 9th AF. B-17G-DL 44-6349 of the 301st BG, 15th AF, can be seen in the background. (via Jack Krause)

Medium bomber specifications

	A-20G	B-26C	B-25H	B-25J	A-26C
Crew:	3	7	3-6	3-6	3
Power Plant:	2 × 1,600 hp R-2600-23	2 × 2,000 hp R-2800-43	2 × 1,700 hp R-2600-13	2 × 1,700 hp R-2600-92	2 × 2,000 hp R-2800-27/-79
Dimensions:					
Span	61 ft 4 in	71 ft 0 in	67 ft 7 in	67 ft 7 in	70 ft 0 in
Length	48 ft 0 in	58 ft 3 in	51 ft 0 in	52 ft 11 in	51 ft 3 in
Height	17 ft 7 in	21 ft 6 in	15 ft 9 in	16 ft 4 in	18 ft 3 in
Wing area	464 sq. ft	658 sq. ft	610 sq. ft	610 sq. ft	540 sq. ft
Weights:					
Empty	15,984 lb	24,000 lb	19,975 lb	19,480 lb	22,850 lb
Gross	27,200 lb	38,200 lb	36,047 lb	35,000 lb	35,000 lb
Performance:					
Max speed	339 mph/12,400 ft	282 mph/15,000 ft	275 mph/13,000 ft	272 mph/13,000 ft	373 mph
Cruise Speed	272 mph	214 mph	230 mph	230 mph	284 mph
Range	1,090 miles	1,150 miles	1,350 miles	1,350 miles	1,400 miles
Armament/	8 × .50 in	12 × .50 in	14 × .50 in	12 × .50 in	6 × .50 in
bomb load	Brownings 2,600 lb bombs	Brownings 3,000 lb bombs	Brownings 1 × 75 mm cannon 8 × 5 m rockets 3,000 lb bombs	Brownings 8 × 5 m rockets 3,000 lb bombs	Brownings in nose, top & ventral turrets 4,000 lb bombs

which it differed in having a strengthened rear fuselage with large loading doors, a stronger cabin floor and more powerful engines. The C-47 was first delivered in October 1938, and the first orders for large-scale production were received in 1940. Douglas at Long Beach, California, built 953 C-47s, and 2,832 C-47As, and Douglas at Tulsa, Oklahoma, built 2,099 C-47As. A further 3,108 C-47Bs and 133 TC-47Bs were built; 36 DC-3 Commercials commandeered from US airlines in 1941 were re-designated C-48, and 51 other DC-3s and 87 under construction for the airlines were also taken over, and re-designated C-49. All other ex-DC-3 Commercials were re-designated C-50, 51, 52 and 68. A total of 221 C-53 Skytrooper troop transport versions and 17 C-117 staff transport models, all based on the DC-3 airline configuration, were built.

C-47s featured in every large-scale paratroop and glider-towing operation. C-47s dropped 4,381 paratroopers over Sicily on 10 July 1943, and were involved in the first airborne invasion of Burma, which began on 5 March 1944, when C-47s towed Waco CG-4A gliders into action. On D-Day, 6 June 1944, in just over two days, C-47s airlifted more than 60,000 paratroopers and their equipment into action in Normandy. C-47s were used again at Arnhem, during Operation MARKET GARDEN in September 1944.

Douglas C-54 Skymaster
At the start of the USA's involvement in the Second World War, no four-engined military transport was immediately available. The Douglas DC-4E had first flown on 21 June 1938, and early in 1942 the DC-4A production line at Long Beach, California, changed over to building C-54 versions for the USAAC. The first 24 off the lines were completed to the original commercial specification, but two-thirds of the total production run of 1,122 C-54s were built at Chicago. C-54s had a crew of six and could carry fifty troops. All C-54s in the Second World War were operated by Air Transport Command on its inauguration in December 1942.

Fairchild AT-13, AT-14, AT-21 Gunner
The first prototype XAT-13 was fitted with a flexible-mounted nose gun and a second .30 in gun in a dorsal power turret, and was primarily used as a bomber crew trainer. A small fuselage bomb bay was also installed.

The XAT-14A became a bombardier trainer after the nose gun and turret were removed. AT-21 gunnery trainers of the same basic type but with a two-gun dorsal turret went into production in 1942. These were largely replaced by training versions of operational models and relegated to target-tug duties.

Fairchild PT-19, PT-23, PT-26
The pre-war Fairchild M-62 tandem-seat monoplane was among the designs obtained by the AAC in 1940 for use in the vast expansion training programme then under way in the USA. A total of 270 175 hp 'Ranger'-powered PT-19s were built before production was switched to the 200 hp L-440-3-powered PT-19A version.

In 1941 demand became so great that trainer production at the Fairchild factory at Hagerstown, Maryland, had to be supplemented by output from four other factories: at Aeronca, Middleton, Ohio; St Louis Aircraft Corporation, Missouri; Howard Aircraft Corporation, St Charles, Illinois; and Fleet Aircraft Corporation, Fort Erie, Ontario. In total, 3,702 PT-19As were built by Fairchild, Aeronca and St Louis, and 873 PT-23 versions, which differed from the PT-19A in having an uncowled 'Continental' R-670 series engine, were also built. These were followed by 256 PT-23A versions which had blind-flying provision.

Fairchild UC-61

A total of 163 Fairchild 24W-41 light transports were intended for the Army in 1941, but all except two were sent to the UK under Lend-Lease. A further 512 UC-61A models with new radio equipment followed, of which 148 were retained by the USSAF.

UC-61B to UC-61J designations were applied to Commercial Model 24A, taken over by the Army, and the 306 UC-61K models built had a 'Ranger' L-440-7 in-line engine in place of the earlier 'Warner' R-500-1 radial engine.

Gliders

Army development of troop-carrying gliders began in 1941. Trials of the Waco XCG-4 were carried out in 1942 and led to large-scale production contracts which eventually totalled 13,906 models from no less than sixteen different assembly lines.

The improved Waco CG-15 Hadrian entered operations rather disastrously in the Allied invasion of Sicily in July 1943, although the

Waco CG-4A gliders with D-Day markings landing at a rough strip. The CG-4A could carry thirteen troops. (USAF)

problems were not attributable to the glider itself. In all, 427 CG-15s were built. Both types took part in every major airborne operation during 1944–5, including the D-Day landings on 6 June, the ANVIL landings in southern France in August 1944, Operation MARKET GARDEN in September 1944, and the crossing of the Rhine in April 1945.

L-series liaison types

At the outbreak of war in Europe in September 1939, the standard Air Corps observation aircraft in service in the USA were the North American O-47 and Curtiss O-52 Owl. By the end of the war the O-49 (later L-1) Stinson Vigilant, Taylorcraft (YO-57, later L-2 aircraft), Aeronca Defender (YO-58, later L-3), Piper J3C-65 Cub (YO-59, later L-4), and Vultee-Stinson O-62 (later L-5) Sentinel liaison types were in use with the Army observation units.

In Washington, DC, in January 1942, at what became known as the 'Puddle-Jumper' conference, a requirement for 4,000 light aircraft for use in low-level reconnaissance, front-line courier duties (and later, spotters for the US Army field artillery) was set out.

A total of 3,000 US liaison aircraft, including nine squadrons in the 9th AF, served in Europe alone. Most were L-4 Cubs and Stinson L-5 Sentinels. By the end of the war 5,409 L-4 Grasshoppers, 250 TG-8 glider trainers and 3,000 Stinson L-5s were built.

Lockheed A-28, A-29 AT-18, B-34/37 Lexington

USAAF interest in the Lockheed Model 18 (Lodestar commercial airliner) in May 1941 led to a contract for one C-56 and three (later increased to thirteen) C-57 versions. The A-29 was developed in 1938 from the

Piper L-4 Grasshopper 43-640 *Georgia Cracker*. By the end of the war some 5,409 L-4 Grasshoppers had been built for the AAF. (USAF)

Lockheed 14 transport, expressly to meet RAF requirements, as the Hudson. With the USA's entry into the war, some were repossessed and used as A-29B photo-reconnaissance models; with the dorsal turret deleted, as bomber crew trainers, and in 1942–3, for antisubmarine duties.

An A-29 carried out the first successful attack on a U-boat by an AAF aircraft in the Second World War. A total of 217 AT-18 Army variants with a Martin dorsal turret were used for air gunner training, and 83 similar AT-18As, with the turret deleted, were used as navigation trainers.

In 1941 most of a second batch of 250 Vega-built B-34/34A (Venturas) for the RAF were retained by the AAC, which used them for overwater patrol duty.

Lockheed C-69 Constellation

The Constellation was requisitioned from the L-49 commercial production lines at Lockheed-California, Burbank, at the time of Pearl Harbor, and designated C-69. The first of 22 C-69s for the AAC was flown on 9 January 1943. At 329 mph it was the fastest transport in the AAF inventory in the Second World War.

Lockheed P-38 Lightning

Originally designed in 1937 as a high-altitude interceptor, the first YP-38 made its maiden flight on 16 September 1940, and the first deliveries of the P-38D Lightning to the AAC followed in August 1941. Beginning in late 1941 a few Lightning I versions with unsupercharged 'Allisons' were supplied to the RAF, but the majority were diverted to the USAAF after Pearl Harbor.

The first unit to operate the P-38 was the 342nd Composite Group, operating from Icelandic bases. By mid-1942, when heavy losses in the bomber groups made it obvious that long-range escort fighters would be required, the P-38F began to be deployed in large numbers in the ETO.

Lockheed P-38H Lightning *Texas Ranger* of the 38th FS, 55th FG, 8th AF, based at Nuthampstead, England, in 1943. It was flown by Lt.-Col. Jack Jenkins. (© Mike Bailey)

Although slightly slower and less manoeuvrable than most single-engined fighters then in service, the Lightning's greater range made it an excellent escort fighter. The P-38J version appeared in August 1943 and was used mainly to accompany US heavy bombers on long-range missions over Germany. A total of 9,535 P-38s were built.

Martin B-26 Marauder

Designed to a specification issued by the AAC on 25 January 1939 for a new high-speed medium bomber, the first B-26 came off the production lines on 25 November 1939. On 25 February 1941 the first B-26 was delivered to the USAAF. On 8 December 1941, the day following the attack on Pearl Harbor, 53 of the first 56 Marauders took off from Langley Field, Virginia, bound for Australia. These B-26A Marauders formed the 22nd BG, and in April 1942 they saw action for the first time, during attacks on New Guinea.

During 1942 B-26As saw wide-ranging service, being employed as torpedo-bombers in the Battle of Midway in June and, based in Alaska, for long-range strikes on the Aleutians. Although these raids were good for morale, the bomb loads were, of necessity, small because of the need to carry extra fuel in bomb bay tanks.

B-26 Marauder ER-V of the 450th BS, 322nd BG, 9th AF, in D-Day invasion markings, 1944. (USAF)

Martin B-26B Marauder *Brinah* of the 320th BG, 12th AF, based in Sardinia in 1944. (© Mike Bailey)

The B-26B, which began production in May 1942, had armour plate around the pilots' area, a ventral tunnel gun, a second nose gun, two blister guns each side of the fuselage below the cockpit and a new Martin-Bell power-operated tail gun.

A high landing speed and an increase in gross weight resulted in many accidents, and for a long time the Marauder gained an unwelcome reputation for being an unsafe aircraft. On the B-26B-10, improvements were made to the flying characteristics by adding a taller fin and rudder and increasing the wing area and wing span.

A total of 1,242 B-26Bs were built at Baltimore, Maryland, and a further 1,235 B-26Cs, which were similar, were built at Omaha, Nebraska.

Marauders began equipping the 8th AF in England in the spring of 1943. Their first mission, on 14 May 1943, ended in disaster when all eleven B-26s failed to return from a low-level strike on Ijmuiden, Holland. During the summer of 1943, Marauders were switched to a high-level bombing role, but success was only finally achieved, late in 1943, when all B-26 groups were transferred to the 9th AF for tactical missions in support of the Allied build-up to the invasion of Europe.

The B-26F had the wing incidence angle increased slightly in an effort to further improve take-off performance. Some 300 were built before minor internal changes altered the designation to B-26G. Some 893 B-26Gs were built before deliveries ceased in March 1945. Altogether, some 5,266 Marauders were built, of which 1,585 were built in Omaha, Nebraska, and 3,681 in Baltimore, Maryland.

Noorduyn UC-64 Norseman

A utility aircraft designed by Noordyn Aviation in Canada, the UC-64 was adopted by the USAAF in 1942 after trials with seven YC-64s. Altogether,

Noorduyn UC-64 Norseman. These Canadian-built utility aircraft did sterling work, and a squadron of twenty were used by the 'Grow Escadrille' to deliver blood and medical supplies and evacuate casualties from France in the summer of 1944. (USAF)

orders for 746 wheeled and ski versions of the C-64A were received from the USAAF during the Second World War.

North American B-25 Mitchell

The result of an AAC requirement for a medium bomber in 1938, North American built the NA-40-1 prototype as a private venture, and successive improvements led to the NA-62. In September 1939 the AAC placed an order for 184 B-25s. The first flying example took to the air on 19 August 1940.

The B-25A, of which 40 were built, introduced self-sealing tanks and armour plate. In 1941 the first B-25As began equipping the 17th BG (Medium). During an anti-shipping strike off the west coast of the USA on 24 December, a B-25A of this group sank a Japanese submarine.

In all, 120 B-25B models, with Bendix electric turrets and the tail gun deleted, were built. In April 1942, the same month that Jimmy Doolittle led the famous B-25 raids on Japan from the USS *Hornet*, B-25Bs of the 3rd BG based in the Philippines were also used against Japanese targets.

A second factory at Dallas, Texas, turned out B-25Ds. Dallas ultimately built 2,290 B-25Ds, while the plant at Inglewood, California, turned out 1,619 of the not dissimilar B-25Cs. North American also built 405 B-25Gs and 1,000 B-25Hs, both of which had a nose-firing 75 mm cannon for anti-shipping strikes in the Pacific.

The B-25H first entered service in the Pacific in February 1944. The cannon were not successful, however, and the type was withdrawn in August 1944. The B-25J, of which 4,318 models were built at Kansas City

North American B-25C Mitchell of the 12th BG, one of fifty-seven to cross the South Atlantic to Egypt in mid-1942, pictured beside the ubiquitous US Army Willys jeep and dutiful groundcrew. (USAF)

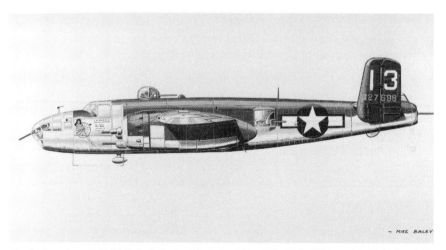

North American B-25J Mitchell *Lucky 13* of the 321st BG, 12th AF, based in Italy in 1944. (© Mike Bailey)

by 1945, introduced four .5 in 'blister' guns, two on each side of the fuselage below the cockpit.

The majority of USAAF B-25Js fought in the south-west Pacific, where they replaced the B-26 in squadron service. During 1943–4, 60 B-25s were stripped and modified to serve as AT-24A-D and TB-25D-J advanced trainers. TB-25Js were finally retired from service in January 1959, and the last transport version was retired in May 1960.

Almost 11,000 examples of the Mitchell were built, including 9,815 which served in the USAAF.

North American BC-1, BC-2, AT-6

In March 1937 North American Aviation of Inglewood, California, submitted their NA-26 design for the AAC design competition to produce a new basic trainer. They were successful, and the company was awarded a contract for 41 BC-1 production versions. Further contracts took the number to 180, and an order for 92 BC-1A versions followed. In 1940 the designation changed from BC-1A to AT-6A, and 85 further models were ordered for use as advanced trainers.

The AT-6 became the standard trainer used by the USAAC and other air arms in the Second World War, and in 1941 a second production line opened at Dallas, Texas, where 912 of the AT-6As built were for the AAF. Dallas also built 2,970 AT-6C models, which differed from earlier ones in having a low-alloy steel and plywood construction.

The last of the main type to be built for the AAF was a proportion of the 4,388 AT-6D models, which reverted to the original construction methods.

North American O-47

Conceived in 1934, this stocky observation monoplane became the standard observation model for Army and national ground units from 1937, and was on the point of being replaced in the role by bombers and camera-carrying fighters when the Japanese attacked in December 1941. None were used in combat in the Second World War, although a few were lost during Japanese attacks in 1941.

North American P-51 Mustang

On 29 May 1942 the first Allison-powered P-51 for USAAF service was flown. It differed from the Mustang I in having four 20 mm cannon in place of the six machine-guns used on the RAF version. In 1942 it was suggested that the Mustang be developed as a long-range fighter fitted with the Rolls-Royce

North American P-51B Mustang *Shangri La* of the 336th FS, 4th FG, 8th AF, based at Debden, England. It was flown by Capt. Don Gentile. (© Mike Bailey)

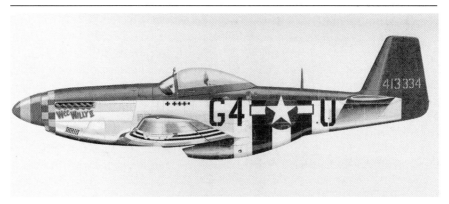

North American P-51D Mustang *Wee Willy II* of the 362nd FS, 357th FG, 8th AF, based at Leiston, England, in 1944. (© Mike Bailey)

P-51B Mustang of the 551st FS, 495th Fighter Training Group, 8th AF. (USAF)

'Merlin' engine. Accordingly, four Allison-engined aircraft were converted to Mustang Xs, with 'Merlin' 61 engines, producing a top speed of 400 mph at 30,000 ft. At the same time, North American began fitting the 1,300 hp Packard-built V-1650-3 'Merlin' to two XP-78 models, later re-designated XP-51B.

In mid-1942 the first twenty P-51s to follow the last Mustang Is were used as tactical reconnaissance aircraft, equipped with two cameras. In 1943 they were used by the 68th Observation Group.

From October 1942 to March 1943, 500 A-36A dive-bomber models fitted with 1,325 hp liquid-cooled V-1710-87 engines boosted for low-level operation, dive-brakes and bomb racks were built. These served in Tunisia and India, and proved so successful that P-51 (and P-47) fighter bombers were used on close-support missions for the rest of the war.

In Europe the first P-51Bs were assigned, in November 1943, to the 9th Air Force for tactical missions. The first Mustang escort mission was flown on 5 December 1943. Eventually, P-51s escorted B-17s and B-24s to Berlin and back. By the end of the war, the P-51 equipped all but one of the 8th AF fighter groups.

The P-51C first flew on 5 August 1943. Similar to the P-51B, it had increased internal fuel capacity and a British-designed Malcolm bulged sliding hood. A total of 1,750 P-51C variants were built. The P-51D appeared in Europe in 1944, having been flown for the first time on 17 November 1943. It had a teardrop canopy with a lowered rear decking, and a change from four machine-guns to six. Later, a dorsal tail fin fairing was added. In all, 7,956 P-51Ds were built, more than any other variant.

By far the greatest contribution made by the Mustang was in Europe, where it was the saving grace for B-17 and B-24 bomber crews. In the Pacific the P-51D provided valuable escort duty for B-29s. In February 1945 P-51Ds flying from Iwo Jima escorted B-29s to attack Japan. On 7 April P-51Ds penetrated Tokyo airspace for the first time.

A few P-51H models reached the Pacific before the end of the war and served operationally. This was the fastest of all Mustangs, having a top speed of 487 mph. Altogether, 15,586 versions were built, 14,490 of which served the USAAF.

Northrop P-61 Black Widow

The XP-61 was not a conventional design, being much larger than the A-70 and almost as big as a medium bomber. It had a tail boom configuration with twin rudders, and a tricycle undercarriage. The long, protruding nose housed SCR-70 radar, and a crew of three were accommodated in a central nacelle, in a gunner's position above and behind the pilot's cabin, with a radio observer (the term used instead of 'radar operator', because of the secret nature of radar) in a compartment aft. Development was quite protracted, and while the first XP-61 flew on 21 May 1942, the first YP-61 was not delivered until 6 August 1943. Early models were painted olive drab and neutral grey, but the P-61's night attire quickly changed to the customary gloss black overall, which led to the aircraft's sinister name.

P-61s equipped eight squadrons in the Pacific, first going into action with the 6th Night Fighter Squadron, 18th NFG, 13th AF, which landed on Saipan on 21 June 1944. The first Black Widow victory was obtained nine days later. During March–June 1944 the 422nd and 425th Night Fighter Squadrons of the 9th AF arrived in England equipped with the P-61A. On 15 July the 422nd NFS flew the first P-61 operation from England, and on the very next night it scored the first 'kill' when it downed a V-1. On 5 August the 425th NFS shot down a V-1, and two days later the 422nd shot down its first manned aircraft. (The 425th had to wait until Christmas Eve 1944 before it could claim its first manned aircraft 'kill'.)

In July–August the 422nd and 425th moved to France for intruder operations, armed with HVAR rockets. At the end of hostilities, 15 of the USAAF's 16 night-fighter squadrons were equipped with the P-61: 8 in the Pacific in three air

Northrop P-61B Black Widow 42-39515. Early models were painted olive drab and neutral grey, but the P-61's night attire quickly changed to the customary gloss black overall which gave the aircraft its sinister name. At the end of hostilities, 15 of the USAAF's 16 night-fighter squadrons were equipped with the P-61. (USAF)

forces, 2 in the CBI, and 3 in the Mediterranean with the 12th AF. In the US ZOI four training squadrons made up the 481st Operational Training Group.

Republic P-47 Thunderbolt

Designed originally as a strategic escort for deep-penetration B-17s and B-24s over Europe in the Second World War, the P-47 also served with distinction in the Pacific. On 6 May 1941 the prototype XP-47B flew for the first time. Built around the 2,000 hp Pratt & Whitney R-2800 radial engine, the Thunderbolt was a real heavyweight, weighing just over 12,000 lb.

On 18 March 1942 deliveries of production P-47B models to the USAAF began. Early models were known as 'Razorbacks' because of their raised rear fuselage leading to the framed cockpit hood. The P-47C's fuselage was extended by some 13 inches to improve manoeuvrability. Some 602 P-47Cs were built. The vast majority of the 12,602 P-47Ds built were fitted with a teardrop moulded cockpit hood for improved rearward vision. Water injection was used to boost engine power at higher altitudes.

On 13 April 1943 the 56th and 78th FGs of the 8th AF in England flew their inaugural mission on the P-47C and P-47D. Known as the 'Jugs' (short for 'Juggernauts', because of their ability to out-dive any other fighter), they flew their first escort mission on 4 May 1943, when the 56th accompanied B-17s to Antwerp.

The final Thunderbolt models were the P-47M, of which 130 were built

Fighter specifications

	P-47B	P-47D-25	P-38J	P-51B	P-51D/K	P-51H/M
Crew:	1	1	1	1	1	1
Power Plant:	2,000 hp R-2800-21	2,300 hp R-2800-59	2 × 1,425 hp V-1710-89/91	1,380 hp V-1650-7	1,490 hp V-1650-7	1,380 hp V-1650-9
Dimensions:						
Span	40 ft 9ins	40 ft 9ins	52 ft 0 ins	37 ft 0 ins	37 ft 0 ins	37 ft 0 ins
Length	35 ft 0 ins	36 ft 1 ins	37 ft 10 ins	32 ft 3 ins	32 ft 3 ins	33 ft 4 ins
Height	12 ft 8 ins	14 ft 2 ins	9 ft 10 ins	12 ft 2 ins	12 ft 2 ins	13 ft 8 ins
Wing area	300 sq. ft	300 sq. ft	327.5 sq. ft	235.7 sq. ft	235.7 sq. ft	235.7 sq. ft
Weights:						
Empty	9,346 lb	10,000 lb	12,780 lb	6,985 lb	7,125 lb	6,585 lb
Gross	13,360 lb	19,400 lb	21,600 lb	11,800 lb	11,600 lb	11,054 lb
Performance:						
Max speed	429 mph/27,800 ft	428 mph/30,000 ft	414 mph/25,000 ft	440 mph/30,000 ft	437 mph/25,000 ft	487 mph/25,000 ft
Cruise Speed	335 mph	290 mph	362 mph	362 mph	380 mph	
Range	550 miles	475 miles	450 miles	400 miles	950 miles	850 miles
Service Ceiling	42,000 ft	42,000 ft	44,000 ft	41,800 ft	41,900 ft	41,600 ft
Armament:	8 × .50 in Brownings 2 × 1,000 lb	8 × .50 in Brownings bombs	11/13 .50 in 1 × .30 in 2 × 1,000 lb	4 × .50 in Brownings 2 × 1,000 lb bombs	6 × .50 in Brownings 2 × 1,000 lb bombs	6 × .50 in Brownings or 10 × 5 in rockets

Republic P-47D Thunderbolt *Penrod and Sam* of the 62nd FS, 56th FG, 8th AF, based at Boxted, England, in 1944. It was flown by Capt. Robert S. Johnson. (© Mike Bailey)

by 1945, and the P-47N, built solely for the Pacific theatre. It had a wing span 18 inches greater than the P-47M, to accommodate two 93 gallon tanks in addition to two drop tanks. With internal fuselage tanks and a 100 gallon belly drop tank, the P-47N had a range of 2,350 miles. Near the end of the war, P-47Ns flew escort for the B-29s bombing targets in Japan.

By August 1945 P-47s had flown on every front, destroying over 7,000 enemy aircraft on the ground and in the air. Altogether, 15,579 Thunderbolts were accepted by the USAAF.

Ryan PT-16, PT-20, PT-21, PT-22

This wartime, low-wing, tandem-seat trainer series was developed from the Ryan S-T, first manufactured by T. Claude Ryan in 1933. Until 1939, when the AAC purchased a single Model STA-1 as the XPT-16, all training aircraft in the service had been of the biplane type. Trials involving 15 YPT-16s late in 1939 were successful, and in 1940, 40 very similar PT-20 versions were ordered.

During 1941 the 125 hp Menasco in-line engine was replaced on the production lines by the 132 hp Kinner R-440 radial, and the 100 models produced became the PT-21. A further 1,023 PT-22 Recruit versions fitted with the more powerful 160 hp Kinner R-540-1 engine followed in 1941–2. They were identical to the PT-21 except that the wheel spats and main leg fairings were deleted.

Seversky P-35

Developed from two privately financed experimental fighters produced by Seversky in 1935, later redesign work produced the AP-1, which was submitted for evaluation by the Army in 1937 and accepted. Seversky delivered 76 P-35s, the last aircraft on the contract, which proved to be the prototype for the Republic P-43 Lancer.

PT-13 Stearman over Randolph Field, Texas. (GG)

By the close of 1941, 48 P-35As were stationed in the Philippines but were destroyed by the Japanese in two days, mostly on the ground.

Stearman PT-13, PT-17, PT-18

The origins of the Stearman Model 75 biplane trainer began with the success of the X-70, which was first flown on 1 January 1934. The US Navy ordered their first Stearman trainer that same year. The Army tested the X-70 in April 1934, and again in October 1934. It was selected as the service's new primary trainer, but it was not until July 1935 that 26 PT-13s (Model 75) were ordered. The production PT-13 flew for the first time in April 1936, and deliveries began in June that year. Altogether, 660 PT-13A/B/C/D aircraft with the 220 hp Lycoming R-680-7 radial engine and 150 PT-18 aircraft using the 225 hp Jacobs R-755-5 engine were delivered during 1937–41.

In 1940, to avoid a shortage of Lycoming R-680 engines, the Army requested the 220 hp Continental R-670-4 and 5 as alternatives on future orders. This brought about a change of designation from PT-13 to (A75 N1) PT-17, and this became the most numerous version. Stearman Aircraft Division, Boeing Aircraft Co., at Wichita, Kansas, delivered 2,942 PT-17s to the Army alone.

Supermarine Spitfire V, IX

The Spitfire Va and Vb also followed the earlier Spitfire II as standard equipment in the three US 'Eagle' Squadrons, nos 71, 121 and 133, which had formed in the UK during October 1940–August 1941, with US volunteers. On 29 September 1942 these were disbanded and transferred to the specially activated 4th FG, 8th AF, at Debden, as the 334th, 335th, and 336th (Pursuit) Squadrons.

On 14 September the 31st and 52nd FGs, which had also been equipped with the Spitfire V since arriving in England in June 1942 (P-39 Airacobras, their intended equipment, having failed to appear), had been assigned to the 12th AF, but they continued to operate from England under the auspices of the 8th AF until 10 October 1942. The 31st and 52nd flew their Spitfire Vs in action under the auspices of RAF Fighter Command, taking part in the Dieppe operation on 19 August, among others (the 52nd flew 83 sorties in the UK).

Late in October the 31st and 52nd Groups were shipped to Gibraltar to re-equip with tropicalized Spitfire Vcs (the discarded Spitfire Vs passing to the 67th Observation Group at Membury, Wiltshire, to be used for training for low-level reconnaissance missions. The 7th PR Group also used a few Spitfire Vs until replacement by the PT XI.)

On 8 November 1942 the 31st and 52nd Fighter Groups flew from Gibraltar to Algiers as part of Operation TORCH, the ground echelon of the 31st landing at Arzeu beach the same day. (The 52nd ground echelon arrived from England after the campaign had ended.) Almost immediately the 31st and 52nd made attacks on German troop and motorized columns in the desert. Later, they flew ground attack and bomber escort missions and took part in the invasion of Sicily (in July 1943). In April–May 1944 both squadrons converted to the P-51 Mustang and were assigned to the 15th AF.

In the summer of 1943 the 14th Photographic Squadron, 7th Photo Group, at Mount Farm, Oxfordshire, began training on the Spitfire V while awaiting its 21 Spitfire XIs. The Spitfire XI also equipped the 10th, 67th and 363rd Tactical Reconnaissance Groups of the 9th AF.

Vultee A-31, A-35 Vengeance

In addition to an order placed by the British Purchasing Commission in 1940, the AAC placed an order in March 1941 for 100 A-31s from Vultee and 200 from Northrop. In December 1941 another 243, designated V-72s, were commandeered from the British cash contract. The principal difference between the A-31 and A-35 was the substitution of .50 in guns in place of the British .303 in guns in the former.

The Vengeance saw limited action in the AAF, many A-31As being relegated to target-towing duties.

Vultee BT-13, BT-15 Valiant

The Vultee Model 54 low-wing monoplane became the most numerous of the basic trainers used in the Second World War. An initial order for 300 was placed with Vultee at Nashville, Tennessee, in 1939, and eventually orders totalling 6,407 BT-13A versions followed. These were followed by an order for 1,125 BT-13B models. All were powered by the 450 hp Pratt & Whitney R-985-AN-1 engine. During 1941–2, 1,693 BT-15 Valiants powered by the 450 hp Wright R-975-11 engine were built.

A-35 Vengeance used by the 8th AF in England. Many A-31A and A-35s were used as target-tugs. (via Mike Bailey)

Westland Lysander

Approximately 24 British-built Westland Lysander TT Mk IIIA target-towing versions were used by the 8th AF in England from mid-1942 to early 1944, when they were replaced by the Vultee A-35.

US aircraft production

Of the 299,293 military aircraft (including 5,254 produced in Canada) built for the US military from 1 July 1940 to 30 August 1945, the AAF received 230,175. These figures include aircraft assigned to overseas air forces under Lend-Lease. Of the 802,161 aircraft engines built during the same period, the AAF received 653,647, or 81 per cent. The grand total of propellers produced in the same period was 807,424.

Aircraft production (aero engines in parentheses)							
	1932	1933	1934	1935	1936	1937	1938	1939
Germany	36	368	1,968	3,183	5,112	5,606	5,235	8,295
Japan	691	766	688	952	1,181	1,511	3,201	4,467
USA	593	466	437	459	1,141	949	1,800	5,856

	1940	1941	1942	1943	1944	1945
Germany	10,247	11,776	15,409	24,807	39,807	7,540
Japan	4,768	5,088	8,861	16,693	28,180	11,066
USA	3,807*	19,433*	47,836*	85,898*	96,318*	46,001*
	(15,513)	(58,181)	(138,089)	(227,116)	(256,912)	(106,350)

* accepted by AAF

Five plants turned out B-24 Liberators during the Second World War. The Ford Motor Company of Dearborn, Michigan, built B-24H/J/L/M models in a plant covering 3,700,000 sq. ft at Willow Run. Here, some of the 1,677 B-24Ms with Emerson nose turrets are coming off the assembly lines. The serial number on the tail of the B-24 (middle) is spurious. (Ford Archives)

In 1939 US output of aircraft from factories was 2,195 aircraft of all types: a quarter of Germany's output, two-thirds of France's, one-third of the UK's and about half of Japan's. By November 1939 the British and French had invested more than $84 million in engine plants alone, and their orders soon reached 14,000 aircraft. On 6 January 1941 Roosevelt outlined the Lend-Lease programme and enunciated the 'Four Freedoms' principle. He asked Congress for approval to extend arms credits 'to those nations which are now in actual war with aggressor nations'. The Lend-Lease Act was passed by Congress on 11 March 1941, when British Commonwealth reserves were almost exhausted.

Roosevelt said: 'This decision is the end of any attempt at appeasement in our land; the end of urging us to get along with the dictators; the end of compromise with tyranny and the forces of oppression.' The Lend-Lease Act made US funds available for Allied aircraft contracts, which were then given Army designations. From March 1941 to25 August 1945 the UK received from the USA an estimated £5,049 million worth of materials. The State Department *Report on War Aid Furnished by the United States to the USSR* (Washington, 1945) lists 14,798 army aircraft allocated to the Soviet Union, of which 14,018 were actually delivered.

Block numbers were assigned to production batches and were frequently changed in series to reflect a slight change in specification or armament. Early A-20G Havocs had four 20 mm M2 cannon and two .50 in machine-guns in the nose, and single guns in the dorsal and ventral positions. A second series had the cannon deleted and replaced with four more .50 in machine-guns. From the A-20G-20- DO block onwards (like 43-9929 pictured), the rear fuselage was widened by 6 in to take a Martin electrically powered dorsal turret with two .50 in guns; other changes increased internal fuel tankage and bomb load. (USAF)

In 1940 some 200,000 people were employed in the US aircraft industry; in 1941 there were 347,000, and in 1942 the total had risen to 471,000. By 1943 it more than doubled, reaching 1,345,600, 478,000 of whom (36.5 per cent of the production force) were women. In 1944 an all-time high was reached with the figure of 2,102,000. Only in 1945 did it fall again, to 1,464,000. By the end of the war a third of all workers in the US aircraft industry were women.

Construction, block and serial numbers

All military aircraft built during the Second World War had a manufacturer's construction number and a corresponding serial number applied by the AAF (a bureau number in the case of the Navy) and stencilled on the aircraft on the production line. The first digit of the serial number signified the year in which the aircraft was ordered (not built): for example, the number '212345' on the aircraft meant that the aircraft was ordered in 1942 – (4)2-12345.

An individual manufacturer's block number and factory letters were also used. For example, in the case of a Liberator D model built by Consolidated in the serial range 42-40218 to 42-40257, this appeared as B-24D-CO-40

B-17s were built at three wartime plants and were identified by their respective block number designations: Boeing Aircraft at Seattle, Washington (B-17-BO); Douglas Aircraft, Long Beach, California (B-17-DL), and Lockheed-Vega, Burbank, California (B-17-VE). These are B-17G-5-VE models from the 42-39758/40057 batch, ordered in 1942 and built by Vega. (Lockheed-California)

(40 being the block number). Block numbers were assigned to production batches and were frequently changed in series to reflect a slight change in specification or armament. Five plants turned out B-24 Liberators during the Second World War, and each was known by its factory letters: CO – Consolidated, San Diego, California; CF – Consolidated (Convair) Fort Worth, Texas; FO – Ford, Willow Run, Michigan; DT – Douglas, Tulsa, Oklahoma; and NT – North American, Dallas, Texas. B-17s were built at three wartime plants and were correspondingly identified as: BO – Boeing Aircraft at Seattle, Washington State; DL – Douglas Aircraft, Long Beach, California; and VE – Lockheed-Vega, Burbank, California.

The system is so comprehensive that it is impossible to list all manufacturers' models here, but corresponding sets of numbers and letters are apparent in the photo captions in this book.

Production problems

In 1941, before the USA entered the Second World War, strikes in the US aircraft industry forced the government to seize two aircraft plants. In 1942 the number of strikes fell, but in 1943 they were on the increase again. War production in 1942 lost over 4 million worker-days because of strike action, and in 1943, 3,752 strikes resulted in the loss of a staggering 13½ million worker days.

The government built a massive aircraft factory covering 3,700,000 sq. ft for the Ford Motor Company near the village of Willow Run, 30 miles west of Detroit, Michigan, and Henry Ford declared that it would produce 1,000 aircraft a day. However, in February 1943 Harry S. Truman, then Chairman of the Senate War Investigating Committee, began an investigation of Willow Run because production of B-24 Liberators was so low. It was not until the end of 1943 that the plant (dubbed 'Willit Run' because of its poor initial output) was producing, on average, 340 Liberators a month. By the end of the war Ford had produced 6,792 Liberators, second only to Consolidated at San Diego, which produced 7,500.

In 1942 the US produced 47,836 aircraft; in 1943 it produced 85,898 aircraft, and in 1944, 96,318 aircraft. Fourteen companies delivered 253,734 aircraft between 1 July 1940 and 31 August 1945, as follows:

North American	41,188
Consolidated Vultee	30,903
Douglas	30,696
Curtiss	26,154
Lockheed	18,926
Boeing	18,381
Grumman	17,428
Republic	15,603
Bell	13,575
Eastern (Gen. Motors)	13,449
Martin	8,810
Chance Vought	7,890
Ford	6,791
Goodyear	3,940

Overseas combat strength of the AAF			
Month End	Group Strength (Total/Overseas)	Total Combat A/C Overseas	First-line Combat A/C Overseas
Nov. 1941		1,024	870
Dec. 1941	(67/18)	1,105	957
June 1942	(114/29)	1,998	1,902
Dec. 1942	(167/69)	4,798	4,695
June 1943	(234/103)	9,001	8,586
Dec. 1943	(269/135)	12,719	11,917
June 1944	(234/203)	20,814	19,892
Dec. 1944	(242/214)	22,876	19,892
Apl 1945	(243/224)	24,122	21,752
Aug. 1945	(213/155)	17,315	15,100

Aircraft acceptances world-wide by the AAF

B-17 January 1940–31 August 1945	12,677
Peak B-17 inventory August 1944	4,574
B-24 January 1940–31 August 1945	18,188
Peak B-24 inventory September 1944	6,043
B-25 production	9,815
B-26 production	5,157
B-29 July 1943–August 1945	3,760
Maximum number of overseas combat groups:	
33 B-17 Groups, September 1944	
45½ B-24 Groups, June 1944	
40 B-29 Groups at end of war	
(21 of these reached their combat status)	
P-47 production	15,579
31 P-47 Groups by end of summer 1944	
(5,595 on hand May 1945)	
P-38 production	9,535
13 P-38 Groups overseas, spring 1944	
P-40 production	13,738
P-39 production	9,585
P-51 production	14,490
(5,541 on inventory Aug. 1945)	
A-20 production	7,230
A-25 production	2,446
Liaison types June 1940–Aug. 1945:	13,558
	(5,611 L-4s/L-14s)
	(3,590 L-5s)
(Peak inventory, liaison a/c:	4,211, June 1944)
Transport aircraft:	DC3/C-47 10,245
C-54	1,089
C-46	3,144

Note: Almost 25 per cent of the grand total of planes accepted by the AAF by August 1945 were trainers – 55,000. During November 1940–February 1943, trainers constituted more than half of the total AAF inventory at any time.

Aircraft in the ETO and MTO theatres (heavy bombers), with tonnage dropped

		ETO	MTO	TOTAL	Total Tonnage
1942	June	0	17	17	
	July	48	42	90	
	August	104	57	161	166
	September	178	64	242	145
	October	296	66	362	308
	November	247	122	369	701
	December	219	150	369	683
1943	January	214	200	414	2,190
	February	255	208	463	1,463
	March	303	255	558	3,126
	April	590	302	892	4,183
	May	705	337	1,042	8,687
	June	846	462	1,308	9,006
	July	856	545	1,401	15,049
	August	907	454	1,361	16,341
	September	971	518	1,489	22,686
	October	1138	416	1,554	13,302
	November	1554	401	1,955	14,287
	December	1686	577	2,263	22,769
1944	January	1817	855	2,672	30,332
	February	1998	901	2,899	31,679
	March	2295	1292	3,587	40,886
	April	2647	1375	4,022	61,360
	May	3137	1499	4,636	96,464
	June	3100	1392	4,492	118,750
	July	3494	1407	4,901	98,341
	August	3662	1571	5,233	105,103
	September	3659	1720	5,379	78,717
	October				71,150
	November				75,805
	December				82,074
1945	January				64,924
	February				107,083
	March				153,541
	April				111,658
	May				464

CHAPTER NINE

Personnel

In December 1938 AAF total personnel stood at 21,125, 1,300 of them officers, and 18,000 enlisted men (with an additional 2,800 officers and 400 men in the Reserve). Two years later the AAFs numbered 101,227 officers and men, and by December 1941 no less than 354,161 officers and enlisted men were in the service. From 1 January 1942 to 30 June 1943, the period of greatest growth, the AAFs expanded to 2,197,114 personnel. In this 18-month period some 1,842,953 personnel were interviewed, classified and assigned to ground or aerial duties.

Up until March 1944 the principal source of flying officers and ground officer specialists was the Aviation Cadet Recruiting Programme. Successful completion qualified men to be commissioned as 2nd lieutenants or appointed flight officers. The programme comprised aircrew trainees – pilots, bombardiers and navigators – and men trained in armament, communications, engineering, meteorology and photography. Altogether, there were seventeen general headings for ground duty, including those already mentioned, plus: aircraft maintenance, wire technician, synthetic training device instruction, parachute rigging, metalworking, welding, supply, and administration. In the air, general duties were divided into pilotage, bombardier, navigation, aerial engineering, radio, and aerial gunnery.

Basic physical requirements included 20/20 vision in each eye without glasses, and perfect colour vision; 20/20 hearing in each ear; a minimum height of 60 in (pilots' minimum 64 in), a maximum of 76 in, and a minimum weight of 105 lb (pilots' minimum 114 lb) and a maximum of 200 lb, depending on height and age. Formal schooling was not required, applicants being given a qualifying examination of short-answer or multiple-choice questions. Applicants also underwent a series of psycho-motor and placement tests at the basic training centre in order to check mental and muscular co-ordination. Scores on these tests determined the particular phase of flying – pilot, bombardier or navigator – in which applicants could be best and most quickly trained. If they failed to meet the minimum standard in any respect, applicants were eligible to apply for aerial gunnery training.

On 8 July 1942 the grade of Flight Officer was established. In 1941 Congress had funded Public Law 999, which provided some conditional training possibilities and gave enlisted flying students the title of Aviation Students. Graduates of the programme were awarded the rating of pilot and warranted as a staff sergeant. In the earliest months of the Second World War, sergeant pilots flew fighter, bomber and transport aircraft, but the prospect of enlisted men flying aircraft was viewed with some scepticism by

UNITED STATES ARMY PAY TABLE (EFFECTIVE JUNE 1, 1942). UNDER PAY READJUSTMENT ACT OF 1942, APPROVED JUNE 16, 1942

Grade	Pay period	Annual base pay	Less than 3 years service	Over 3 years service	Over 5 years service	Over 6 years service	Over 9 years service	Over 10 years service	Over 12 years service	Over 15 years service	Over 17 years service	Over 18 years service	Over 21 years service	Over 23 years service	Over 24 years service	Over 27 years service	Over 30 years service	Rental With dependents	Rental No dependents	Subsistence (30-day month) With dependents	Subsistence (30-day month) No dependents
General of A. of U. S.		$13,500	$1,125.00	$1,125.00	$1,125.00	$1,125.00	$1,125.00	$1,125.00	$1,125.00	$1,125.00	$1,125.00	$1,125.00	$1,125.00	$1,125.00	$1,125.00	$1,125.00	$1,125.00	(2)	(2)	(2)	(2)
General [1]		8,000	666.67	666.67	666.67	666.67	666.67	666.67	666.67	666.67	666.67	666.67	666.67	666.67	666.67	666.67	666.67	$120	$105	$42	$21
Lieut. Gen. [2]		8,000	666.67	666.67	666.67	666.67	666.67	666.67	666.67	666.67	666.67	666.67	666.67	666.67	666.67	666.67	666.67	120	105	42	21
Major General		8,000	666.67	666.67	666.67	666.67	666.67	666.67	666.67	666.67	666.67	666.67	666.67	666.67	666.67	666.67	666.67	120	105	42	21
Brig. Gen.		6,000	500.00	500.00	500.00	500.00	500.00	500.00	500.00	500.00	500.00	500.00	500.00	500.00	500.00	500.00	500.00	120	105	42	21
Colonel	6	4,000	333.33	350.00	350.00	366.67	383.33	383.33	400.00	416.67	416.67	433.33	450.00	450.00	466.67	483.33	500.00	120	105	42	21
Lieut. Col., Less than 30 yrs. ser.	5	3,500	291.67	306.25	306.25	320.83	335.42	335.42	350.00	364.58	364.58	379.17	393.75	393.75	408.33	422.92		120	105	63	21
Lieut. Col., Over 30 yrs. ser.	6	4,000	333.33	350.00	350.00	366.67	383.33	383.33	400.00	416.67	416.67	433.33	450.00	450.00	466.67	483.33	500.00	120	105	42	21
Major, Less than 23 yrs. ser.	4	3,000	250.00	262.50	262.50	275.00	287.50	287.50	300.00	312.50	312.50	325.00	337.50					105	90	63	21
Major, Over 23 yrs. ser.	5	3,500												393.75	408.33	422.92	437.50	120	105	63	21
Captain, Less than 17 yrs. ser.	3	2,400	200.00	210.00	210.00	220.00	230.00	230.00	240.00	250.00								90	75	42	21
Captain, Over 17 yrs. ser.	4	3,000									312.50	325.00	337.50	337.50	350.00	362.50	375.00	105	90	63	21
First Lieutenant, Less than 10 yrs. ser.	2	2,000	166.67	175.00	175.00	183.33	191.67											75	60	42	21
First Lieutenant, Over 10 yrs. ser.	3	2,400						230.00	240.00	250.00	250.00	260.00	270.00	270.00	280.00	290.00	300.00	90	75	42	21
Second Lieutenant, Less than 5 yrs. ser.	1	1,800	150.00	157.50														60	45	42	21
Second Lieutenant, Over 5 yrs. ser.	2	2,000			175.00	183.33	191.67	191.67	200.00	208.33	208.33	216.67	225.00	225.00	233.33	241.67	250.00	75	60	42	21
Warrant Officers (J.G.)		1,800	150.00	157.50	157.50	165.00	172.50	172.50	180.00	187.50	187.50	195.00	202.50	202.50	210.00	217.50	225.00	60	45	42	21
1st Mates & Asst. Engrs. AMPS.		1,950	162.50	170.63	170.63	178.75	186.88	186.88	195.00	203.13	203.13	211.25	219.38	219.38	227.50	235.63	243.75	60	45	42	21
Ch. War. Officers (except Masters, AMPS).		2,100	175.00	183.75	183.75	192.50	201.25	201.25	210.00	218.75	218.75	227.50	236.25	236.25	245.00	253.75	262.50	75	60	42	21
Masters, AMPS.		2,400	200.00	210.00	210.00	220.00	230.00	230.00	240.00	250.00	250.00	260.00	270.00	270.00	280.00	290.00	300.00	90	75	42	21
Ch. War. Officers (especially designated by S/W)		2,400	200.00	210.00	210.00	220.00	230.00	230.00	240.00	250.00	250.00	260.00	270.00	270.00	280.00	290.00	300.00	90	75	42	21
Ch. War. Officers (especially designated by S/W)		3,000	250.00	262.50	262.50	275.00	287.50	287.50	300.00	312.50	312.50	325.00	337.50	337.50	350.00	362.50	375.00	105 [3]	90 [3]	63	21
Master or First Sergeants			138.00	144.90	144.90	151.80	158.10	158.10	165.60	172.50	172.50	179.40	186.30	186.30	193.20	200.10	207.00				
Tech. Sergeants			114.00	119.70	119.70	125.40	131.10	131.10	136.80	142.50	142.50	148.20	153.90	153.90	159.60	165.30	171.00				
Staff Sergeants—Technician 3rd Gr.			96.00	100.80	100.80	105.60	110.40	110.40	115.20	120.00	120.00	124.80	129.60	129.60	134.40	139.20	144.00				
Sergeants—Tech. 4th Gr.			78.00	81.90	81.90	85.80	89.70	89.70	93.60	97.50	97.50	101.40	105.30	105.30	109.20	113.10	117.00				
Corporals—Tech. 5th Gr.			66.00	69.30	69.30	72.60	75.90	75.90	79.20	82.50	82.50	85.80	89.10	89.10	92.40	95.70	99.00				
Privates First Class.			54.00	56.70	56.70	59.40	62.10	62.10	64.80	67.50	67.50	70.20	72.90	72.90	75.60	78.30	81.00				
Privates			50.00	52.50	52.50	55.00	57.50	57.50	60.00	62.50	62.50	65.00	67.50	67.50	70.00	72.50	75.00				

[1] Entitled to personal money allowance of $2200.00.
[2] Entitled to personal money allowance of $500.00.
[3] Total pay and allowances not to exceed $458.33.

Flight Pay: 50% of base pay, longevity pay and overseas pay.
Overseas Service: 10% of base pay; for submarine and aviation duty longevity pay is included in the computation.
Warrant officers, enlisted men, 20%.
Parachute Pay: Officers, $100 monthly, enlisted men, $50.

the War Department, and this led to the Flight Officer Act, Public Law 658. As a result, those sergeant pilots produced by the Staff Sergeant Pilot Programme were promoted as top-flight officers. Upon graduation, aviation (flying training) cadets who had not qualified for commissions as 2nd lieutenant could be appointed flight officers, with a status equivalent to that of warrant officer, junior grade. Promotion from flight officer to 2nd lieutenant was permitted.

In order to be rated as any of the various types of flying personnel, officers, warrant officers, flight officers and enlisted men on duty with the AAF had to meet certain qualifications. Most pilot personnel qualified by successfully completing a prescribed course of instruction at an AAF advanced pilot school. However, pilots could receive a rating upon the recommendation of a board of officers on the basis of meeting one of the following requirements:

1. previous aeronautical ratings held or previous aeronautical instruction passed within a specific past period; certain requirements of flying time; completion of a flight test;
2. a rating as service pilot currently held; certain requirements of flying time; determination by the board of qualifications and readiness for assignment to the combat duties appropriate for a pilot who had graduated from an AAF advanced flying school;
3. graduation from a course of instruction for pilots in armed forces of friendly foreign nations, or the accumulation of certain required flying time with the armed forces of friendly foreign nations.

Officer specialities

Pilots

There were nineteen types of pilots among rated personnel, from glider to four-engine:

Senior Pilots required not less than five years' service as rated pilots with aviation components of the military or naval services, and not less than 1,500 hours logged time according to War Department records.

Command Pilot rating could be attained by any rated pilot who had certain combinations of the following: 10, 15 or 20 years active duty or service with air components of the military or naval services, and 2,000–3,000 hours or more logged time according to War Department records. Time flown in heavier-than-air military aircraft as a pilot, co-pilot, or when not at the controls but acting in capacity of command pilot in unit operations of two or more aircraft was credited at 100 per cent. All other flying time in military heavier-than-air aircraft was credited at 50 per cent. Lighter-than-air time was credited at 25 per cent. Flying time in non-military aircraft of 400 or more horsepower was credited at 100 per cent.

Service Pilot rating could be attained by individuals aged between 18 and 45 who had passed physical tests and who possessed outstanding qualifications for the performance of service pilot duties, as defined in AAF Regulation 35-23. Completion of a flight test and professional examination, a certain amount of flying time and a recommendation by a board of officers was required.

GRADES AND INSIGNIA

Rank	*Shoulder Insignia*
General	
Lieutenant General	
Major General	
Brigadier General	
Colonel	
Lieutenant Colonel	(Silver)
Major	(Gold)
Captain	
First Lieutenant	(Silver)
Second Lieutenant	(Gold)
Warrant Officer (chief)	(Brown)
Warrant Officer (j.g.)	(Brown)
Flight Officer	(Blue)

	Sleeve insignia
Master Sergeant, First Sergeant (1st Grade)	
Technical Sergeant (2nd Grade)	
Staff Sergeant (3rd Grade)	
Sergeant (4th Grade)	
Corporal (5th Grade)	
Private First Class (6th Grade)	
Private (7th Grade)	**no chevrons**

Source: *The Officer's Guide*, Military Service Publishing Co., Harrisburg, Penn., July 1943; *AAF: The Official Guide to The Army Air Forces*, Pocket Books, New York, 1944

Senior Service Pilot rating could be attained by a rated service pilot with 1,500 hours logged time according to War Department records, and five years experience as a licensed pilot with the CAA.

Liaison Pilot rating was granted only to officers, warrant officers and enlisted men assigned to air observation of the Field Artillery.

Glider Pilot rating required successful completion of a prescribed advanced course of glider pilot training at an AAF special service school. Individuals could be rated Glider Pilot if they held ratings as Command Pilot, Senior Pilot, Service Pilot or Senior Service Pilot, had flown as pilot of tactical type gliders for three hours or more and had made at least ten landings, passed a flight test, and were recommended by an examining board.

Rated personnel (other than pilots)

There were seven types of bombardiers and navigators;

Airbase commander;

Aircraft Warning Officers;

Anti-Aircraft Artillery Officers;

Aircraft Engineering – aircraft maintenance engineers, inspectors and aeronautical engineers;

Aviation Engineers – inspection, mechanical, surveying, construction, camouflage and mapping engineers;

Armament and Ordnance – including torpedo, bombsight and mine specialists; bomb disposal and other ordnance officers;

Administrative – adjutant, publications and inspection officers, non-tactical unit commanders;

Chaplains;

Chemical – aviation chemical warfare specialists;

Communications – including signal, message centre, crypto-analytic and pigeon officers, radio, telephone, telephoto, radar and telegraph engineers;

Finance, Budget and Fiscal Officers;

Intelligence – historical, public relations and prisoner of war interrogation officers, photo interpreters;

Legal – judge advocates, legal assistance and claims officers;

Operations – personal equipment, flight control, priorities and traffic, and weight and balance officers;

Medical – fifty-three types, including surgeons, nurses, veterinarians, sanitation engineers, dieticians, physical therapy aides and varied medical specialists;

Mess Officers;

Personnel – military personnel and civilian personnel officers, classification and assignment officers, psychologists;

Photographic – including ground and aerial photographers, motion-picture producers, technicians, laboratory supervisors;

Provost Marshal – including military police and prison officers;

Radar – airborne and ground officers;

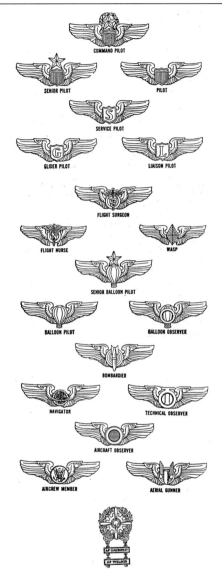

'Wings' are 3 inches for uniform coat and 2 inches for shirt. In the ETO, 'wings' were sometimes mounted on a blue, rectangular 'Combat Crew' patch. It is probably apocryphal, but it is said that the patch was introduced because EM ground crew acquired aircrew 'wings' and, on pass, wore them on their uniform to impress their 'girls'. However, it was more likely used to denote that the individual was on a combat crew. Gold braid bordering the patch indicated that the individual was a member of a lead crew.

AAC Technician badge (bottom). AAF enlisted technicians and mechanics were authorized to wear a distinctive silver badge indicating the skills in which they were qualified. Qualifications: at least six months service with the AAF, and either graduation from an authorized course in technical training or evidence of capability in one or more of twenty-four specialities for which the badge was designated.

Source: The Officer's Guide, Military Service Publishing Co., Harrisburg, Pennsylvania, July 1943; *AAF: The Official Guide to the Army Air Forces,* Pocket Books, New York, 1944.

Special Services – including physical fitness and orientation officers;
Statistical Officers;
Supply – quartermaster, army exchange, salvage, laundry, technical, freight, petroleum, procurement and renegotiation officers;
Weather – forecasters, climatologists, oceanographers.

Enlisted specialities

Pilots – Liaison Pilots (this rating had been discontinued by mid-1944), Glider Pilots (EM between the ages of 18 and 26 years of age with 125 hours flying time, either in a glider or powered aircraft, were eligible) and Service Pilots;★
Aircrew – gunners, photographers, radio operators, aerial engineers;
Administrative – financial, typing and mail clerks; interpreters, translators and investigators; business machine operators; supply technicians in communications, ordnance, engineer and quartermasters' equipment;
Aircraft Warning – controllers, aircraft observers, information centre operators;
Anti-aircraft – including gunners, repairmen, heightfinders, listeners, searchlight men;
Armament and Ordnance – power turret, bombsight, munitions and armament technicians;
Bandsmen – twelve types, classified by instrument;
Chemical – toxic gas handlers, decontaminating equipment technicians;
Communications – including codes, cryptographic, pigeon, signal and facsimile technicians, radar mechanics and radar repairmen, radar operators, radio operators, telephone and telegraph technicians;
Draftsmen – draftsmen and photogrammetrists;
Duty and Instruction – including military police guards, athletics instructors, technical instructors, aircraft handlers;
Engineer, Utility and Repair – including geodetic computers, surveyors, laundry technicians; construction men, including bricklayers, camouflagers, riggers, carpenters;
Maintenance – including supercharger, power plant and fabric and dope specialists; electrical instrument, autopilot and fire control specialists; gyro, optical, hydraulic and mechanical instrument technicians; machinists; parachute and propeller specialists; sheet metal workers, welders, woodworkers;
Medical – laboratory, supply, optical and dental technicians; pharmacy and veterinary specialists;
Marine – including able seamen, mates, oilers, engineers;
Miscellaneous – including dog trainers, tyre rebuilders, entertainment directors, physics laboratory assistants;
Photographic – including camera and motion-picture technicians, photographers and projectionists, laboratory assistants;
Reproduction and Printing – lithographic and printing specialists;

★ The only enlisted personnel who could apply for aircrew training were enlisted men of the AAF who were combat crew members returned from overseas theatres after completion of a prescribed number of combat missions or in accordance with War Department regulations.

Service and Repair – including shoe repair, leather and canvas workers, painters, refrigeration mechanics, demolition specialists, water supply technicians;

Trainer Equipment – navigation trainers; instrument flying trainers, altitude chamber and flexible gunnery specialists;

Transportation – automotive equipment operators and repairmen, diesel mechanics, motor and tractor specialists;

Weather – forecasters, observers; equipment, radio-sonde men.

Staff organization

Wing & Higher Levels		Staff Sections In Groups
A-1:	Personnel (Policies & Plans)	S-1
A-2:	Intelligence	S-2
A-3:	Operations and Training	S-3
A-4:	Supply (& Maintenance)	S-4

Women in the US Air Forces

On 15 May 1942 President Roosevelt signed a bill creating the Women's Army Auxiliary Corps (from the summer of 1943, re-designated the Women's Army Corps). To enlist as an Air WAC, a woman had to be aged between 20 and 49 and be a citizen of the USA. She could be married or single, but must be without children under fourteen years old. As regards education, two years at high school and a satisfactory aptitude rating were sufficient.

By January 1945, 29,323 women were serving in the AAC, and female officers carried out more than sixty types of duty. They included: medical and hospital technicians; personnel; photography; drafting; radio operators; radio and electrical repair; telephone operators; gasoline motor and light machinery operators; instrument repair; general clerical; typing clerical; statistical and financial; stenography; tabulating machine operators; teletype writer operators; drivers; and supply and stock clerks.

Air WACs served in more than 200 job categories, ranging from aerial photographer to weather observer. They served in the aircraft warning service on the east and west coasts of the USA, releasing 6,000 unpaid women volunteers for other duties. Air WACs accounted for almost half of the Army's entire WAC personnel. Only twenty Air WACs qualified as aircrew for non-combat flights. Women mechanics totalled 1,200.

In January 1945, 32,008 WACs were serving in the AAF in the USA, 8,904 of them in Training Command, and 7,315 overseas, including 2,755 in ATC, 2,835 in the ETO, 457 in the MTO, and 694 in the FEAFs.

The WASP

The 318th AAF Flying Training Detachment was formed in November 1942 at Howard Hughes Field in Houston, Texas, and was the brainchild of the famous American aviatrix, Jacqueline Cochran. She helped persuade the Army to create a training unit to prepare women pilots to ferry military aircraft from manufacturers to embarkation points, just as women pilots in the Air Transport

Francie Meisner with her instructor, Herman Fuchs, during training on the PT-13 Stearman at Avenger Field, Sweetwater, Texas. WASPs performed outstandingly in the Second World War, ferrying aircraft, towing targets at gunnery school and serving as flight instructors at flight schools. (Francie Meisner Park)

Auxiliary were doing in the UK. (Originally, from 1943, when they were allowed into Training Command, women ferried only *training* airplanes.)

So successful was the school that in June 1943 Gen. Arnold ordered the WFTD and WAFS to amalgamate under Col. Cochran into the Women's Air Force Service Pilots, better known as the WASP. Comprised of female pilots who were Civil Service employees rather than military members of the AAF, the WASPs performed outstandingly. In all, 25,000 women applied to join the WASP; 1,830 were admitted, and 1,074 completed their indoctrination. (The elimination rate for WASP applicants in 1943 was 26 per cent; 47 per cent in 1944.) A total of 37 WASPs were killed in accidents, and 36 were injured. WASPs also towed targets at gunnery school and served as flight instructors at flight schools.

The WASP was disbanded on 20 December 1944, when the AAFs were facing a surplus of male aviators. Women pilots had flown 77 types of aircraft, including single- and twin-engined fighters, C-54 and C-46 transports and B-24 Liberators. In 27 months up to December 1944, ferry pilots completed 12,650 movements over 9,224,000 miles. At the end, 916 women pilots were on duty with the AAF, including 620 in Training Command, and 141 in the ATC.

Nurses
By 1944 more than 6,500 nurses were assigned to the Army Nurse Corps: 6,000 served at AAF station hospitals, the other 500 were flight nurses assigned to air evacuation of the wounded.

Class 44-W-10, the last WASP class, 20 December 1944. WASP was disbanded at this time because the AAFs were facing a surplus of male aviators. (Francie Meisner Park)

Civilians
By September 1942 the AAF had 58,125 female employees. By June 1943 the figure was 151,125.

American Indians in the AAF

American Indians, mostly from California, joined the AAFs in great numbers: 30 American Indians won the DFC, 70 received the Air Medal, and an Osage won the DFC. At least one posthumous Silver Star was awarded, to an American Indian pilot flying a B-24, who made a direct hit on a Japanese convoy off New Guinea even though his right arm had been shot off. A Paiute of the 77th Pursuit Squadron pulled a pilot out of an aircraft which crashed in flames.

One of the most distinguished American Indian pilots was William R. Fredersburg, a Menominee from Wisconsin, who flew with the 8th AF in England. One Seneca pilot flew twenty-five missions with the 8th AF before being listed MIA over Hungary in 1944.

Black Americans

The armed forces had agreed that 10.6 per cent of the total service personnel should be black. However, the AAFs took only 6.1 per cent (145,327) at the peak (November 1943), and only 0.3 per cent of the officers were non-white. The vast majority were draftees, who maintained aircraft, loaded bombs and generally carried out the most menial of duties. By August 1945 there were 139,559 blacks (6.2 per cent) in the AAF.

In 1940 Congress forced a reluctant Gen. Henry Arnold to accept blacks and admit them to flight training, although on a racially segregated basis, in keeping with War Department policy.

The Army Expansion Act of 1939 brought into existence the all-black 99th Pursuit Squadron in January 1940. The 99th Pursuit Squadron was trained at the traditionally Negro Tuskagee Institute in Alabama. The Tuskagee Programme eventually contributed 673 fighter pilots, 253 twin-engine (medium bomber) pilots, 58 field artillery liaison officers and 132 navigators.

The 99th Pursuit, renamed the 99th Fighter Squadron, was joined by the 100th, 301st and 302nd Fighter Squadrons, which constituted the 332nd Fighter Group of the 12th AF in Italy after February 1944. Its commander was Lt.-Col. Benjamin O. Davis Jr. In 1941 he and his father and three others, all chaplains, were the only black officers in the US military. The only other black American AAF unit was the 477th Bombardment Wing (Medium), but this unit never saw combat.

Flying first P-40s and later P-51s, black airmen in the 332nd FG were credited with the destruction of 108½ enemy aircraft in the air and another

Men of a black aviation ordnance unit loading 250 lb bombs for the bombers. (USAF)

150 on the ground. On escort missions, they never lost or abandoned a bomber. The 332nd FG was awarded a Distinguished Unit Citation, and its pilots received one Silver Star and 150 Distinguished Flying Crosses.

US engineer (aviation) regiments

In 1939 the AAF operated 69 airbases. Four years later, this number had risen to 1,400 bases world-wide. In every theatre of war, USAAF groups operated either from existing airfields and airstrips or ones specially constructed by the Allied nations and the US Army Aviation Engineer Battalions.

The 21st Aviation Engineers were established on 4 June 1940 from the 21st Engineers (Gen. Service) Regiment, which served in the First World War, and was composed of 800 officers and enlisted men. By 1 November 1943 the Aviation Engineers totalled about 80,000 men, of whom more than 65,000 were overseas. Between mid-1940 and 1943 the Aviation Engineers built 500 bases world-wide. A peak strength in personnel was attained in February 1945, with a complement of 117,851 officers and men.

At the beginning of the war, twelve battalions of Engineer Aviation regiments were scattered throughout the world, from Hawaii to the Pacific. Detachments of the 804th EAB, for instance, were on Christmas Island, helping construct an airfield for the south Pacific ferry route, and on Canton Island, beginning an Army airfield. Between December 1941 and December 1942, the number of battalions was increased from 12 to 51, three-fifths of them overseas. Eventually, bases were constructed throughout the Solomons–New Guinea, Alaska, the Aleutians and China-Burma-India (where up to 100,000 indigenous workers were used to construct a single air base).

Early in January 1942, following the attacks on Hawaii by the Japanese Air Force, the 804th AEB hurriedly laid a turf landing strip at Kualoa Field and put down steel matting. Also in 1942 the aviation engineers laid out airstrips on Bataan, until they were overrun (two companies of the 803rd were captured). Company A reached Corregidor, where for three months its men tried to keep Kindley Field in operation. On 7 August 1942 the invasion of Guadalcanal yielded the first base captured from the enemy, when Henderson Field was established. The 807th EAB had been in Alaska since June 1941, and work started on an airfield at Umnak Island. Steel matting was laid in January 1942.

After the North African campaign, in November 1942 an engineer command was finally established for the Northwest AAFs. During the winter of 1943–4, fifteen heavy bomb groups of the 15th Air Force were based in the Foggia area of Italy. In June 1944 the 9th AF made full use of engineering aviation battalions in Normandy, Gen. Lewis Brereton having the pick of 8th AF engineering battalions. (A 9th AF Engineering Command was activated on 1 July 1944, with a strength of 17,000 officers and men in sixteen aviation engineer battalions.) The first units landed on UTAH and OMAHA beaches, and a landing strip was built at St Laurent-Sur-Mer, near OMAHA, on D-Day + 3, to enable transports to fly in supplies and evacuate the wounded. One hundred C-47s landed daily for the first six weeks. An advanced landing ground at Pierre du Mont was finished and used by P-47s, the first aircraft to be based in France since 1940.

The Cleveland Cletrac M2 7-ton high-speed tractor, seen here towing a GP trailer, was used by the AAF for towing aircraft and heavy equipment. (Charles W. Warren)

Airborne aviation engineer battalions

These descended by parachute to patch up captured aerodromes with hand tools, reinforced by glider-borne engineers with light equipment such as light tractors, rollers and mixers, and so on. Sixteen airborne battalions had been organized by the end of 1943 and were used in North Africa, Burma and New Guinea.

On Christmas Day 1943 the 900th Airborne Engineering Battalion were airlifted to Shingbwiyang to construct the first airfield behind enemy lines in Burma. On 5 March 1944 this unit, together with the Chindits and Commandos led by Gen. Orde Wingate and Col. Philip G. Cochran, descended by gliders at night. On 17 May 1944 the same happened at Myitkyina, Burma, when Company A of the 879th Airborne Engineers were landed by transport gliders.

Aviation engineer battalions (CBI)

In the CBI, all five aviation engineer battalions (823rd, 848th, 849th, 858th and 1883rd) which reached the theatre in 1942–4 were black units. Late in 1943 airfields for B-29s in southern Bengal were constructed at Kharagpur, Chakulia, Piardoba and Dudhkundi as part of the MATTERHORN project to base B-29s in the CBI. Roads were also constructed. Early in 1945 Ledo Road (later Stilwell Road) was opened.

Aviation engineer battalions, Marianas

In the south Pacific the 811th EAB, 13th AF, largely built Tontouta, the most important air base on New Caledonia, while the 810th (black) Battalion built Plaines des Gaiac's at the northern end of New Caledonia in time for it to be used by fighters for the Battle of the Coral Sea, 7–8 May 1942. In 1943

Men of an Engineering Aviation Battalion wearing GI steel helmets fill a US bowser with aviation fuel from captured German jerry cans at an advanced landing strip in France, June 1944. The P-47 Thunderbolts are from the 378th FS, 362nd FG, 9th AF. (USAF)

airfields were built on the atolls of the Gilbert and Ellis Islands by aviation battalions supported by Navy Seabees. Late in 1943, on Makin Island, the 804th AEB ensured that Starmann Field was ready to support the heavy bombers of the 7th AF which took part in the assault on Kwajalein.

The biggest project of all was in the Marianas, where the largest air bases ever were constructed. Runways alone were 8,500 ft long by 200 ft wide. By mid-May 1944 twelve VHB (B-29) groups were to be based there for raids on Japan. Eventually, six airfields (and an air depot, Harmon Field on Guam, HQ XXI BC and a Forward HQ) were constructed: North Field and Northwest Field on Guam, Kobler Field and Isley Field on Saipan, and North Field and West Field on Tinian. Altogether, there were finally six 8,500 ft runways on Tinian, including four (with forty-seven hardstands/taxiways) at North Field by 5 May 1945. (Later, Iwo Jima was converted into a giant airbase for staging B-29s for long-range fighter aircraft. At the end of the war, other 20th AF units were in place in the Ryukyu Islands.)

The first B-29s to land in the Marianas were those of the 73rd VHB Wing, in August 1944, at Isley Field, Saipan. The airfield was finally completed on 2 February 1945, the same day the first runway at Guam was completed. (The first B-29 mission from the Marianas was in late February 1945.) Altogether, five wings – the 73rd, 313th (North Field, Tinian), 314th (North Field, Guam), 58th (West Field, Tinian), and the 315th (Northwest Field, Guam) – and the 509th Composite Group (North Field, Tinian) were based in the Marianas.

By mid-July 1945, 166,345 personnel were based in the Marianas, of whom 59,910 were in the five wings/special units, assigned to XXI BC. By July 1945, 33 Aviation Engineer battalions (927th Engineering Aviation

B-29 *Censored* of the 39th BG taxies out at North Field, Guam. This group flew its first mission to Maug, in the northern Marianas, in April 1945. (USAF)

B-24 Liberator *Patched Up Piece* of the 20th Combat Mapping Squadron, 5th AF, at a Pacific landing strip. A steam roller and the usual jeep can also be seen. (USAF)

Regiment) were on Guam, with the 933rd EA Regiment on Okinawa (secured 31 July 1945), and the 935th EA Regiment on Ie Shima (home of the 301st Fighter Wing from July 1945). If the war had continued a few more months, 93 aviation engineer battalions (some of whom were veterans of the European theatre) would have been in the western Pacific.

CHAPTER TEN

Uniforms, Clothing and Protective Dress

Uniforms

Officers and enlisted men's service uniforms, winter and summer, were basically of the same design, although officers' service uniforms were darker and made of higher-quality materials.

Officers normally wore the 'no. 1' service uniform, which consisted of a no. 51 olive drab, dark-shade service coat and trousers ('greens'), while light-

Capt. John H. Diehl Jr, 44th BG, 8th AF, has captain's bars on his no. 1 uniform (bars were known as 'Hershey Bars'), with officer's tan collar and tie, and garrison cap with gold-and-black piping on the curtain edges. His pilot's wings are mounted on a blue 'Combat Crew' patch above ribbons, L–R: Air Medal, with three Oakleaf Clusters, US Defence Service Medal and the European-African-Middle Eastern Campaign ('ETO' or 'Spam') Medal. (via Steve Adams)

Group and wing commanding officers of the 2nd Bomb Division, 8th AF, in 'greens' and 'pinks'. Brig.-Gen. Leon Johnson (sitting, 2nd from right), and Col. Fred Dent, CO 44th BG (standing, left), are wearing the Distinguished Unit Citation ribbon over their right breast. The 3 inch wings worn by all the officers include Command Pilot and Service Pilot ratings, although Col. Jack Wood (seated, left) is wearing 2 inch wings. Brig.-Gen. Ted Timberlake (seated, 2nd left) and Brig.-Gen. James P. Hodges, CG, 2nd Bomb Division (to his left), are wearing A-11 GI watches. (USAF)

shade drab (shade no. 54) wool serge was used in the EM's Class A or 'dress wear' uniform. Light OD trousers, the same shade as the enlisted men's, could be worn by officers in garrison. Most officers, though, wore khaki chino cotton or wool trousers in garrison. In bright sunlight the trousers appeared a pinkish khaki and the no. 51 OD coat a deep dark green, earning the nickname 'pinks and greens'. Officers' summer uniforms were khaki shade no. 1, a light tan. Most field uniform components were of the greener OD shade no. 7. Leather components were russet (reddish) brown. Shirts included the no. 33 OD shade officer's wool shirt or OD shade no. 50 officer's cotton shirt. (The EM's shirts were the same, except the shoulder straps of the officers' were deleted.) The dark OD officer's wool overcoat was basically similar to the enlisted version, but made of higher-quality wool, with bone buttons.

From 1943 some US troops in England were supplied with contracted British-made jackets similar to British battledress. Gen. Eisenhower asked that an improved version with concealed buttons and sharper appearance be developed for the European and Mediterranean theatres as both a service and field jacket. It was standardized in November 1942 as the OD shade no. 54 wool field jacket, or

'M1944'. Known universally throughout Europe as the 'ETO' or 'Ike' jacket, it became more popular as a service jacket than a field item. In the USA it could be worn only by personnel returning from the European and Mediterranean theatres of war until they were issued with the standard wool coat.

Headgear

Generally, the EM wore the garrison cap, or 'flight cap' as it was commonly known. Officers normally wore the no. 51 officer's wool service cap, which had a crest and peak, or the forage (or 'envelope-style') no. 51 officer's wool garrison cap with folded crown crest. From 1933 EM were authorized to wear the garrison cap, but officers had worn it since 1925, 'for use in flying missions'. They wore the radio/intercom headset over the garrison cap. The service cap could not be worn in flight with a headset over it because of the 'stiffness' of the cap, which prevented the headset from fitting comfortably over the ears. However, a pre-war uniform regulation allowed Air Corps officers to delete the service cap's 'front spring stiffening' (or grommet) so that the headset could be worn over it in flight.

This effect was further enhanced by soaking the cap overnight (preferably in seawater) and subjecting it to as much abuse as possible, even to the extent

Francie Meisner Park, WASP, in the Santiago-blue wool and gaberdine beret and duty uniform (Eisenhower jacket and slacks) of the service, the colour of which was 'invented' by Jacqueline Cochran who loved the blue waters at Santiago, Chile. After WASP was disbanded the Santiago blue dye was destroyed, never to be duplicated. In summer the WASPs wore 'tans'. Gen. Hap Arnold secretly planned to replace Army Air Corps 'pinks' and 'greens' and wanted blue – the blue the US Air Force wears today. (Francie Park)

Capt. Leonard K. 'Kit' Carson, 357th FG, 8th AF, who finished the war with 18½ victories. He is wearing the RAF C-Type helmet and British-made Mk VIII goggles with tinted lenses, B-3 life preserver, and an early US A-14 oxygen mask with web strap, as opposed to the rubber strap. (Merle Olmsted)

93rd BG B-24 crew at Alconbury, England, 1942. The difference in 'old bold' airmen, distinguished by the 'fifty-mission crush' cap worn by the captain (3rd from right), and the young, inexperienced 'kids' (centre), still wearing their 'stiff' caps, is very evident. Significantly, the latters' HS-33 radio headphones are placed around the backs of their necks, while the captain still wears his over his service cap. All are wearing the B-3 life vest. The gunners are wearing the early, heavy B-3 high-altitude 'Alaskan suits', whose collar, cuffs and waist skirt were trimmed with fleece, and A-3 trousers, all made of lightweight seal-brown ¼ inch shearling. The gunners are wearing A-6 winter shoes. All four officers are wearing rubber overshoes over their officer's shoes. These were US Army issue originally, and adopted by the AAF when they arrived in England because of the ubiquitous mud. The first gunner is wearing a B-2 flight cap, the second two wear B-6 winter flight helmets, and the gunner (far right) wears a wool A-4 'Beano' cap. (USAF)

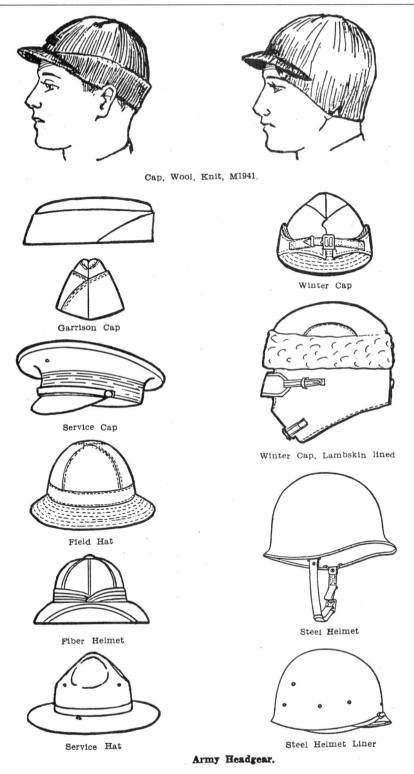

Cap, Wool, Knit, M1941.

Garrison Cap

Service Cap

Field Hat

Fiber Helmet

Service Hat

Winter Cap

Winter Cap, Lambskin lined

Steel Helmet

Steel Helmet Liner

Army Headgear.

Source: *The Officer's Guide*, Military Service Publishing Co., Harrisburg, Penn., July 1943

of running it over with a jeep if necessary!★ Once this procedure had been carried out, the cap was known to all and sundry as the 'fifty-mission crush', which was considered *de rigueur* in some combat theatres. It is by no means certain, but legend has it that removal of the spring could *only* take place after the wearer had flown an acceptable number of combat missions. Veterans, or 'old, bold ones', were therefore easily distinguishable from the 'new kids'.

Flight clothing

In 1928 AAC pilots were issued with Type B-7 flight suits and A-2 boots lined in shearling, with a small pocket, nicknamed 'moccasins', Type B-3 leather helmets, goggles for low-altitude flying, or face masks were issued for higher-altitude tests. Other innovations of the era included the A-4 gloves, called 'aviator two-finger gloves' because two of the fingers were enclosed in the same space. In 1928 the summer Type A-3 flight suits with patch pockets on the knees and breasts were issued, and continued in limited quantities until 1944.★★

The first olive-green, lamb leather 'sport fashion' A-1 flight jacket had been

A-2 jackets in all their splendour. The crew of *Mac's Sack*, 392nd BG, 8th AF, bid their farewells to the crew of *Big Fat Mama* at Wendling, 26 January 1945. (Myron Keilman)

★ Osprey Military Elite Series, US Army Air Force no. 2, Gordon Rottman and Francis Chin (Osprey, 1994).
★★ *Cowboys of the Sky*, Gilles Lhote and Jeff Clyman (Avirex, 1988).

Maj. James Stewart, pilot, operations officer and Hollywood movie star, wearing a B-3 jacket and garrison cap, with fellow officers in A-2s. The AAF branch of service wings and propeller can be seen on the two shirt collars visible. (John McClane Coll.)

perfected in 1925 and standardized in 1927. It was closed with buttons, since the zipper was not invented until 1928. On 29 September 1930 the laboratories of the Clothing Branch of the AAC began working on a project for a new 'summer' leather flight jacket. On 9 May 1931 the A-2 flight jacket, made of dark-brown horsehide and lined with light-brown spun silk, was finally standardized. It had an 'officer's collar' with snaps underneath, epaulettes, two patch pockets and knit cuffs and waistbands. The name of the pilot, printed on a piece of lighter leather, was stitched on the breast, and the jacket was emblazoned with hand-painted unit insignia on the right and left breasts.★

By 1939 the Type A-2 leather flying jacket and Types D-1 (later worn by ground crews only), B-3 and B-6 sheepskin flight jackets were standard among air crew members. Although not authorized for use outside the US, the A-2 (summer) jacket was universally worn by fighter and bomber aircrew, who had them embellished with hand-painted nudes, mission tallies and inspiring names showing the origins of the aircraft they flew. The B-3 winter flying jacket and the A-3 winter flying trousers appeared in April 1934, when Maj. E.L. Hoffman, Chief of the Equipment Branch, noticed after numerous tests that sheepskin flight suits called 'Alaskan suits' were ideal for Air Mail and Army pilots. The first US pilots to use the A-2 and

★ *Cowboys of the Sky*, Gilles Lhote and Jeff Clyman (Avirex, 1988).

Col. Jack Wood, 2nd Combat Bomb Wing CO and ex-389th BG CO (left), in OD no. 54 wool serge service coat (with Command Pilot's Wings) and trousers, known as the 'no. 1' uniform. Col. Robert Miller (right) is wearing 'pinks' and A-2 jacket with the 44th BG 'Flying Eightball' patch over his left breast. Miller took over the 389th BG after leaving the 44th BG. (Russ D. Hayes)

B-3 flight jackets in combat, in November 1941, were the famous American Volunteer Group in China. To help prevent a pilot being killed by Chinese in the event of a bale-out, a Chinese Nationalist flag was added to the back of the leather jacket, and a message known as a 'blood chit' explained in Chinese that the aviator was a US pilot and an enemy of the Japanese and that the rescuer would gain a reward if he delivered him safely to his unit. A red lining in the jacket indicated that the pilot had notched up five victories. From 1942 onwards it became customary for flight personnel in all theatres of war to have silk escape maps sewn inside the linings of their jackets.*

By 1942 aircraft were flying at altitudes of over 20,000 ft and temperatures inside were between minus 30°F and minus 50°F. Special clothing was therefore needed to remove the threat of frostbite and allow the crew to function inside the aircraft. Crewmen wore regulation flying helmets and goggles, long woollen underwear underneath their regulation GI trousers and shirt, an electrically heated flying suit, and finally, an alpaca-lined B-10 suit or

---

* *Cowboys of the Sky*, Gilles Lhote and Jeff Clyman (Avirex, 1988).

B-17E waist gunners wearing B-3 jackets, A-3 trousers and B-2 flight caps ('the Gunner's Cap') man their hand-operated .50 in machine-guns (the remaining .50s were all power-operated) for the camera. The suits, first issued in 1935, were made of lacquered oil, gasoline and water-resistant seal-brown shearling, ¼ inch thick. The jackets are immediately distinguishable from the later, lighter-weight B-6 jacket, as they have a single, angled patch pocket (the B-6 had two slash pockets at the waist). The ammunition boxes (note the two spares) were later replaced by belt feeds, and the waist positions were staggered to ease congestion in the compartment. The sliding hatches which cover the waist windows have been pushed to the rear. (Boeing)

fleece-lined leather jacket and trousers. Where possible, crews wore two pairs of gloves or mittens (a rayon or other light pair inside heavier, gauntlet-type ones, either A-9s, A-12s or electric gloves). Mittens were better than gloves as they allowed fingers to come in contact with each other and help keep them warm. Socks and underwear had to be kept clean. After they became soiled by body oils and excretions, they lost much of their insulation value.

To protect the feet, crews wore wool, rayon and silk socks inside fleece-lined winter shoes (flying boots). Shoes were available in various styles. The most commonly used in the Second World War were the 10 inch high A-6 winter flying shoes, which were standardized on 27 March 1937. These were made of seal-brown, lacquered, ¾ in shearling, with non-skid soles of black rubber, and they could also be worn over electrically-heated shoes or special inserts. When crew were evacuating an aircraft in distress, many shoes literally flew off as soon as the parachutist hit the slipstream or pulled

Lt. Paul Kimble's crew in the 372nd Squadron, 307th BG, 13th AF, at Sansapar in the Pacific, wear long-sleeve cotton khaki summer shirts with tan summer uniform trousers, standard issue in hot-climate zones. (Elmer Vogel)

Air gunners in the crew of *Shoot Luke*, 93rd BG, Hardwick, England, 1943, get their Service Dress, or 'Class A' uniforms ready to wear on a three-day pass. Technical Sgt. William Mercer (writing a letter home) wears the OD shade no. 54 wool serge coat (a pair of rubber overshoes under his bed), while Staff Sgt. Floyd Mabee (on the bed) sews on a button. Staff Sgt. James Cowan (reading a newspaper) is wearing a 'Parsons' M-1941 field jacket. George Foster (standing) does up his dark-green necktie on a khaki shade no. 1 cotton shirt, as worn by Mahlon Cressey (shining his shoes). Adam Hastak (tying up the laces on his russet-brown, high quarter service shoes), wears an OD no. 54 wool shirt and khaki necktie. (USAF)

his ripcord, and by the time he hit the ground he might well have frostbitten feet.

Flying boots were totally unsuitable for walking long distances and were an obvious give-away in enemy-occupied territory. US air crews showed a preference for British-type flying boots. These had a concealed hacksaw blade, which could be used after baling out to cut away the leggings to reveal a conventional shoe which made evasion more straightforward.

Electrically heated flying suits

Electrically heated one-piece flying suits developed by the General Electric Co. were standardized on 4 April 1941 as the E-1 and F-1. Manufactured with heated gloves and heated shoe inserts, these permitted crews to fly for long periods at extreme altitudes without getting cold. The light-grey E-1 suit was used in aircraft such as the B-24 and B-25 which had a 12 volt battery system, while the light-blue ('blue bunny') F-1 was used with the B-17's 24 volt system.

On 13 August 1943 the 24 volt four-piece F-2 electric suit was standardized. The F-2 consisted of an elastic grip jacket and trousers inserts made of OD wool blanket material and an unheated outer jacket and trousers.

B-17 gunners in high-altitude gear and chestpack parachute harnesses. The gunner sitting on the boxes (which probably contain 'Chaff' packets) near the spare aircraft radio set wears an AN-H-16 winter helmet (which only differs from the A-11 in having fur inside), a 1944 ANS-31 summer suit over his electrically heated suit, and A-6A winter flying shoes (straps were added in 1944 at the top and instep, to prevent the boot coming off during bale-out). The gunner (middle) wears the B-10 jacket with mouton collar and A-9 suit over his electric suit, and a pair of F-2 electric gloves, an A-14 oxygen mask and a pair of RAF Mk VIII goggles with tinted lenses on his A-11 intermediate helmet. The gunner (right) is wearing an F-2 electric suit and life preserver. An aviator's kit bag is on the left, and a 'Gibson Girl' radio for the life raft, with parachute, rests on the floor to the right. (via Mike Bailey)

B-24 *Betta Duck*, 34th BG, waist gunner at his position in F-2 electric suit, with extremely rare white fur collar, and gloves, A-11 winter helmet, RAF Mk VIII goggles with tinted lenses, A-14 oxygen mask and 6 ft extension oxygen tube, chest parachute harness, and B-4 life preserver. The intercom jack box is visible below the gun mount. (via Mike Bailey)

The two-piece F-3 electrically heated flying suit appeared early in 1944 (replaced by the F-3A in October 1944) and was designed to be worn over long underwear and underneath the A-15/ B-11 suit. The F-2 consisted of a dark OD cotton and rayon twill jacket and A-9 bib-type alpaca-lined overalls. The F-2 would protect in temperatures as low as minus 40°F and the F-3 in minus 60°F.

Body armour

Early in October 1942 an investigation by Brig.-Gen. Malcolm C. Grow, the 8th Air Force Chief Surgeon, prepared a study that analysed the kinds of wounds suffered by bomber crewmen. It revealed that approximately 70 per cent of the wounds incurred by 8th AF combat crew were due to relatively low-velocity missiles. This resulted in the development of body armour, or 'flak suits' as they became known, consisting of armoured vest and apron assemblies. The first 600 were made by the Wilkinson Sword Company of the UK, which had specialized since 1772 in the manufacture of swords. After experimentation, on 4 March

This B-17 gunner on *Meat Hound* shows the various stages of dressing for a high-altitude mission. First he dons his long-sleeve white wool/cotton blend undershirt and long underwear, then a white silk scarf and F-1 'blue bunny' electrically heated suit (used with the B-17's 24 volt system), white glove inserts, E-1 or F-1 electric gloves, A-6 winter flying shoes, B-6 winter helmet, B-7 goggles, A-10 oxygen mask, and finally, his B-3 jacket and A-5 trousers, parachute harness and B-3 life preserver. The belted .50 in rounds were included purely at the request of the photographer. (USAF)

1943 armoured flak vests were worn by ten crews in the 91st BG on a combat mission. The armoured vest consisted of heavy canvas covered with overlapping two-inch squares of 20-gauge manganese steel, protecting the chest and back from low-velocity shrapnel and ricocheting missiles. They certainly saved the life of a radio operator aboard one ship when a 20 mm shell fragment struck his vest just above the hip but only dented it. The whole suit weighed 20 lb and was cumbersome in the aircraft, but one other life at least was saved by the suit on a later raid, when a 20 mm shell exploded just 2 ft from a bombardier's chest. It peppered the vest, but the bombardier was unhurt.

Large-scale production in the USA began, and by 1 January 1944 approximately 13,500 suits had been produced for the 8th and 9th AFs. Five main US types were available: the Armour Flyers' Protective M-1 vest with armoured front and back panels, weighing 18 lb 2 oz; the M-2 Vest, armoured in the front only, and intended for crewmen occupying armour-plated seats, weighing about 9 lb; the M-3 Tapered Sporran, attached to the front of other armour for crewmen in a sitting position where the lower part of the body was unprotected, weighing 4 lb 12 oz; the M-4 Full Sporran, protecting all frontal area of body, and usually worn

B-24 gunners manning their .50 in machine-guns wear C-Type Sporrans (not normally worn by gunners) and A-Type armoured flak suits, B-3 leather jackets, A-3 caps and HS-33 radio headsets. The man behind is wearing a 'blue bunny' electrically heated suit. (USAF)

by gunners, weighing 7 lb 8 oz; and the M-5 Thigh Sporran, attached to the front of either the M-1 or M-2, and consisting of three pieces hinged together, giving protection to the lower front torso, thighs and crotch area.

Crewmen normally wore the suits when approaching the target area. A ripcord at the centre of the M-series suit allowed the entire suit to fall off when pulled. The suits were not personal issue, but were delivered to the aircraft before the flight and picked up afterwards for inspection.

Helmets

The Surgeon, 1st Bomb Division, became an early advocate of the use of the GI M-1 infantry steel helmet. In January 1943 the 306th BG at Thurleigh developed a modification in the headgear which, subject to wide modifications made by other groups, came into general use under the designation M-3. It carried hinged ear protectors to permit the use of earphones, and provided additional protection for the neck. Of 28 individuals struck by missiles while wearing the M-1, 15 (53.6 per cent) escaped uninjured, 5 (17.8 per cent) were severely wounded, and 8 (28.6 per cent) were killed. Of 64 individuals struck while wearing the M-3, 39 per cent were uninjured, 21.9 per cent wounded severely, and 39.1 per cent were killed.

US 'Snowdrops' (Military Police) wearing white-painted M1 helmet liners, British cross-over straps, web belts and holsters (painted with white spirit-based emulsion), with brass fittings, and white/midnight-blue MP arm brassards. The British 'Bobbies' are from the Norfolk Constabulary. The US officers in 'pinks' and 'greens' wear 'hash marks', or bars, on the left cuff of their service uniform. Each bar represents six months active service overseas, as do the AAF colonel's First World War chevrons. (Norfolk Constabulary Hist. Coll.)

The M-4 'Grow' helmet was cut away around the ears to allow free use of the intercom and radio headsets, and thus could be worn over the winter flying helmet. Tests showed that it could deflect a .45 bullet at 6 ft.

The T-8, made from manganese steel with welded ear flap hinges to cover the cut-outs at the ear positions, was introduced to try to provide a more compact and lighter helmet than the M-3, and to give more protection than the M-4 series.

The average fatality rate for the M-1 and M-3 was 33.8 per cent; for the M-4, 17.4 per cent.

Other clothing

Ground mechanics wore the D-1 jacket and B-1 trousers, in use from 1940. Made of seal-brown ⅜ in thick shearling, they were similar in design to the winter flying B-6 jacket and A-3 trousers. In late 1943 the lighter-weight D-2 jacket and B-2 trousers, made of alpaca-lined OD shade no. 7 boat cloth, were introduced. In milder weather, mechanics used the QMC-issue OD herringbone twill one-piece suit, which came into standard use in 1941.*

---

* Osprey Military Elite Series, US Army Air Force no. 2, Gordon Rottman and Francis Chin (Osprey, 1994).

A close shave! A waist gunner shows the hole in his M3 flak helmet and B-6 flying helmet made by a flak burst. (USAF)

A three-man team clad in GI steel helmets and B-3 jackets man a water-cooled .50 in Browning machine-gun used for airfield defence. (USAF)

Groundcrew in one-piece coveralls and A-3 caps unload unused bombs from this 392nd BG, 8th AF, Liberator after its return from a mission, 9 September 1943.

Officers in M-1941 field jackets (a later version of the 'Parsons', issued to ground troops as a result of a specification laid down by Gen. Parsons, Commander, US Army III Corps, in early 1940), khaki cotton and wool serge trousers, and garrison and service caps. (Bill Cameron Coll.)

Officers' clothing for wear overseas

The list of clothing which follows is suggested for each officer when going on overseas duty. The destination and nature of duty after arrival will each have an influence on the requirements and where they can be foreseen should receive consideration. Additional information will be furnished at Ports of Embarkation and staging areas. For certain countries additional

Groundcrew in the 392nd BG pose in front of their Liberator, *We'll Get By*, wearing D-1 groundcrew jackets, and in the case of the EM (far right, kneeling), the B-3 and F-1 A-3 mechanic's caps. The D-1 differed principally from the B-3 in having pockets higher up, so that tools could be slipped in more easily. The jackets and trousers are made of light-weight (¼ in), seal-brown shearling. Because of a shortage, flight crews started wearing groundcrew's B-1 trousers (to go with the D-1 jacket), sometimes adding a pocket. (via Robert Foose)

These officers in the 467th BG, at Clastres, France, in September 1944, are wearing khakis and different tops. Col. Albert J. Shower, the CO (centre) wears a garrison cap, and a flight jacket similar to the the Type B-13, but with no pockets (probably privately commissioned), with Senior Pilot Wings and 'bird colonel' insignia on the epaulettes and right shirt collar. His deputy, Lt.-Col. Herzberg (far left), and Maj. Ned Ogden, the Group Intelligence Officer (far right), are wearing officer's raincoats. The operations officer (2nd from left) is wearing the alpaca-lined B-10 with mouton-lined collar, and Lt.-Col. Walter R. Smith, Group Operations Officer (2nd from right), is wearing the customary leather A-2 and his flight suit trousers over his 'pinks'. (Albert J. Shower)

Albert Gehrt, Allen Bryson and Sol Greenberg, air gunners in the 453rd BG, 8th AF, at Old Buckenham, England, pose cheekily for the camera wearing their long-sleeve white wool/cotton blend undershirts and long underdrawers, chest-type parachute harnesses, B-8 goggles, A-6 flying boots and A-11 flying helmets, while Sol Greenberg packs a .45 pistol in an M-3 holster. In the Pacific, crews normally wore only underwear like this under summer flying suits. (Sol Greenberg)

clothing will be necessary, due to climate. Certain items will vary according to assignment. An officer assigned to a headquarters in London, for example, would require more than one blouse, whereas an officer assigned to a combat unit might get along with one.

Notes

The summer uniform has not been authorized for use in England. Extra clothing for Arctic regions may be obtained from the Quartermaster at Port of Embarkation. Officers should not draw Arctic clothing unless ordered to do so.

For travel by air to destinations overseas the weight allowance is frequently announced in instructions contained in travel orders or otherwise. It will rarely exceed 77 pounds and may be as little as 55 pounds. The balance of the authorized weight allowance may follow by transport. The 55 pound limit applies for air travel to the United Kingdom, the South Pacific and Southwest Pacific theatres.

Equipment for overseas. The articles listed below apply generally to officers of all the arms and services. However, there are special requirements for certain of the arms and the individual should ascertain his exact requirements and add them to this list. These items of equipment are issued to the officer on memorandum receipt. They should be guarded carefully and their continued serviceability preserved. In some theatres replacement will be difficult. The individual will be the only sufferer in such an event.

Clothing for wear overseas (contained in The Adjutant General's School Bulletin, November 1942)

1 cap, service, wool
1 cap, garrison, wool (overseas)
2 caps, cotton, khaki (overseas)
1 blouse, wool, elastique
2 pairs slacks, wool (1 pink, 1 dark)
1 pair slacks, wool (enlisted OD)
2 shirts, field, wool
4 pair slacks, cotton, khaki
1 short coat (preferable to overcoat)
1 field jacket
1 pair leggings, canvas
2 complete extra sets of insignia
1 belt, waist, khaki
8 pair shorts, underwear
8 undershirts
12 pair socks, cotton, tan
1 pair shoes, service, high
2 pair shoes, low
1 pair slippers
4 shirts, cotton, heavy khaki
4 shirts, cotton, light khaki
4 wool tan ties
4 cotton tan ties
24 handkerchiefs
1 set toilet articles
2 pair garters
1 cigarette lighter
2 cans lighter fluid (cannot be taken by
   air travel)
6 bars of soap and supply of towels
Don't forget the lighter! Matches are
   almost unobtainable.

Extra clothing for Iran, Iraq, Egypt,
   North Africa, India and Australia
1 blouse, tropical*
1 pair slacks, worsted *
3 pairs shorts, cotton, khaki (buy
   them here, they are hard to get
   overseas)
3 shirts, cotton, short sleeves, khaki (for
   use with khaki shorts)
3 pairs socks, wool, long (for use with
   khaki shorts)
1 sun helmet
1 pair sun glasses, best quality

Extra Clothing for Arctic Regions
1 hat, rubberized
1 overcoat, parka type
1 sweater, worsted, turtle neck
2 undershirts, wool knit, arctic
1 pair trousers, jersey lined
4 pair socks, wool, arctic
1 pair gloves, wool O.D. arctic
1 pair mittens, horsehide, lambskin lined
1 shoe pacs, 16 in, rubberized bottom,
   leather top
1 parka, double texture rubberized
1 jacket, field, arctic
1 sweater, sleeveless
2 pair drawers, wool knit, arctic
1 pair trousers, double texture, rubberized
1 toque, face
1 pair goggles, polarized

Equipment
Quartermaster

1 (NS) 74-H	Helmet, Bodies, MI
1 74-K-60	Knife, M-1926
1 (NS) 74-L	Liner, Helmet, MI
1 74-F-63	Fork, M-1926
1 (NS) 74-H	Headband, Helmet, MI
1 74-P-260	Pouch, first aid, packet
1 (NS) 74-N	Neckband, Helmet, MI
1 24R-110	Roll, bedding, waterproof
1 74-B-53	Bag, canvas
1 74-S-312	Spoon, M-1926
1 74-B-265	Belt, pistol
2 74-P-225	Poles, tent, shelter half
1 27-B-678	Blankets, wool, OD
10 74-P-125	Pins, tent, shelter, wood
1 74-C-62	Can, meat, M-1932
2 74-T-100	Tent, shelter half
1 74-C-80	Canteen, M-1910
1 74-P	Packet
1 74-C-300	Cover, canteen
1 37-M-1505	Mask, gas, diaphragm
1 74-C-354	Cup, canteen, M-1910

Ordnance

1 pistol, auto, cal. .45
2 clips, extra, for cal. .45
1 holster for cal. .45 auto
21 rounds, ammunition, cal. .45

* this is merely suggested since blouses are worn by the British after working hours

CHAPTER ELEVEN

Equipment: Arms, Ordnance and Weapons

Bombs

The two main heavy bomber types used by the Army Air Forces were the B-17 and B-24. Depending on distance to target, the B-17 carried a mission bomb load of between 4,000 and 6,000 lb, and the B-24 between 5,000 and 8,000 lb. The B-29's maximum bomb load was 20,000 lb.

Fifteen of the eighty different types of ordnance available to the AAF were normally carried. These included the 'conventional' types – general purpose, high explosive, incendiary and fragmentation – and 'stand-off', or controllable bombs (which the US Navy had been experimenting with since 1937).

General purpose bombs

These cause destruction by blast and vacuum pressures when they explode above ground, and by earth shock when they explode below ground. These bombs are of the AN-M series and resemble each other closely. They differ mainly in size, weight, and weight of explosives. Light-case bombs have such light cases that about 80 per cent of the total weight is explosive.

Armour-piercing bombs are used against heavily armoured targets and against structures of stone or reinforced concrete. They have an extra-heavy case and a sharp nose. HE comprises about 5–15 per cent of their weight. Semi-armour-piercing bombs are similar, but cannot penetrate such heavy armour or concrete. HE comprises about 30 per cent of their weight. Armour-piercing and semi-armour-piercing bombs use a tail fuse only.

Fragmentation bombs are used chiefly for attacks on personnel, light materiel and aircraft on the ground. For more concentrated attacks, fragmentation bombs are used in 100 lb and 500 lb clusters.

GP bombs could also be used for demolition or penetration. In 1944 a 1,600 lb armour-piercing bomb was used by the 8th Air Force against V-1 and V-2 rocket sites and underground concrete bunkers. Some 1,220 of these bombs were dropped before VE Day.

Rocket bombs

Capt. Edward Terrell of the Royal Navy developed a 4,500 lb bomb, powered by a rocket motor in the tail, that was designed to penetrate 20 ft of

Bomb loads, showing the increase in tonnage carried, 1942–4. (USAF)

concrete before exploding. Its weight prevented it being carried in the bomb bay of a B-17 or B-24, but two of these so-called 'Disney' bombs could be carried under each wing of a B-17. 'Disney' bombs were first used on 10 February 1945 when nine B-17s of the 92nd BG dropped eighteen of them on E-boat pens at Ijmuiden in Holland. One hit was recorded, and further trials were ordered, but the Allies' sweeping victories in the Low Countries and the vast distance to suitable targets in Norway brought the 'Disney' missions almost to an end.

High explosive bombs

The HE generally used in bombs and fuses included TNT; Amatol (a mixture of ammonium nitrate and TNT); Explosive D; Composition B (RDX); Torpex; Tetryl (used as a booster and burster in chemical bombs); mercury fulminate (used in detonators for bombs and shells); lead azide (sometimes used in place of mercury fulminate), and Primer Mixture (composed of ground glass mixed with a sensitive explosive).

HE bomb weights were predominantly 100, 250, 500, 1,000, 2,000 and 4,000 lb. The 1,000 lb bomb's metal components weighed about 435 lb and carried a HE charge of about 530lb. The 2,000 lb bomb had about 56 per cent HE content. Some 77.4 per cent of the light metal-cased 4,000 lb

	ETO	MTO	Total Against Germany	Total Against Japan	Total Against Germany and Japan
1941 Dec	-	-	-	36	36
1942 Jan	-	-	-	20	20
Feb	-	-	-	47	47
Mar	-	-	-	68	68
Apr	-	-	-	128	128
May	-	-	-	184	184
Jun	115	-	115	295	410
Jul	357	-	357	299	656
Aug	135	414	549	409	958
Sep	215	482	697	459	1,156
Oct	334	771	1,105	564	1,669
Nov	612	1,195	1,807	752	2,559
Dec	417	1,076	1,493	855	2,348
Total 1942	1,713	4,410	6,123	4,080	10,203
1943 Jan	739	1,983	2,722	859	3,581
Feb	705	1,719	2,424	1,147	3,571
Mar	1,530	2,773	4,303	1,644	5,947
Apr	1,130	5,053	6,183	2,033	8,216
May	2,688	7,297	9,985	2,344	12,329
Jun	2,468	8,596	11,064	1,845	12,909
Jul	4,366	13,846	18,212	4,041	22,253
Aug	5,072	12,584	17,656	4,333	21,989
Sep	8,519	13,942	22,461	4,212	26,673
Oct	6,015	7,625	13,640	5,013	18,653
Nov	8,309	9,480	17,789	5,921	23,710
Dec	14,114	13,564	27,678	11,291	38,969
Total 1943	55,655	98,462	154,117	44,683	198,800
1944 Jan	14,015	19,097	33,112	7,885	40,997
Feb	22,566	11,595	34,161	9,912	44,073
Mar	26,539	17,440	43,979	12,255	56,234
Apr	38,540	29,856	68,396	13,537	81,933
May	56,874	46,075	102,949	14,715	117,664
Jun	85,648	36,287	121,935	10,499	132,434
Jul	63,062	41,769	104,831	10,034	114,865
Aug	67,766	40,280	108,046	9,458	117,504
Sep	52,175	29,285	81,460	12,849	94,309
Oct	52,860	22,108	74,968	12,329	87,297
Nov	51,413	26,695	78,108	15,025	93,133
Dec	60,501	26,506	87,007	18,528	105,535
Total 1944	591,959	346,993	938,952	147,026	1,085,978
1945 Jan	54,474	14,539	69,013	19,335	88,348
Feb	80,348	32,661	113,009	23,919	136,928
Mar	118,003	41,120	159,123	41,088	200,211
Apr	69,242	44,365	113,607	44,007	157,614
May	368	151	519	47,180	47,699
Jun	-	-	-	50,893	50,893
Jul	-	-	-	53,665	53,665
Aug	-	-	-	26,869	26,869
Total 1945	322,435	132,836	455,271	306,956	762,227
Grand Total	971,762	582,701	1,554,463	502,781	2,057,244

Tons of Bombs Dropped December 1941 to August 1945

Source: *Carl A. Spaatz and the Air War in Europe*, Richard G. Davis (Centre for Air Force History, Washington DC, 1993)

A 'Disney' bomb is visible beneath the right wing of this B-17G 43-38832 of the 306th BG at Thurleigh, Bedfordshire. (Richards Coll.)

bomb's total weight was made up of high explosive. All of these bombs, except the 4,000 lb bomb which was carried exclusively by the B-29, were carried by B-17 and B-24 aircraft, mostly internally, although on occasion in 1943, B-17s carried two 500 lb or 1,000lb bombs on external wing racks. Soviet 225 kilo (about 550 lb) bombs were also carried during operations from shuttle bases in Russia in 1944. B-29s operating from the Marianas dropped 1,220 4,000 lb bombs on Japanese targets in the final six months of the war.

Incendiary bombs

Magnesium-based incendiary cluster bombs like the 2 lb M52 and 4 lb M50 were used in Europe by the AAFs. These were designed to burn for six to eight minutes at temperatures of 2,300°F. In 1943 B-17s and B-24s began dropping 100 lb (34 × 4 lb M50s) and 500 lb (110 × 4 lb M50s) cluster bombs, but these became widely scattered as soon as they hit the slipstream, and accurate bombing of targets with these devices was impractical. In January 1944 the M17 cluster bomb, fused to explode at 5,000 ft above ground, appeared in Europe and proved much more effective. The 500 lb (110 × 4 lb M50s) cluster bomb was the most commonly used by the 8th and 15th Air Forces. B-29s carrying M17s and the 22 lb M19 (36 × 6 lb M69 jellied oil) cluster bombs dropped them in vast quantities during fire raids on Japanese cities.

CLASSIFICATION	WEIGHT	NOMEN-CLATURE	COLOR MARKINGS BODY	COLOR MARKINGS BANDS	HE WEIGHT	FUZES NOSE	FUZES TAIL	SHACK-LES	MINIMUM SAFE BA	TARGETS AND REMARKS
GENERAL PURPOSE	100	AN-M30	LUSTERLESS OLIVE DRAB	(1½") YELLOW BAND AROUND NOSE AND TAIL	54	AN-M103	AN-M100A2 or M112A1	B-7 or B-10	1500	Railroad equipment, trackage, small buildings, ammunition dumps, planes on ground, hangars
	250	AN-M57			123	AN-M103 or M118	AN-M101A2 or M113A1		2000	Railroad equipment, trackage, RR terminals, ammunition dumps, destroyers, subs, transports
	500	AN-M64			262	M118			2500	Steel railroad bridges, subways, concrete docks, light cruisers
	1000	AN-M65			530	M119	AN-M102A2 or M114A1	D-6	3000	Reinforced concrete bridges, steel RR bridges, piers, approach spans, medium cruisers
	2000	AN-M66			1061				3000	Massive reinforced concrete and suspension bridges, heavy cruisers, battleships, dams
LIGHT CASE	4000	AN-M56	OLIVE DRAB		3245	AN-M103	AN-M102A2	B-10	3000	Raze areas equal to a city block or more
SEMI-ARMOR-PIERCING	500	AN-M58A1			145	STEEL PLUG	AN-M101A2	B-7 or B-10		Armor plate, lightly armored vessels, reinforced concrete
	1000	AN-M59			303		AN-M102A2			
ARMOR-PIERCING	1000	AN-Mk33			144	NONE	AN-Mk228	B-10		Heavily armored naval vessels
	1600	AN-Mk1			215					
DEPTH	350	AN-Mk47			252	AN-Mk219 or AN-M103	AN-Mk224 AN-Mk234 (LATERAL)	B-7 or B-10		Submarines and surface craft
	650	AN-Mk29			464					
FRAG. PARACHUTE	23	AN-M40	GRAY	*See Below	2.7	AN-M120A1	NONE	N-3	80	Personnel—If detonated at proper angle, almost 100% casualties over 120 ft. radius
FRAG. FIN	20	AN-M41			2.7	AN-M110A1			800	Tanks—Running gear, 60-90 ft.; light tank, direct hit 200 ft.; structural damage, 3-4 ft. Planes—Motor, 60 ft.; wings and tanks perforated, 200 ft.; structural damage, 3-4 ft. Telephone wires—100 ft., some cut by side spray
CLUSTER	500	M26				M111A2				
CHEMICAL MULTI-PURPOSE	100	M47A2	GRAY		68	M108	BURSTER M4	B-7 or B-10		Irritating physiological effect on personnel, neutralize areas, contaminate materiel
	115	M70			64	AN-M110A1	BURSTER M10			HS produces irritating physiological effect. WP produces screening smoke or incendiary effect
INCENDIARY	4	AN-M50A1		1 PURPLE	1.8	NONE	STRIKER UNIT			Usually in 5 bomb clusters; includes 1 AN-M50XA1 (150 gr. BP burster charge)
PRACTICE	100	M38A2	BLUE		2.6	NONE	M1A1		2500-3000	Training—22 gage, light sheet metal body, filled with about 80 lbs. of dry sand. Actual weight, 98 lbs.
FLARES (PARACHUTE)	44	M24	GRAY	BLUE		NONE	FRICTION IGNITER		4000-25,000	Target lighting; dropping rate, 11.6 ft./sec.; burns 3-3.5 min.; yellowish tint, 1,000,000 candle power
	53	AN-M26				M111A2				Target lighting; dropping rate, 11.6 ft./sec.; burns 3-3.5 min.; 800,000 candle power
	16	M8A1				NONE				Emergency landings; can be used for bombing. Burns 3 min.; soft yellow, 400,000 candle power
TORPEDO	2100	Mk13-2			600	EXPLODER MECHANISM	NONE			Effective range, 6000 yds.; speed about 40 mph; has 93-98 hp steam and gas turbine engine

*BANDS: (NOSE, TAIL AND CENTER) 1 GREEN, NON-PERSISTENT; 2 GREEN, PERSISTENT; 1 PURPLE, INCENDIARY; 1 YELLOW, SMOKE; 1 RED, IRRITANT SMOKE (Vomiting Gas)

Source: *Bombardiers' Information File*
Aerial bombs.

M47 70 lb bomb

Developed by the US Army Chemical Warfare Service, the M47 contained a petroleum, crude latex, caustic soda and coconut oil mix which burned longer and gave better fire spread than previous incendiary devices. It was used from late 1943.

The early version was followed by the most widely used of all incendiaries, the 100 lb M47A2, which contained a jellied oil, giving a fire spread of 40 yd. The M47A2 version was dropped in large numbers in 1945 during the fire-bombing campaign against Japanese cities.

The M47A1 used the same 49 in × 8 in thin-walled steel cylindrical body, but the filling included 93 lb of white phosphorous. M47A1s were predominantly used in Europe during the final six months of the war.

M76 500 lb 'pyrotechnic gel' bomb

This was the largest of all the incendiaries, and contained a mix of jellied oil, heavy oil, petrol, magnesium powder and sodium nitrate. It saw only small-scale usage in Europe.

Class C fire bombs

These consisted of fighter aircraft drop tanks filled with Napalmgel. They were used towards the end of the war in Europe. Napalmgel (or 'napalm', as it is more widely known) is petrol thickened with a compound made of aluminium, naphthenic and palmitic acids, to which a 1 lb all-way white phosphorous fuse was added for ignition. The most commonly used were 108 US gallon composition paper tanks, and six per aircraft were carried by B-17s and B-24s.

Assembly unit of the Azon bomb. (USAF)

Fragmentation bombs

The 260 lb M81 anti-personnel bomb was the most widely used fragmentation bomb in the Second World War, while the 128 lb M1 (6 × 20 lb M41) was the most numerous cluster type used in both Europe and the Pacific. The 540 lb version was also used in the final months of the war in Europe.

Controllable bombs

Azon VB-1 (vertical bomb):   The VB-1 was a 'stand-off' glider bomb, consisting of a 1,000 or 2,000 lb GP bomb with radio-controlled movable tail fins. After release, a flare in the tail ignited and kept it in view of the controller in a 'mother ship', who steered the bomb, in the horizontal plane only, by radio. It was used experimentally by the 8th AF in the ETO and by the 15th AF in the MTO in the summer of 1944, mainly against bridges in France and Italy. Four special B-17s dropped twenty-four 1,000 lb Azon bombs on the Avisio bridge in the Brenner Pass, and four direct hits were claimed, but overall, the Azon project was a failure in Europe and was abandoned in June 1944.

At about this time Gen. James H. Doolittle, the US Air Force Chief in the Pacific, revealed that his bombers had also tried bombing by means of radio-controlled glide bombs. Like the Azon bombs, his 160 knot 'Torpeckers' had met with little success. Seven glide bombs had been used

42-13603, the prototype Northrop XB-35, which first flew on 25 June 1946, was considered for operational use in the Second World War as a glide bomb. (Northrop)

against positions on the island of Truk in the Pacific, and all had been destroyed at will by the Japanese defences.

Late in 1944 the Azon was employed in Burma against bridges. The 7th BG in the CBI claimed twenty-seven bridges with 459 Azon bombs, and direct hits with 10–15 per cent of those dropped.

Glide bombs: The experimental GB-1 'Grapefruit' glide bomb was developed by fitting small wings and empennage to a 2,000 lb GP M34 bomb, and was launched from the external wing racks of B-17s. On 28 May 1944 the 384th BG, 8th AF, launched 116 GB-1 bombs on targets at Cologne, but none even hit the city. The weapon did not see widespread use.

The GB-4 'Batty' combined radio-control and visual-observation version was produced using a GB-1 with the Azon bomb, and the GB-8 version was controlled visually by rudimentary television. Both the GB-4 and GB-8 were launched experimentally from B-17s in the last few months of the European war, but were largely unsuccessful.

The biggest 'glide bombs' of all were war-weary 8th AF B-17 'drones' packed with 20,000 lb of Torpex or 10 tons of RDX, which were launched from Fersfield, Suffolk, against German V-1 and V-2 sites in the late summer of 1944. Code-named PROJECT A or APHRODITE, B-17s, stripped of all removable equipment, were fitted with radio equipment and flown manually by two pilots who baled out after take-off, and the drone was then guided to its target by a control aircraft, or 'mother ship', usually a B-34 (ex-RAF Ventura). The project was abandoned after several crashes, near misses (and the loss of a US Navy ANVIL drone which killed Lt. Joe Kennedy Jr and his co-pilot on 11 August 1944, when their PB-4Y Liberator exploded prematurely). On 4 August, for instance, four APHRODITE B-17s were despatched against a V-1 site in the Pas de Calais, each loaded with 10 tons of RDX. None reached their intended targets: two were shot down, and the other two crashed and exploded, one after the crew had baled out. Two days later, two more drones were launched. One crashed into the Channel, and the other exploded just after the crew had baled out over East Anglia.

JB-2 (V-1) flying bombs: In August 1944 a Chinese copy of a captured German V-1 which landed in England was test-flown, and the first JB-2 was test-flown in October. Gen. 'Hap' Arnold immediately ordered a thousand for use against Japan, but none had been used when the Pacific war ended.

Northrop Corporation intended to build a flying bomb (JB-1, for 'Jet Bomb') based on their B-35 Flying Wing, but this, and the proposed AAF JB-3 air-to-air missile, never left the drawing boards.

Mines
In the Pacific B-29s of the 313th Bomb Wing carried out highly successful aerial mining of Japanese home waters and shipping lanes. US Navy 1,000 lb and 2,000 lb mines (magnetic, acoustic, pressure-magnetic and low-frequency acoustic) were dropped by B-29s in Japanese home waters by parachute from altitudes of up to 8,000 ft. Typically, loads were 12,000 lb (12 × 1,000 lb mines) or 14,000 lb (7 × 2,000 lb mines) per B-29.

Pumpkin bombs
A small number of these 5,000 lb HE bombs were used by B-29 crews practising to use the atomic bombs.

Atomic bombs
Two completely different atomic bombs were designed and produced at Los Alamos, New Mexico, under the codename MANHATTAN PROJECT, led by J. Robert Oppenheimer and his team of Allied scientists. 'Little Boy' was a uranium device. It was 10½ feet long × 29 inch diameter, it weighed 9,700 lb, and its explosive yield was the equivalent of 12,500 tons of TNT. 'Fat Man' was a plutonium device. It was 10 feet 8 in long × 5 feet in diameter, it weighed 10,000 lb, and its explosive yield was the equivalent of 22,000 tons of TNT.

Bombsights

Two main types of US precision bombsights were used – the Norden M-Series, and the Sperry S Series, which was suitable for use in radar-guided bombing.

'Pickle Barrel!' A bombardier in the 91st BG signals that his bombs have landed smack on the target. Often the reverse was true. On the left is the bomb selecting mechanism. (USAF)

The Norden bombsight was developed by consulting engineer Carl L. Norden, a Dutch-born expert on gyroscopes, in response to a request by the US Navy in 1921. The Navy needed a gyro-stabilized base for their existing Mk 3 bombsight to enable it to be used at high altitude. Norden's device appeared in prototype form in 1923, but was only good for targets that remained stationary. The improved Mk 11 gyro-optical sight followed in 1924 and incorporated a timing device to indicate the precise moment for bomb release, but it was not tested until 1928. After many setbacks, in 1931 the famous Mk 15 appeared. Results achieved in tests by the Navy were impressive, and the Air Corps ordered the Mk 15. The crowning refinement was the Automatic Flight Control Equipment which, during the bomb run, allowed the bombardier to take over flying the aircraft from the pilot, giving him lateral control of the aircraft through the Norden bombsight's connection to the A-5 or C-1 autopilot. In 1935 the Mk 15 was tested by two of Col. Henry Arnold's B-10 groups on the west coast of the USA. Results were impressive but

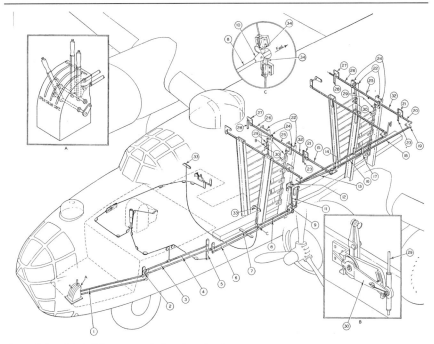

Consolidated B-24 Liberator main bomb rack release system.

exaggerated, and soon stories of being able to put a bomb in a pickle barrel from 10,000 ft were rife.

When the USA entered the Second World War, the standard precision bombsight was the Norden M series. The Mk 9 was introduced late in 1943. (By the end of 1943 about 2,000 Norden bombsights a month were being produced. By September 1945, 43,292 M-series bombsights had been produced.) The Norden was estimated to be six to eight times more accurate than the Mk XIV bombsight used by the RAF.

Early in the European war, before the USA's entry, only about 5 per cent of all British bombs landed within a mile of their aiming point under combat conditions. In 1940 RAF Bomber Command could manage an average monthly delivery of bombs on German targets of 1,128 tons. This increased to almost 6,000 tons in 1942, when the USAAF joined the offensive. In 1943 the monthly tonnage was 26,000 tons, by 1944 it was 131,000 tons, and in 1945, 170,000 tons. Not all fell on the intended targets, of course. For instance, during the period 1 January 1943–1 October 1943, only 24 per cent of bombs dropped by the 8th AF fell within 1,000 ft of the MPI; in the period 1 October 1943–1 March 1944 this figure had risen to 40 per cent. The USAAF expected that 40 per cent of its bombs would be dropped within 500 yd of the MPI.

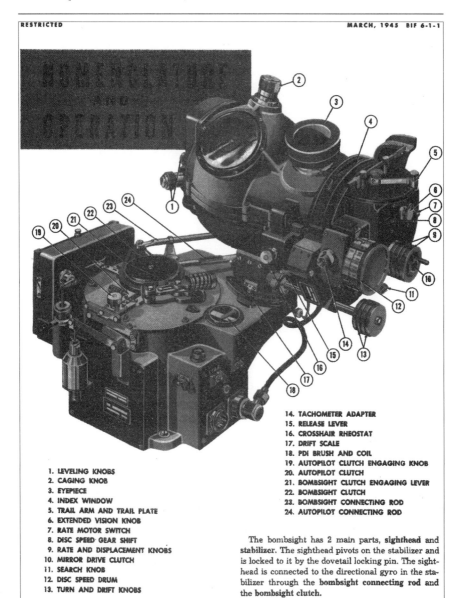

14. TACHOMETER ADAPTER
15. RELEASE LEVER
16. CROSSHAIR RHEOSTAT
17. DRIFT SCALE
18. PDI BRUSH AND COIL
19. AUTOPILOT CLUTCH ENGAGING KNOB
20. AUTOPILOT CLUTCH
21. BOMBSIGHT CLUTCH ENGAGING LEVER
22. BOMBSIGHT CLUTCH
23. BOMBSIGHT CONNECTING ROD
24. AUTOPILOT CONNECTING ROD

1. LEVELING KNOBS
2. CAGING KNOB
3. EYEPIECE
4. INDEX WINDOW
5. TRAIL ARM AND TRAIL PLATE
6. EXTENDED VISION KNOB
7. RATE MOTOR SWITCH
8. DISC SPEED GEAR SHIFT
9. RATE AND DISPLACEMENT KNOBS
10. MIRROR DRIVE CLUTCH
11. SEARCH KNOB
12. DISC SPEED DRUM
13. TURN AND DRIFT KNOBS

The bombsight has 2 main parts, **sighthead** and stabilizer. The sighthead pivots on the stabilizer and is locked to it by the dovetail locking pin. The sighthead is connected to the directional gyro in the stabilizer through the **bombsight connecting rod** and the **bombsight clutch.**

The Norden bombsight.

8th AF BOMBING ACCURACY

Average per cent of bombs dropped which fell within 1,000 ft and 2,000 ft respectively, of pre-assigned MPIs on visual missions under conditions of good to fair visibility

	Within 1,000 ft				Within 2,000 ft			
Period	1st Div. (B-17)	2nd Div. (B-24)	3rd Div. (B-24/B-17 from 8/44)	8th AF	1st Div. (B-17)	2nd Div. (B-24)	3rd Div. (B-24/B-17 from 8/44)	8th AF
1943								
January February March	18	–	–	18	36	–	–	36
April May June	13	–	11	12	32	–	29	30
July August September	13	–	19	16	31	–	48	38
October November December	25	32	27	27	46	58	47	48
1944								
January	34	23	41	35	61	48	60	58
February	42	26	46	39	76	49	77	69
March	31	20	39	31	64	36	70	58
April	34	21	32	29	62	43	58	55
May	44	34	33	37	68	64	62	65
June	49	32	35	40	81	62	65	71
July	42	26	44	37	73	56	77	69
August	54	36	42	45	84	65	72	75
September October	29	32	46	38	61	56	72	65
November December	24	24	25	25	54	44	47	48
1945								
January	29	34	24	29	59	61	56	59
February	50	57	40	49	80	81	69	77
March	40	45	30	38	76	73	58	69
April	64	58	52	59	91	79	80	85

This PFF bombing attack by B-24s of the 389th BG on a V-1 site at Belloy-sur-Somme resulted in 90 per cent of the bombs exploding within 2,000 ft of the MPI and 5 per cent within 1,000 ft, but the small NO-BALL site was not hit. (USAF)

Blind bombing/navigational devices

Gee

This British navigational device involved a special aircraft radio receiver working on pulsed signals received from three ground stations. It was limited to a range of about 400 miles. By late 1942 Gee had been rendered almost ineffective by German jamming, and it was replaced by Oboe. Gee-H was a development of Gee, giving more precise fixes to aircraft, and Micro-H was a further development of the Gee system using ground stations' signals, but combined with H2X for bombing.

Oboe

This British technique adopted by the AAFs got its name from a radar pulse which sounded like a musical instrument. Two ground stations were used,

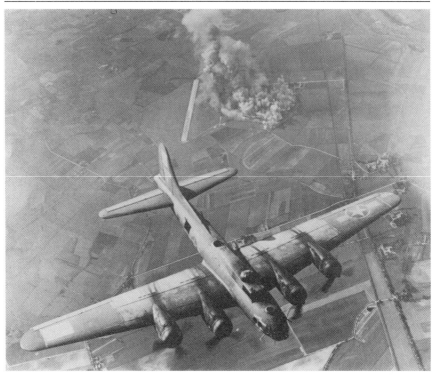

On occasion, bombing under ideal conditions produced near perfect accuracy. On 9 October 1943 the 8th AF bombed the FW190 factory at Marienburg, and 60 per cent of the bombs dropped by the 96 Fortresses exploded within 1,000 ft of the MPI; 83 per cent fell within 2,000 ft. Eaker called it 'a classic example of precision bombing'. (USAF)

but in contrast to Gee, an aircraft's position was assessed at the ground stations, which operated on re-radiation of radar signals directed at the aircraft. Its range was 280 miles.

H2S

This British airborne radar provided a map-like image on a cathode ray tube (radar scope screen). It employed a revolving scanner antenna in a radome beneath the nose of a bomber or in the position once occupied by the ball turret on heavy bombers.

City areas on coastlines or estuaries were chosen as targets when using H2S because of the clear distinction between water and land on radar screens. This technique allowed a large increase in raids during the test period in late 1943 and early 1944.

About 80 per cent of 8th AF missions in the last quarter of 1944 used some type of radar bombing devices, either for navigation or targeting. About half of all blind bombing missions were 'near failures or worse'. When using non-visual techniques in total overcast conditions, just 39.8 per

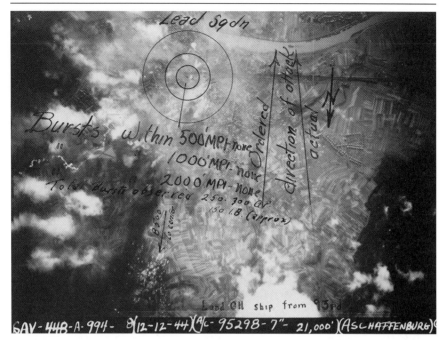

This strike photo of an attack by the 448th BG on Aschaffenburg on 12 December 1944, led by a 93rd BG Gee-H lead ship, and which has subsequently been plotted following the critique, reveals that none of the GP bombs dropped actually landed in the target area. (USAF)

cent of all bombs dropped by the 8th AF landed within 3 miles, and 58.5 per cent within 5 miles. Only 0.2 per cent landed within 1,000 ft in total overcast. In ⁴/₁₀–⁵/₁₀ cloud cover, 48.5 per cent landed within 1 mile, and 4.4 per cent within 1,000 ft; in ⁶/₁₀–⁷/₁₀ overcast conditions, 36.5 per cent fell within 1 mile and 2 per cent within 1,000 ft; with ⁸/₁₀–⁹/₁₀ cloud cover, 22.5 per cent fell within 1 mile, and 1 per cent within 1,000 ft.*

The 8th AF Analysis Section estimated that bombing in good visual conditions was six times more accurate than with Gee or with a beacon combination with H2X called Micro-H, and 150 times more accurate than with H2X through complete overcast conditions (the 8th dropped 49.7 per cent of its bombs with non-visual methods, the 15th AF, 18.5 per cent). By 1945 bombing accuracy in Europe had risen to 44 per cent of all bombs falling within 1,000 ft of the target and 73 per cent within 2,000 ft.

AN/APS-15 ('H2X', 'Mickey')
Usually known as H2X, this was a US-developed version of H2S. The first use of H2X was made on the mission to Wilhelmshaven in October 1943.

---

* 8th AF Operations Analysis Section *Report on Bombing Accuracy*, 8th AF, 1 September–31 December 1944.

Sets were available in sufficient numbers by late 1943 to mount the first major raids to test its effectiveness, and it became the standard device for bombing through overcast conditions. Using H2X on D-Day, 1,365 8th AF bombers dropped 2,798 tons of bombs through cloud behind the beachheads thirty minutes before the landing.

AN/APQ-13

Developed by the Radiation Laboratory at Massachusetts Institute of Technology (in conjunction with Bell Telephone and Western Electric) this was a development of the AN/APS-15 ground-scanning radar to serve as a navigational aid in B-29s. It consisted of a partially retractable radome (later a teardrop unit designed at the Denver Modification Centre) located between the two bomb bays, containing a revolving scanner which swept through 360°, and two or more fixed beacons on land or sea. The aircraft radar operator or navigator queried the beacons and, by triangulation, located the aircraft at a fixed point. Once the aircraft's position was known, the navigator could plan the route to the other known position – the target. However, in early bombing operations over Europe, AN/APQ-13 proved to be inaccurate and unreliable.

AN/APQ-7 'Eagle'

For attacks on oil refineries, B-29s of the 315th Bomb Wing based on Guam were stripped of all armament except the tail turret, and AN/APQ-7 'Eagle' radar bombsights were installed. The 'Eagle' was developed at Massachusetts Institute of Technology's Lincoln Laboratories specifically for long-range bombing to replace AN/APS-15 types. The electromagnetic scanner, which gave a higher degree of resolution, was housed in an 18 ft aerofoil section beneath the fuselage which swept from side to side through approximately 60°, the beam being formed in the forward path of the aircraft.

A much higher frequency was used with AN/APQ-7, giving a clearer presentation of ground images on the radar scope. The aircraft's radar gave the navigator accurate data on the location of the bombardier. Using maps of the target area, the navigator took the information from the radar system and calculated the course to the target.

SCR-729

This was a Philco-built airborne interrogator fitted at the radio operator's position in B-29 aircraft and used on early 58th Wing B-29s in the Pacific. All B-29s carried SCR-695 'Identification, Friend or Foe' equipment.

Weaponry

Browning .50 in M2 machine-gun

The standard machine-gun on all US fighters and bombers was the .50 in (12.7 mm) Browning M2. First produced in 1921, this was basically an enlarged version of the .30 in M1917A1. It was produced in greater numbers than any other US machine-gun in the Second World War:

With fifty missions to his credit, Sgt Ralph E. Miller of Oklahoma, waist gunner of 9th AF Marauder *Mild and Bitter*, loads his guns in the rear fuselage of the aircraft. He wears an A-3 cap and a rare leather first-aid pack. (USAF)

365th FG P-47D-RE 44-20571 on a snowbound airfield next to a four × .50 in AA quad mount, normally mounted on half-tracks, used for airfield defence. One of these quads shot down and killed George Preddy of the 328th FS, 352nd FG, 8th AF, on Christmas Day 1944. (USAF)

Field-modified twin .50 in Browning installation in the waist gun position of a 350th BS, 100th BG, B-17. The towns listed are from the time the gunner, Corporal Jerome E. Ferroggiaro, spent fighting in the Spanish Civil War. 'RHEUDELL' perhaps refers to the Indian waist gunner, 'Paddy' Blaizier. An open waist hatch was a very cold place to be at altitude, and the wind deflector helped. (Thorpe Abbotts Memorial Museum)

Republic P-47 Thunderbolt, armed with eight .50 in machine-guns in the wings, and underwing .5 in rockets. (USAF)

(Browning .50 in M2 machine-gun, continued)
Length: 57 in
Weight of gun: 64 lb
Weight of barrel: 10 lb
Length of barrel: 36 in
Overall length of gun: 56.125 in
Muzzle velocity: 2,750 ft per second
Maximum range: 7,200 yd
Effective range: 1,200 yd
Rate of fire: 800 rounds per minute

Browning .30 in machine-gun
The .30 in calibre Browning was used in early fighters and bombers, but had been discarded by bomber groups in Europe and the Pacific by early 1943:
Length: 40 in
Weight: 21 lb
Muzzle velocity: 2,600 ft per second
Effective Range: 300 yd
Rate of fire: 1,350 rounds per minute

M-2B 20 mm cannon
The 20 mm M-2B cannon was fitted to fighter aircraft and used as tail defence on the B-29 bomber:

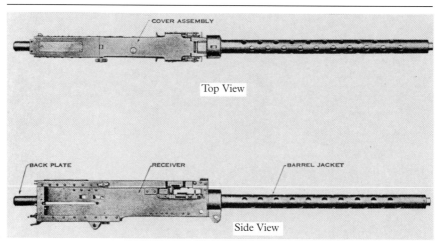

Browning M2 .50 calibre machine-gun.

Length: 94 in
Weight: 102 lb
Muzzle velocity: 2,850 ft per second
Effective Range: 700 yd
Rate of fire: 650 rounds per minute
37 mm M-4 and M-9 cannon
Length: 89.5 in
Weight: 213 lb
Muzzle velocity: 2,000 ft per second
Rate of fire: 150 rounds per minute

75 mm M-4 cannon
The 75 mm M-4 cannon was standard armament on some models of the B-25 and other aircraft. Its effective range was 2,000 yd.

Ammunition

A round of .50 in calibre ammunition was 5.47 in long and weighed 1.71 oz; the 0.30 in round was 3.34 in long and weighed 2.1 oz.

Classification and identification
Ball – cartridge, ball, calibre .50, M1 & M2 (standard) and M1923 (limited standard); for use against personnel and light materiel targets;
Armour-piercing – for use against armoured vehicles, concrete shelters and similar bullet-resisting targets;
Incendiary;
Tracer – for observation fire and incendiary purposes; the tracer contained a chemical composition that burned from the rear forward, giving the illusion of a stream of fire.

The .30 in machine-guns could be mounted in sockets in the nose of the B-17E and B-17F models of the Fortress for operation by the bombardier and navigator. Three sockets, including one non-standard fitting in the roof, can be seen in this B-17F, pictured in the USA. Note also the early ring-and-bead sight atop the Browning, and the empty side magazine. The gunner is wearing a B-3 jacket and HS-33 headset. (USAF)

An armourer in the 56th FG uses an empty ammo box to carry out maintenance on a .50 in Browning machine-gun which is fitted with a ventilation jacket to stop the heat from the barrel coming into contact with the wing. (USAF)

All .50 in calibre ammunition had bullets with copper-coloured metal jackets. Armour-piercing, tracer and incendiary ammunition could be distinguished by the nose of the bullet, which was painted black for armour-piercing, red for tracer or light-blue for incendiary rounds for a distance of approximately ⁷⁄₁₆ in from the tip. Dummy ammunition was identified by a hole in the body of the cartridge case.

Colour bands painted on the sides and ends of the packing boxes further identified the various types of ammunition. The following bands were used:
cartridge, armour-piercing – blue on yellow
cartridge, ball – red
cartridge, ball and tracer, in metallic link belt – yellow, red, and green stripes (yellow on left, red in centre, green on right)
cartridge, blank – blue
cartridge, dummy – green
cartridge, tracer – green on yellow
cartridge, incendiary – red on yellow

Defensive armament

When daylight attacks by the USAAF began in August 1942, Luftwaffe fighter pilots, who attacked mostly from above and behind, found that US defensive firepower was extremely effective.

Field modifications to this B-17E, *The Last Straw*, in the 19th BG shows an early attempt to improve the forward firepower of the Fortress in the Pacific.

Two B-17 waist gunners stand guard with their .50 in Brownings amid expended shell cases. The gunner nearest the camera has a first aid kit strapped to his lower chestpack parachute harness. The staggered waist gun arrangement was less cramped than on earlier B-17 models. The open hatches used on the B-17Fs and early B-17Gs were later glazed over, and the guns fired through mountings set in the glass. (USAF)

The B-17E, which first flew on 5 September 1941, and the B-24D, first delivered from Consolidated's San Diego plant on 23 January 1942, were equipped with the power-operated Bendix and Martin mid-upper turret respectively, a tail turret, and a hand-held single .50 in machine-gun mounted at each waist window. Each turret contained two .50 in machine-guns. B-17Es delivered to the ETO were equipped with two .50 in 'cheek' guns mounted through the side windows of the nose to be operated by the navigator. At first, the bombardier operated a lightweight .30 in machine-gun fitted with a removable magazine, which could be fired from any of three sockets in the Plexiglas nose. This gun proved ineffective and was replaced by one, sometimes two, belt-fed .50s.

The B-24D/E model had two .50 in flexible machine-guns mounted in the Plexiglas nose, and, later, a third gun was added, in a window on the left-hand side of the aircraft, forward of the navigator's position. Often, modifications made in the field increased the firepower still further, and a twin gun was mounted in place of the single gun in the bomb aimer's sighting panel.

All the nose-mounted guns in the B-17 and B-24 had to be operated by the bombardier and navigator as the situation demanded. Whichever mountings were used, the guns offered only a very poor field of fire. The Luftwaffe soon found that the frontal area of the US bombers offered very little in defensive firepower, and despite the dangers of very high closing

Waist gunner watching from the port hatch of a B-17 (the gun mount allowed the gunner to swivel his weapon inside and outside the window opening) during a photo-reconnaissance mission over New Guinea. He is wearing a pair of sunglasses, 'comfort cable'-type, with green lenses, and a .45 pistol in an M-3 shoulder holster. (USAF)

B-17F-10-DL showing the cheek gun, tail, mid-upper and ball turret positions. A radio hatch gun was also mounted in an attempt to improve firepower, but was largely ineffective. (McDonnell Douglas)

speeds, an approach from the front was considered the best method of shooting them down.

On the early B-24D models, which lacked a gun position underneath the aircraft, improvised .50 in gun mountings had to be installed in the rear entry hatch until ventral turrets (or 'ball' turrets, as they were popularly known) were fitted during production. (The B-17 was fitted with a ventral turret from the beginning.)

2nd Lt. William Zarhrte of Wisconsin wearing B-7 goggles, manning the flexible nose gun of a B-26 Marauder. The gun to his lower right is a fixed weapon which is fired by the pilot from the flight deck. (USAF)

Ford-built B-24H showing the Emerson nose turret and the company's distinctive 'wavy demarcation line' which separated the OD upper surface and grey lower surface. (Different B-24 manufacturers also had distinctively shaped black anti-dazzle panels atop the noses.) In the bombardier's window, the white heater tube known as the 'Elephant's pecker', which heated the bombsight and optical glass, can be seen. The open entry port is to allow ammunition to be fed into the nose guns, covered here for protection against the elements. (USAF)

B-17G *Wicked Witch*, 91st BG, 8th AF, showing the chin turret installation which added much needed frontal firepower to help combat head-on attacks by the Luftwaffe. (USAF)

Turrets

Other than remote-controlled turrets fired electrically from sighting stations on the aircraft, there were six basic types on AAF bombers: nose turrets, chin turrets, ball turrets, tail turrets, upper turrets and training types.

In 1942 many B-24Ds for use in the Pacific were modified at the Hawaiian depot so that a tail turret could be installed in place of the Plexiglas nose. The all-electric Emerson nose turret was introduced on the B-24H in June 1943. (For details of the other turrets used on the B-24, see the entry for the Consolidated B-24 Liberator aircraft in Chapter Eight.)

From the 113th B-17E onwards, a Sperry ball turret was installed on all Fortresses. Protection from below on 179 B-24D models was provided by a Bendix power turret with periscopic sights, but this was replaced by a single hand-held tunnel gun. The final 93 B-24D-CO models, and all subsequent B-24 production (except the first five B-24G models), carried the Briggs/Sperry retractable ball turret, a necessity because of the B-24's low ground clearance. The final production version of the B-17 was the B-17G, with an added Bendix two-gun, power-operated 'chin' turret under the nose for defence against direct frontal attack.

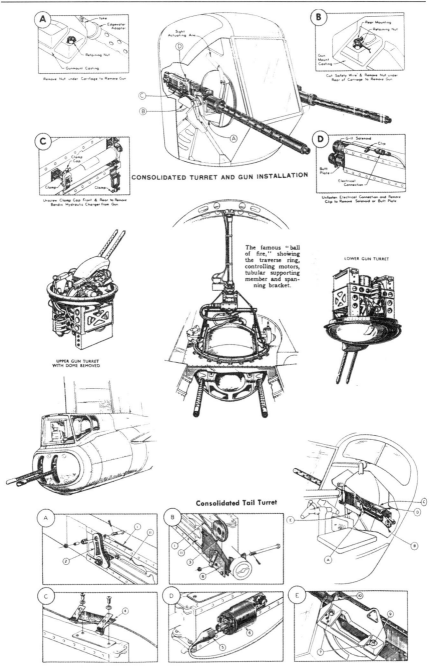

Gun turrets used on US bombers. Top: Consolidated tail turret. Centre: Sperry ventral turret (popularly known as the 'ball' turret), as used on the B-17E from the 113th and subsequent model, and the B-24 (retractable Briggs/Sperry ball turret). Left: Upper gun turret used on the B-29. Right: Lower gun turret used on the B-29. Left, below: B-17 tail gun installation. Bottom: Consolidated tail turret.

REMOTE CONTROL TURRET SYSTEM (B-29)

The 4 turrets and tail mount of the B-29 all operate by remote control. The gunners sit at **sighting stations** inside the fuselage and manipulate their gunsights. Computers, connected to the sights, automatically figure deflections for any fighter within range.

A system of control transfer enables gunners to take over control of more than one turret for a single gunsight. For every turret there is a gunner who has **first call.** The nose gunner is given first call on the upper and lower forward turrets. This affords him the greatest possible fire power with which to meet a frontal attack.

If he doesn't need the lower turret, he can let one of the side gunners take it over. For instance, he might be using the upper turret to shoot at an enemy coming in high, while at the same time another hostile plane may be coming in low. In such a case, he would give one of the side gunners control of the lower forward turret. Similarly, he can release control of the upper forward turret to the top gunner.

In the nose sighting station there are 3 units of gunnery equipment that are of concern to you, the bombardier:

1. **Control box** with the necessary switches for operating the turrets and gunsight.
2. **Gunsight** and controlling equipment.
3. **Transfer switches.**

An auxiliary switch on the control box starts the compressor motors that operate the gun chargers. A **computer standby switch** turned to the IN position cuts the computing mechanism into the forward turret circuits.

To operate both forward turrets, turn both transfer switches to IN and press down on the **action switch.** The guns in both turrets then follow your gunsight and fire when you press the trigger.

YB-40 Fortress gun ship

In May 1943 specially adapted Fortress gun ships fitted with sixteen machine-guns, including two top turrets (the existing one plus a Martin turret over the radio room), were introduced in the ETO as 'destroyer escorts' for conventional Fortresses. The first YB-40 was converted from the second Boeing-built B-17F-1 by Lockheed, and

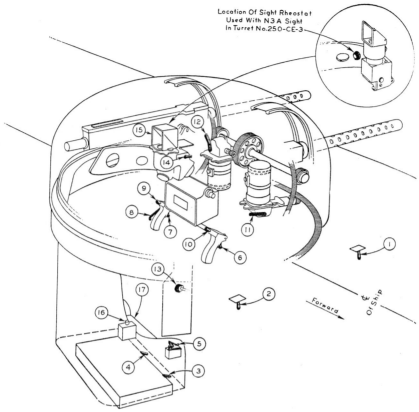

Location Of Sight Rheostat
Used With N3A Sight
In Turret No.250-CE-3

1 L.H. Turret Power Switch	10 High Speed Switch
2 R.H. Turret Power Switch	11 Azimuth Clutch Lever
3 Elevation Power Switch	12 Elevation Clutch Lever
4 Azimuth Power Switch	13 Sight Rheostat
5 Gun Switch	14 Sight Light Switch
6 R.H. Gun Trigger Switch	15 N6A Sight
7 L.H. Gun Trigger Switch	16 Extension Light
8 Dead Man Switch	17 Gunners Seat
9 Microphone Switch	

Location of units in Martin turret.

Douglas Aircraft converted the remaining YB-40s (service test conversions) at Tulsa (42-5732/42-5744). Thirteen YB-40s were assigned to the 327th Squadron, 92nd BG, 8th AF. Sixty-nine YB-40 sorties were flown between 29 May and the end of July 1943. These proved three things: that the additional machine-guns on each YB-40 did not add materially to the combined firepower a group formation could provide; that only stragglers were regularly attacked by the Luftwaffe, and the YB-40s were unable to protect these from concentrated attacks; and that the extra armour plating installed

Early models of the B-17G series had the conventional tail gun installation, as used in the B-17F series. Later variants had the Cheyenne tail gun modification, which gave the twin .50 in machine-guns an improved field of fire. Visibility was also improved, and the ring-and-bead sight was replaced by a reflector gunsight. The Cheyenne installation was used in the B-17G-90-BO, B-17G-50-DL, B-17G-55-VE and subsequent batches. (Boeing)

XB-40 'gun ship' 41-24341, pictured on 14 November 1942 after leaving the Boeing modification centre. (Boeing)

around the tail and waist gun positions (the latter having power-boosted, double waist guns with paired ammunition feeds), and additional ammunition, made the YB-40 a very heavy aircraft, and it could not keep up with conventional B-17s, especially after the bombs had been dropped on the target.

Gunsights

The ring-and-bead gunsight used in the First World War was used only on hand-held guns. Reflector-type and computing-type gunsights were used in turrets and fighter aircraft. The sight projected a sight reticle image on a transparent reflector plate which, at infinity, moved with the gunner's eye. Thus, although the gunner's head might be in continual movement in turbulent conditions, the sight line and target remained together.

The Bendix 'chin' turret was operated electrically by remote control from the bombardier's seat directly above it, and moved 96° to either side in azimuth, 26° above and 46° below horizontal in elevation. The bombardier's seat remained stationary: as he turned the gunsight, the guns swung around beneath. The bombardier's control unit, housing the Sperry N-8 or N-6A gunsight, pivoted out from its stowed position on his right and locked in place in front of him.

The Emerson nose turret on the B-24H and other power-operated turrets also used the N-8 or N-6A optical gunsight. The gunsight moved in azimuth about 75° either side of the aircraft's centre line, and in elevation from 50° below horizontal to 60° above. It had two speeds: normal tracking, and high. It was protected by armour plate, and bulletproof glass plate which moved with the guns. The N-8 was also used in the hand-held 'Cheyenne' tail turret of B-17s.

Computing sights

The Sperry K-15 computing sight, which permitted accurate deflection shooting, was fitted in some power-operated turrets towards the end of the war. The basic principle of the computing gunsight was that the gunner moved his gunsight directly, either by hand or through power drive, so as to follow the target. The gunsight computed the correct angle, and advanced the gun bores by that amount. The principle of the Sperry K-type 50 in calibre sight was simplified for mass production. Instead of moving the sight crosshairs directly, the gunner controlled the guns, and the sight crosshairs followed.

B-29s used Sperry K-3 and K-4 automatic computing sights mounted in power turrets as an integral part of the Gen. Electric Fire-Control System. Three flexible connections from the turret to the sight provided the sight with the necessary information for its computing. Two were connected in the back of the sight. One revolved as the guns were driven around (in azimuth) and the other revolved as they went up and down (in elevation). In this way, the sight could measure the angle of the guns and the speed the turret moved in order to calculate the deflections.

The four turrets and tail mount of the B-29 all operated by remote control. The gunners sat at sighting stations inside the fuselage and manipulated their gunsights. A system of control transfer enabled gunners to take over control of more than one turret from a single gunsight. For every turret there was a gunner who had first call. The nose gunner was given first call on the upper and lower forward turrets. This afforded him the greatest possible firepower with which to meet a frontal attack.

B-29s of the 315th Wing were fitted with a AN/APG-15 tail turret with a radar of about 2,000 yd range, designed by Gen. Electric. It was prone to breakdown and considered a failure. As enemy fighter opposition diminished, it was possible to improve the speed of the B-29 by deleting gun turrets and sighting blisters. These stripped-down versions were designated B-29B.

In daylight, even during the last three months of the war, Japanese fighters would occasionally dive into the B-29 formations, dropping phosphorous bombs, or trying to ram the B-29s, but the Superfortress gunners were more than a match for them. On the 7 May 1945 mission, for example, B-29 gunners shot down 34 Japanese fighters. US fighter escorts were positioned out in front, and stayed there, forcing the Japanese fighters to attack from the rear, where the compensating gunsights of the B-29s took care of most of them.

Specialized equipment

Computers
The E-6B computer was designed to be used for nearly all computations in navigation and bombing. The Automatic Bombing Computer, which was used with the M-series bombsight, enabled bombardiers to allow for wind, and automatically indicated the drift angle and dropping angle for any heading of the aircraft. The C-2 computer or the AN computer was used to allow for bombing altitude. The G-1 computer enabled bombardiers to find the true airspeed. The J-1 Sighting Angle Computer gave a sighting angle for a 30 or 50 second bombing run.

C-1 Autopilot
This automatically controlled the aircraft in straight and level flight, or manoeuvered it in response to the fingertip control of the pilot or

B-17 navigator in garrison cap with gold-and-black piping, wearing HS-33 (HB-7 headset/AN-B-H-1 receivers) radio headset, B-4 life preserver and garrison cap. An E-6B computer is tucked into the charts box. (via Mike Bailey)

This combat cameraman holding a K-20 camera wears F-2 electric gloves, A-14 oxygen mask, an M-3 flak helmet and M1/M3 flak suit over his electric suit for protection. In his right hand he holds an SW-141 intercom unit. (USAF)

bombardier. The autopilot's vertical flight gyro could detect any flight deviations of an aircraft from level flight the instant they occurred, and just as instantaneously, operate the controls to correct them. The autopilot control panel was located in the pilot's compartment and contained the switches, lights and knobs used to operate and adjust the autopilot.

Cameras

Camera bombing helped the bombardier improve his ability to identify targets. For low or medium altitudes, the simplest equipment for camera bombing was the A-4 35 mm bomb-spotting camera. With this camera, the bombardier took a picture through the bombsight optics at the time he would have released the bomb. For high-altitude camera bombing, the best equipment was a combination of the B-7 camera intervalometer (a device used to transmit electrical impulses at uniform timed intervals to externally connected equipment) with either the K-22 or K-24 camera mounted in the aircraft's camera well. The bombardier preset the the ATF on the camera intervalometer. When the aircraft was at the simulated bomb release point the bombsight's automatic release mechanism started the camera intervalometer, which tripped the camera when the preset time expired.

Radio countermeasures

Chaff ('Window')

This consisted of metallic foil strips, of varying lengths depending on the radar to be jammed, dropped in huge quantities to reflect radar signals and give enemy operators false readings. It was first used by the RAF in July 1943, by the 8th AF in December 1943 and the 15th AF in March 1944.

AN/APQ-9 and AN/APR 4 ('Carpet III')

The AN/APQ-9 (transmitter) and AN/APR 4 (search receiver) were used to jam signals operating on the 300–1,000 MHz range (the frequencies of German fire-control radars). The system was first used by the 8th AF in October 1943 and the 15th AF in August 1944.

A 1944 study indicated that formations protected by 'Carpet' averaged 1.5 per cent losses, compared to 14.1 per cent losses in unprotected formations. By the end of the war, three-quarters of the bombers in Europe were fitted with 'Carpet'.

AN/APT-2 and AN/APT-5

These transmitters for spot-jamming German early warning radar transmissions were fitted extensively to bombers in the ETO during the last twelve months of the war in Europe.

Crew equipment

Oxygen systems

As you ascend into the atmosphere, the air pressure drops, and the higher you go, the less dense the atmosphere becomes. At 18,000 ft the pressure is only 7½ lb per sq. in, or half that at sea-level. With increasing altitude, the air also gets colder, up to 35,000 ft. Decrease in pressure on the body results in oxygen want (anoxia), expansion of trapped gases, and decompression sickness, or aero-embolism.

US oxygen systems were of two general types: the demand system and the continuous flow system. As its name suggests, the continuous flow system supplied oxygen in a constant flow. To ensure delivery of the proper mixture for each altitude, crewmen had to adjust a dial manually on the A-9A regulator to correspond with the altimeter reading. The demand system, developed by Dr R. Lovelace and the Aero Medical Laboratory at Wright Field, became standard use during 1942 and was automatic. It furnished oxygen when the aircrewman breathed, and in just the right amount at each altitude. Every time he drew a breath, oxygen was supplied with the proper mixture of air. All aircraft had demand oxygen equipment. The A-11 regulator, used for passengers, was automatic.

The demand system included a demand-type mask, diluter-demand regulator, a pressure gauge, and a ball- or blinker-type flow indicator. In addition, a portable recharger hose was supplied at each crew position in heavy bombardment aircraft for recharging portable (walk-around) oxygen equipment from the oxygen system of the aircraft. The A-4 cylinder and A-13 regulator had a duration of 3–8 minutes; the D-2 cylinder and A-13 regulator, 20–50 minutes, and the A-6 cylinder and A-15 regulator, 15–40 minutes. Also, two bale-out oxygen cylinder assemblies, the Type H-1 and Type H-2, were available.

Two types of demand oxygen masks, both with built-in microphones for inter-crew or radio communication, were available: the Type A-10A and the Type A-14. The A-10A was prone to icing and uncomfortable to wear, and

The low-pressure, continuous-flow oxygen system was used early in the war by the AAF and featured an A-8B mask with two sponge rubber discs in the turrets of the face piece and in the re-breather bag. The unit is worn here by Lt. (later Col.) Bill Cameron in OD gaberdine B-1 summer cap and A-2 jacket. When exposed to freezing temperatures, the discs were squeezed to free them of moisture to prevent ice blocking them, but the A-8B easily froze at altitude and was replaced in 1943 by the A-9 mask. Pilots and flight crew wore a T-30 throat microphone around the neck, over the larynx, to enable radiotelephone voice communication. (Bill Cameron Coll.)

was revised in 1942. By 1943 the A-14 had become standard equipment on high-altitude aircraft. Both were used with the demand-type regulators, the A-12 or AN-6004-1 regulator for permanent installations with the aircraft, and the A-13 or A-15 regulator for portable use. The demand regulator was essentially a diaphragm-operated flow valve which opened by suction when you inhaled and closed when you exhaled. Types A-12 and AN-6004-1 were provided with two manual controls for use under special conditions: the 'auto mix' or oxygen control lever, and the emergency valve. Crews were urged to use oxygen on all flights above 10,000 ft, on all flights above 8,000 ft if the duration was more than four hours, and from the ground up on all night flights.

Personal safety equipment

Parachutes

Backpack-type parachutes included the Type B-7 (AN6512), on which the chest straps and leg straps had bayonet or snap fasteners, the Type B-8 flexible backpack with bayonet fasteners on the chest straps and leg straps,

B-24 waist gunner wearing an A-11 winter flying helmet, F-2 electric gloves, B-4 life preserver and A-14 oxygen mask. A type A-3 oxygen indicator on a panel in the aircraft told the recipient how much pressure was being exerted in the system. A warning light would glow when the pressure reached 100 lb. (USAF)

and the Type B-9 flexible backpack with a single-point, quick-release harness. To operate the quick-release harness, the crewman had to turn the cap clockwise through 90°, pull the safety clip and strike the cap a sharp blow with the hand.

Seat-type parachutes included the Type S-1, S-2 AN6510 and AN6511. The harness incorporated a back and seat pad. The chest and leg straps had snap or bayonet fasteners. The Type S-5 was the same as the S-1, except it had a single-point, quick-release harness.

Attachable chest-type parachutes (Group 1 Assemblies) included the Type QAC (AN65113-1), which could be put on quickly; it consisted of a square pack, attached to the harness by D-rings; the harness had snap fasteners on the chest and leg straps; the Type QAC (AN6513-1A) was similar, except it had a barrel-type pack.

Attachable chest-type parachutes (Group 2 Assemblies) included the Type A-3, which resembled the Type QAC, except the harness, which had bayonet fasteners; the Type A-4 resembled the Type A-3, but had a single-point, quick-release harness.

P-47 Thunderbolt pilot in A-4 summer flying suit, B-3 life preserver, B-3 summer gloves, RAF C-Type helmet, RAF oxygen mask with built-in microphone, B-7 goggles, Low Quarter GI service shoes, and S-1 seat parachute with cushion, which he sits on in his aircraft. US fighter pilots tried to obtain British-made helmets and boots when possible, as they were more comfortable than US ones. (USAF)

Rear view of a B-24 tail gunner in his turret, wearing a B-8 back parachute pack. A yellow-painted oxygen walk-around bottle is stowed on the right. (USAF)

Bomber flight crew, wearing B-4 life preservers and carrying their chest parachute packs and flak helmets, leave their briefing room and walk out to their aircraft, mid-1944. (USAF)

Lt. Abe L. Dolim, 94th BG navigator, pictured in March 1945 after completing his second combat tour, wearing a B-15 jacket with mouton-lined collar, B-3 life preserver and 'fifty-mission crush' cap with the 2⅜ inch high coat of arms gilt cap badge. EM wore a smaller version which was attached to a 1¹¹⁄₁₆ inch diameter disc. (Abe Dolim)

B-3, B-4, B-5 Pneumatic Life Preserver Vests: These were yellow, inflatable life preservers with mouth inflator valves, sea-marker packets and a carbon dioxide inflator, worn on the chest over all flying clothes and under the parachute harness. The sea-marker packet was cemented to the life vest. When 'friendly' aircraft approached, the packet was released by pulling down on the tab. The dye formed a large, green slick which lasted three to four hours. The improved B-5 was standardized in December 1944 to replace the B-3 and B-4.

Life rafts: In addition to the personal life preservers, two or more A-2, A-3 or A-3A four-man or E-1, E-2 or E-2A six-man life rafts were normally carried aboard bombers. These contained a signal kit (an M2 or AN-M8 pyrotechnic pistol and six flares), emergency drinking water (seven cans), sea marker (three cans), life raft rations (seven cans) and twenty-three other accessories (everything from aluminium oars and a bailing bucket to sun protection ointment and religious books).

For personnel such as fighter pilots, the AN-R-2 and AN-R-2A one-man life rafts were stowed in a seat pack attached to the parachute harness and inflated after the jumper struck the water. M3 and M8 smoke grenades were used to attract attention from the air when planes were forced down over sparsely settled regions; the M3 gave off a dense, red smoke for two minutes, and the M8 gave off grey smoke for three-and-a-half minutes.

CHAPTER TWELVE

Health and Survivability

Each of the operational stations had a serviceable dispensary/sick quarters building with bed space for twenty-five to forty-five patients. Mildly ill or slightly injured personnel were kept in the sick quarters beds until fit for duty, usually for no more than five days. The more seriously ill were evacuated to the 2nd or 30th General Hospitals, but these were over 60 miles from any station. Emergency cases which could not be hauled long distances were treated at one of thirteen RAF or nearby Emergency Medical Hospitals.

Death and disease

Death could be caused in the air from the effects of enemy fighters and flak, either directly or as a result of shock brought on by wounds, blood poisoning and other factors, such as anoxia (oxygen starvation). Professional treatment was, of course, only available once the aircraft had returned to its permanent base, and it was not uncommon in Europe for badly wounded men, who would not survive the journey home, to be pushed out of the aircraft with their parachutes on, in the hope that the enemy would treat them and save their lives.

In the tropics, the AAF units had to contend with alaria, dengue fever, scrub typhus, diarrhoea, dysentery ('Karachi crouch' and 'Delhi belly'), schistosomiasis, boils, abscesses, tropical ulcers, fungus infections ('Guinea crud' and 'jungle rot'), furunculosis and filiriasis. In the Libyan desert, sandstorms and inundations were a hazard to men and aircraft. In other regions a wide range of conditions prevailed, from the freezing wastes of Alaska and the Aleutians to the sun and stench of Bengal and the dehydration, monsoon, fever, khamsin and williwaw of North Africa.

Fraternization brought its own problems. Venereal disease, particularly, was prevalent. One AAF manual said:

In the tropics venereal diseases are common among prostitutes and most native women as well. In addition to syphilis and gonorrhea, large numbers of them are infected with chancroid, lympogranuloma venereum, and granuloma inguinale. Don't give them a chance to give it to you. The treatment of these diseases is longer than their names.

These diseases were not solely confined to the tropics, as high rates of VD were recorded in Europe too, as shown opposite. A total of 35,477 cases (rate 48.7) of sexually transmitted diseases were recorded by white (32,451,

A very badly wounded gunner receives an infusion from a plasma bottle and other treatment immediately after his aircraft has landed back at base after a mission over enemy territory. (USAF)

rate 45.5) and coloured (3,026, rate 208.5) personnel in the US Air Forces in western Europe from July 1942 to June 1945.

Venereal disease by commands, January–June 1945		
	Cases	Rate
8th Air Force	4,009	48.50
9th Air Force	6,030	71.00
IX Troop Carrier Command	1,198	62.84
First Tactical Air Force	477	51.70
Air Service Command	1,957	81.28
USSTAF, Miscellaneous	726	57.48
Total	14,397	61.07

Source: *Medical Support of the Army Air Forces in WWII*, Mae Mills Link and Hubert A. Coleman (Office of the Surgeon-General, USAF, Washington DC, 1955).

Combat tour

In their early attempts to deal with victims of combat exhaustion and stress, 8th AF flight surgeons found that the absence of a fixed, limited tour of combat missions contributed to their anxiety or emotional breakdown. Col. Grow, Surgeon of the 8th AF, recognized in 1942 that the morale of combat crew personnel in the ETO was 'not all that it should be to obtain the maximum efficiency in operational missions'. A major cause for the low morale, he said, was the fact that combat crews realized they could, at least theoretically, be wiped out within twenty missions if the average loss of 5 per cent per mission, then a conservative estimate, was not reduced. He therefore urged that combat crew members be released from operational duty upon the completion of fifteen missions.

Apparently, no immediate action was taken on this recommendation and as a result, morale was at a very low ebb during the winter of 1942–3. Mounting losses in VIII Bomber Command meant that by the end of January 1943, casualties had exceeded replacements, with only 24 bomber crews arriving in England to replace 67 lost on missions that month. When B-17s were despatched to Schweinfurt and Regensburg on 17 August 1943, 60 were lost and many others written off in crashes in England – an unacceptable 19 per cent loss rate. On 6 September 45 B-17s failed to return from a raid on Stuttgart. The worst day, 'Black Thursday', occurred on 14 October, when another 60 B-17s were lost, again on a mission to Schweinfurt.

The Central Medical Establishment, in a study entitled *Morale in Air Crew Members, 8th Bomber Command*, dated 9 March 1943, recommended the establishment of a definite and fixed combat tour of duty. General Ira Eaker, Commander of the 8th AF, directed that bomber crews should fly a tour of twenty-five combat missions and fighter pilots should complete 150 missions or 200 operational flying hours before being taken off combat operations. A DFC was awarded to all crew members who completed their tour of duty. Approximately 75 per cent of them were returned to the US ZOI. The others were retained in the theatre as instructors or staff assistants.

The personnel of the XIII Bomber Command who were recommended for return to the USA in June and July 1944 had flown an average of 525–590 combat hours. In August 1944, regardless of the fact that psychological breakdowns were closely related to the operational intensity of that time, the combat tour of duty in England was extended to thirty-five missions, on the grounds that individual missions appeared less hazardous. But were they?

On 7 August 1944 the 492nd BG, 8th AF, was withdrawn from combat after losing 54 B-24s between May and July 1944. This was the heaviest loss for any B-24 group for a three-month period. On 27 September 1944 the 445th BG, 8th AF, lost 25 out of 33 bombers shot down, and 5 more crashed over France and England. Only five made it back to England. It proved the highest group loss in 8th AF history. There were 236 empty seats in the mess halls at Tibenham that evening. Altogether, the 445th lost 117 men killed in action, and 45 officers and 36 EM had been made prisoners of war. Two months later, on 26 November, 16 out of 28 Liberators in the 491st BG, whose target was Misburg, were shot down in the space of just fifteen minutes.

In 1944 Col. Charles B. Thornton of Gen. Arnold's Statistical Control Unit tried to demonstrate mathematically that a crew member flying from

Combat Sorties Flown, Europe December 1941 to August 1945			
	ETO	**MTO**	**Total**
1941 Dec	-	-	-
1942 Jan	-	-	-
Feb	-	-	-
Mar	-	-	-
Apr	-	-	-
May	-	-	-
Jun	-	70	70
Jul	-	166	166
Aug	324	255	579
Sep	423	576	999
Oct	534	1,519	2,053
Nov	629	2,544	3,173
Dec	543	2,166	2,709
Total 1942	2,453	7,296	9,749
1943 Jan	767	4,330	5,097
Feb	976	3,362	4,338
Mar	1,564	6,478	8,042
Apr	989	12,963	13,952
May	3,915	12,724	16,639
Jun	4,104	13,248	17,352
Jul	5,531	24,370	29,901
Aug	5,826	21,532	27,358
Sep	9,294	20,659	29,953
Oct	7,463	14,124	21,587
Nov	9,624	15,856	25,480
Dec	13,876	19,948	33,824
Total 1943	63,929	169,594	233,523
1944 Jan	15,183	28,992	44,175
Feb	24,425	20,568	44,913
Mar	31,950	24,798	56,748
Apr	43,434	30,645	74,079
May	67,979	42,539	110,518
Jun	96,096	33,947	130,043
Jul	74,878	33,987	108,865
Aug	77,976	37,968	115,944
Sep	57,384	26,359	83,743
Oct	52,596	22,607	75,203
Nov	52,299	26,055	78,354
Dec	61,089	28,347	89,436
Total 1944	655,289	356,812	1,012,101
1945 Jan	47,477	16,914	64,491
Feb	68,365	31,348	99,713
Mar	111,472	35,408	146,880
Apr	79,402	41,495	120,897
May	5,565	646	6,211
Jun	-	-	-
Jul	-	-	-
Aug	-	-	-
Total 1945	312,381	125,811	438,192
Grand Total	1,034,052	659,513	1,693,565

the UK had a 'better than 60% chance of completing his tour and a better than 50% chance of living even if he was shot down'. These figures gave an 80 per cent chance of survival. However, a postwar analysis of six bombardment groups flying missions in Europe found that of the 2,051 crewmen who began a cycle of twenty-five missions, by the time of the last mission, 1,295 had been killed or reported missing, and another 197 were ill or recovering from wounds. Policies differed from one theatre to another. In the CBI there was no fixed tour length at all. In the Mediterranean, crews had to fly between 50 and 60 missions, and fighter pilots had to fly 300 hours or more. In the Pacific 500–600 hours constituted a tour of duty in either bombers or fighters. In July 1944 B-24 personnel in the 5th AF who had been in the theatre for 12.7 months flew 43 missions and 543 combat hours. During 14 months in the theatre, some pilots flew 58 strikes and 856 combat hours. In 1945 B-24 crews flew 42 sorties and 392.2 combat hours in 12.8 months. The survival rate of a tour of duty by combat personnel of V Bomber Command through January 1945 was 79.6 per cent for light bombers, 66.62 per cent for medium bombers and 83.8 per cent for heavy bombers. The attrition rate per 1,000 hours flown was the greatest among the heavy bombers in 1944 (7.7), second among medium bomber personnel (6.9), third among light bomber personnel (3.39), fourth among fighter personnel (1.09), and lowest for transport personnel (0.038).

Flying fatigue

As early as December 1942 evidence of mental stress, ranging from simple flying fatigue to serious psychological disorders, began to appear in some of the units of the 8th and 12th AFs. Flight surgeons, aided by psychiatrists and psychologists, kept a close watch for the first signs of battle fatigue.

Upon the recommendation of of their flight surgeons, enlisted men and officer crewmen had separate 'rest homes' to which they were sometimes sent when combat fatigue was diagnosed. Members of combat crews were sent to rest homes, free of transportation charges, for an average period of seven days rest and recreation, with a daily allowance. These homes were established on the recommendation of the 8th AF Surgeon, Col. Grow, to prevent breakdowns and promote morale and efficiency. In November 1942 one home provided accommodation for only twenty-five 'guests'. From 1 August 1944 to 31 December 1944, seventeen AF 'rest homes' accommodated 6,581 officers and 6,809 EM.

In the Mediterranean theatre, 'rest camps' began to function in December 1942, but only a very limited number of flying personnel could be sent to them. Despite combat conditions, numbers of breakdowns due to flying stress were remarkably low, according to a report by the surgeon on 20 January 1943. On the other hand, the flying personnel of the 15th Bombardment Squadron and the 14th Fighter Group (P-38) (which suffered a 31 per cent loss of its personnel killed or missing in action) had to be relieved from duty and returned to the USA in January and February 1943 because of generalized flying fatigue.

8th AF rate of loss (killed and MIA) per operational heavy bomber mission, January–June 1944 (prepared by Lt.-Col. Robert E. Lyons, Chief, Biometrics Division, Office of the Air Surgeon)*

Mission No.	Number Starting#	Number killed and MIA
1	2,051	93
2	1,927	139
3	1,775	94
4	1,651	46
5	1,585	117
6	1,451	74
7	1,360	56
8	1,291	75
9	1,203	76
10	1,117	60
11	1,047	54
12	990	36
13	942	61
14	873	28
15	831	20
16	794	37
17	748	31
18	708	20
19	680	21
20	654	20
21	623	12
22	605	6
23	588	7
24	564	3
25	559	9
Total		1,195

Figure arrived at by subtracting the number killed and MIA plus those otherwise 'lost' between missions, from the preceding mission.
The period covered was a period representing intense operational activity. The flying personnel used in this study were members of the 91st, 94th, 305th, 306th, 381st and 384th BGs (all B-17 units).

* Source: *Medical Support of the Army Air Forces in WWII*, Mae Mills Link and Hubert A. Coleman (Office of the Surgeon General, USAF, Washington DC, 1955).

In England cases of extreme flying fatigue were sent to the 5th General Hospital, where treatment was given by the psychiatrists of the 8th AF on detached service at this hospital. (During the first eight months of 8th AF operations, only thirty-five cases of flying fatigue occurred.) In 1943 steps taken towards the formation of a uniform policy regarding treatment and disposition of neuropsychiatric cases among Air Force personnel included

8th AF 'Life Table' for group of 1,000 flyers starting sorties, lost at specific rates in successive missions, and completing tour at end of twenty-five missions (prepared by Lt.-Col. Robert E. Lyons, Chief, Biometrics Division, Office of the Air Surgeon.★ Rates obtained from experience of 8th AF and smoothed)

Mission	Loss rate % lost in specified mission	Number lost in specified mission	Number surviving specified mission out of 1,000 starting 1st mission
Start			1,000
1	6.2	62	938
2	6.0	56	882
3	5.7	50	832
4	5.5	46	786
5	5.3	42	744
6	5.0	37	707
7	4.8	34	673
8	4.6	31	642
9	4.5	29	613
10	4.3	26	587
11	4.1	24	563
12	4.0	23	540
13	3.8	21	519
14	3.7	19	500
15	3.5	18	482
16	3.4	16	466
17	3.3	15	451
18	3.2	14	437
19	3.1	14	423
20	3.0	13	410
21	2.9	12	398
22	2.8	11	387
23	2.7	10	377
24	2.6	10	367
25	2.5	9	358

Source: *Medical Support of the Army Air Forces in WWII*, Mae Mills Link and Hubert A. Coleman (Office of the Surgeon General, USAF, Washington DC, 1955).

the creation of Group Flying Evaluation Boards, empowered to review cases involving physical and psychological disability and 'lack of moral fibre'. (In Europe 3,067 neuropsychiatric cases resulted in removal from flying, of which, 1,042 were permanent.)★

★ *Medical Support of the Army Air Forces in WWII*, Mae Mills Link and Hubert A. Coleman (Office of the Surgeon General, USAF, Washington DC, 1955).

The incidence in fatigue among flying personnel during the war in the Pacific varied considerably from time to time, though it was always a serious problem. In the summer and autumn of 1942 and the first six months of 1943, combat crews were required to expend efforts considerably beyond the acknowledged limits of endurance, because of the tactical demands placed upon them and the lack of sufficient replacements. The Assistant Air Force Surgeon, 5th AF, stated in February 1943 that 45–60 per cent of the flying personnel of four bombardment squadrons were suffering from severe pilot fatigue. In a fighter squadron, 45 per cent were suffering from staleness and the early stages of pilot fatigue, while in another fighter squadron, 37 of 47 pilots showed some degree of fatigue. In the 13th AF at the same time, the Surgeon stated: 'the main cause of flying fatigue has been plain and simple overwork, operational demands have been heavy, all units have constantly been well below T/O strength and replacements have never arrived in the quantities promised. Flight surgeons have been forced to close their eyes to the condition of aircraft members and all accepted standards of physical fitness for flying have had to be junked.'*

Removal from flying

There were three major occupational disorders peculiar to flying personnel: aero-otitis, frostbite and anoxia (the last two occurring almost entirely in the heavy bombardment units). In Europe, for instance, aero-otitis accounted for 8,345, frostbite for 3,452 and anoxia 403 removals, making a total of 12,200 removals. The major non-occupational medical disorders accounted for a total of 18,799 temporary removals from flying status.

The total number of temporary removals from flying as a result of all causes was 108,953, of which aero-otitis media accounted for about two-thirds. It also resulted in the permanent removal from flying of thirty-four personnel. In addition to anxiety reactions (1,042), air sickness accounted for 124 permanent removals, old wounds 59, sinusitis 59, frostbite 35, and defective vision 24. In administration, inefficiency resulted in 405 personnel being permanently removed, 766 because they were no longer required, 145 because of misconduct, and 45 at their own request.**

Leaves and furloughs

Leaves were often issued upon the completion of 10–15 missions. In North Africa and the Mediterranean in 1942, temporary relief of flying personnel was in most cases impossible owing to the lack of replacements. Leave in the

---

*   *Medical Support of the Army Air Forces in WWII*, Mae Mills Link and Hubert A. Coleman (Office of the Surgeon General, USAF, Washington DC, 1955).
** Ibid.

Charles Weaver, pilot, his leg in plaster, and his crew chief, 357th FG, 8th AF, pose in front of his Mustang at Leiston, England. (Merle Olmsted)

5th and 13th Air Forces in the Pacific, for instance, was granted about every three months, while in the 8th Air Force in Europe, the interval varied from two to five months.

Late in the war a policy was adopted whereby 30 days (later 45) TDY in the US ZOI would be given to qualified personnel who agreed to return to the theatre for another year, or fly another combat tour. In the Pacific, advances made it increasingly difficult to send men to Australia for leave. The 5th AF tried to give non-combat men a week's leave in Australia for every six months in New Guinea. Most waited 10 months, some as long as 18. Innovative as ever, General LeMay, in 1945, tried to get two luxury liners to sail to the Marianas to be used as floating rest camps for his B-29 crewmen, but lack of shipping prevented it.

Losses

During 1944 alone the US Strategic and Tactical Air Forces in the ETO and MTO lost 6,925 bombers (3,465 to flak, 2,341 to fighters). From this total, the 8th AF lost 4,470 aircraft (2,211 to flak, 1,715 to fighters), and the 15th AF lost 2,455 aircraft (1,254 to flak, 626 to fighters).* During 1942–5

---

* Compiled from *AAF Statistical Digest, WWII*, pp. 255–6.

Cockpit interior of a B-24D Liberator showing flak curtains which were fitted during production behind the pilots' seats, the left one occupied on this occasion by Gen. Carl A. Spaatz. Armour was installed here and in the waist and bulkhead sections to reduce possible damage from enemy fighter attacks from the rear, but was deleted on subsequent models as tactics changed. (USAF via Mike Bailey)

B-24J-1-FO Liberator *Miss B-Haven* of the 448th BG, Seething. Thick boilerplate obtained from British sources has been fixed to both sides of the pilots' compartment for added protection, while the Plexiglas in the front and side windows of the cockpit has been replaced by armoured glass. (Ford-built Liberators often had, on the flight deck, 'coffin'-style armoured seats which enclosed the head and body of the pilot, but this innovation proved unpopular and was later deleted.) A 'bubble'-style blister window has been installed to improve the navigator's all-round vision. Below the Emerson turret is the 'fishhook' *Carpet* antenna. (USAF)

B-17s in the ETO flew 291,508 sorties in Europe, losing 4,688 of their number in combat. By comparison, B-24s flew 226,775 sorties for the loss of 3,626 of their number; B-26s flew 129,943 sorties for the loss of 911 aircraft; B-25s, 63,177 sorties for the loss of 380; A-20s, 39,492 for the loss of 265; and A-26s flew 11,567 sorties for the loss of just 67 aircraft.

Fighter losses in the ETO were as follows: P-47s, 423,435 sorties, 3,077 combat losses; P-51s, 213,873 sorties, 2,520 lost; P-38s, 129,849 sorties, 1,758 lost; P-40s 67,059 sorties, 553 lost; P-39s, 30,547 sorties, 107 lost.

From December 1941 to August 1945 US combat losses in the Pacific war totalled 8,700 aircraft. XX Bomber Command, XXI Bomber Command and the 20th AF, from 5 June 1944 to 15 August 1945, flew 27,611 bombing sorties for the loss of 402 B-29s.

Air Force casualties in all theatres, December 1941–August 1945

Theatre	Total Cas.	% of Total cas.	Killed	Wounded	MIA	Officers	EM
ETO	63,410	52.0	19,876	8,413	35,121	28,190	35,220
MTO	31,155	25.6	10,223	4,947	15,985	12,754	18,401
POA	2,476	2.0	926	882	668	922	1,554
FEAF	17,237	14.2	6,594	3,005	7,638	4,842	12,395
CBI	3,332	2.7	1,263	494	1,575	1,723	1,609
Alaska	682	.6	451	53	168	269	413
20th AF	3,415	2.8	576	433	2,406	1,575	1,840
Other	160	.1	152	1	7	140	20
Total	121,867	100.0	40,061	18,238	63,568	50,415	71,452

Source: AAF Statistical Digest, December 1945, pp. 49–59.

Prisoners of war

A total of 90,000 US airmen were taken prisoner of war by Germany and 15,000 by Japan. (In the USA 371.683 German prisoners were held in POW camps.) Generally, the treatment afforded PoWs by Germany was good. Germany was a signatory of the 1929 agreement devoted to the treatment of PoWs, which became known as the Geneva Convention. Captured aircrew were sent first to Dulag Luft Interrogation Centre, then to the Stalags and Oflags (officers' camps) scattered throughout Germany, Poland and the Greater Reich for incarceration until the end of the war.

Japan signed the Geneva Convention, but it was never ratified by the Japanese Government. In January 1942 Japan said it would abide by the convention, but it rarely did so. On the 60 mile Bataan death march, 10–12 April 1942, an estimated 5,200 US PoWs, including 104 US Army and Navy nurses, died. Of the US Army and AAF prisoners held captive in Japan, 40.4 per cent died in captivity. Torture and maltreatment of prisoners by the Japanese military authorities was commonplace, and in the last few days of the war at least one B-29 crew was beheaded after capture.

In comparison, 1.2 per cent of US Army and AAF prisoners died during incarceration by the Germans. However, US fliers were called '*Terrorflieger*' by large parts of the population in Germany, and towards the end of the war, it was not uncommon for crews to be lynched by civilians, and on occasion, murdered in cold blood by the military.

Total losses

Total US aircraft losses (all services) in the Second World War numbered 59,296 aircraft; 9,949 of these were bombers and 8,420 fighters. The final human toll for the US Army and Air Force for the Second World War was 234,874 killed, 565,861 wounded. The total number of Americans who died in the war was 406,000 – 91,000 less than in the American Civil War and 290,000 more than in the First World War.

Non-combat losses

These were as hard to endure as losses in combat. Aircraft accidents in Europe, for example, accounted for 1,806 deaths, or 65.9 per cent of the total number of deaths from disease and injury (2,734). Motor vehicle accidents accounted for 341, accidental explosions 125, firearm wounds 113, drowning 34, heart disease 34, suicide 24, and other causes 257 deaths.★

In the Pacific, the 5th AF labelled 16 April 1944 'Black Sunday' after 31 fighters, which were returning safely from an attack on the Tadji area, were fatally cut off from their home bases by a barrier of fog and cloud. In India-China, the black days occurred in the ATC on 6–8 January 1945, when a storm over the Himalayas caused the loss of nine transport aircraft.

Generally, if the mission was worth the cost, aircrews could endure the hazards. Bombs on canneries in the Kuriles, and endless neutralizing strikes against Marcus, Truk, Navru, Ponape and others did not inspire B-25 and B-24 crews of the 7th AF.

Certain aircraft gained the reputation for being 'killers' at certain times of their development or during combat tours. The B-26 Marauder was quite often referred to as the 'Widow Maker' or the 'Baltimore Whore' because 'it had no visible means of support' (a reference to its small wing area). At one time, all personnel in the 320th(M) BG, 9th AF, except the CO and his Executive, asked – either formally or informally – to escape from B-26 flying to a safer form. P-38 crashes in 1942 led to requests to transfer to bombers. During 1942–3 the B-24 had the sorry distinction of being the 2nd AF's

★ *Medical Support of the Army Air Forces in WWII*, Mae Mills Link and Hubert A. Coleman (Office of the Surgeon General, USAF, Washington DC, 1955).

238 THE USAAF HANDBOOK 1939–1945

problem plane. In 1943 alone, 850 men were killed in 298 accidents. The 34th BG lost 7 B-24s and 43 crewmen in six weeks at Salinas, California.

The B-17 had the lowest accident rate of all US bombers and fighters operating in the US ZOI. In England the B-17 had a lower accident rate than the B-24, and B-24 accidents were also more serious. A six-month survey of bomber ditching in the ETO and MTO revealed that 22 per cent of B-17s broke up, compared to 62 per cent of B-24s, and 6 per cent of B-17 crews drowned, compared to 24 per cent of B-24 crews. Overall, 38 per cent of 8th AF B-17 crew members who ditched survived, compared to 27 per cent of B-24 crew members. One report in the US Strategic Bombing Survey concluded: 'the B-17 was a more efficient combat aircraft than the B-24 from a viewpoint of bombing accuracy, life of aircraft, tons dropped for each effective sortie, and losses'.

CHAPTER THIRTEEN

Morale, Medals and Awards

Morale

Effect of losses on morale

Heavy losses always affected morale, and the signs manifested themselves in many ways, from a high abort rate to, at the very least, severe bouts of intoxication. The loss of key personnel, especially near the end of tours of duty, was another factor.

As noted in Chapter Twelve, losses could sometimes affect entire groups. Disaster at the hands of the Luftwaffe at Vicenza on 28 December 1943 was a major factor in the withdrawal of the 512th Bomb Squadron, 15th AF, from combat two days later. Losses to XIII BC during the Balikpapan oil campaign in Indonesia (30 September 1944–3 October 1944) brought the morale of the survivors 'close to breaking point', according to Gen. Kenney. In England the 'Bloody Hundredth' and the 492nd BG in particular gained notoriety after sustaining heavy losses.

At certain times in their history, many groups earned an unenviable reputation for being 'unlucky'. Sobriquets such as this were sardonically applied to those who felt sorry for themselves and their 'ill luck', but the cause was usually bad formation flying or poor leadership, rather than misfortune.

Boosts to morale

The greatest morale boost of 1942 occurred in the Pacific on 18 April. Lt.-Col. (later Gen.) James H. Doolittle earned the Medal of Honor for leading an audacious carrier-borne strike by sixteen Mitchell bombers with crews hand-picked from the 17th BG and the 89th Reconnaissance Squadron in low-level attacks on Tokyo and three other cities. Doolittle had planned to fly the B-25Bs off the deck of the *Hornet* while some 450 miles from his targets, but the aircraft carrier was spotted while it was still some 823 miles distant. Ten hours earlier than anticipated, the Mitchells were flown off and crews told to land in China as planned.

Most aircraft crash-landed in China, but several crews were captured, and three airmen were executed by the Japanese. The bomb loads were, of necessity, small, but at home, news of the 'Tokyo Raiders' had the desired effect. Morale soared, while the Japanese were forced to plan counter-attacks on the US Fleet.

Revenge was sweet on Sunday 18 April 1943, when P-38G Lightnings of the 339th Fighter Squadron, commanded by Maj. John W. Mitchell, succeeded in intercepting and shooting down the Mitsubishi transport carrying Admiral Yamamoto, the architect of the 6 December raid on Pearl Harbor. The interception, 550 miles from their base at Guadalcanal, was made possible by the use of long-range drop tanks.

Other adverse effects on morale

Groups that were well led usually showed few outward signs of low morale. The overall efficiency of the group – which had one purpose only: to get bombs accurately on target – depended entirely on its commander and his attitude towards training, and on the policies which he laid down with regard to the general running of his HQ and the four squadrons under his command. Much also depended on his accurate assessment of the key personnel assigned to his command, both at HQ and squadron level. Groups which showed lassitude, poor performance and a marked decline in discipline – which in turn led to high losses and a corresponding fall in morale – had their commanders posted away and replaced by a specially chosen officer, quite often a 'West Pointer', to knock the outfit back into shape.

Curtis E. LeMay, when 305th BG Commander, 'demanded the best from each man. If the man did not "produce", he would fire him. He was a believer in exactness in flying, abiding by the book as far as possible, but wanted the job done. He would not tolerate laziness of any type and he didn't want any "unlucky" person on his team. He would fire a person for being "unlucky" as quick as incompetent.'*

Col. Albert J. Shower, CO of the 467th BG, was the only bomb group commander in the 8th AF to bring his group to England and retain command of it until the end of hostilities. He would order parades every Saturday morning, when possible, and he drove his men hard, but the fact that the 467th's bombing accuracy was unsurpassed throughout the 8th AF speaks for itself. On 13 May 1945 his group had the honour of leading the victory fly-past over the 8th's HQ at High Wycombe.

Every army the world over since time immemorial has had its 'grousers and groaners', and the AAF was certainly no exception. Inhospitable surroundings, lack of comfort, food (and the lack of it), monotony, absence or slowness of promotion and lack of direction are just some of the factors that, singularly or collectively, can contribute to general malaise in a crew, squadron, group or even command. On occasion, it was a case of 'better the devil you know . . .': this was certainly true during the German breakthrough in the Ardennes in December 1944, when 'groundpounders' in AAF groups were selected to be sent to the front as replacements for the infantry. Many then realized that life on a muddy, remote air base, even with its lack of plumbing and its freezing huts – was not so bad after all.

From time to time, certain types of crews and units, groups, and even air forces, had a tendency to be 'uncharitable' towards their peers in other types

---

* Cliff Pyle in *Castles in the Air*, Martin W. Bowman (PSL, 1984).

of aircraft and in other air forces. B-24 crews of the 13th AF resented toiling in the shadow of the 5th AF. In 1942 8th AF men sardonically referred to the 12th AF destined for North Africa as 'Junior': an upstart. Men, aircraft and supplies earmarked for the 8th found their way to the 12th, and the phrase 'You can't have that, it's for Junior' became widespread.

Relationships between the 8th and 9th AF B-24 groups in 1943 were not particularly good; they were even worse within the 8th, between the B-24 crews and the B-17s crews. The latter dubbed the B-24 'the crate that ours came in' and 'banana boat', while the B-17 was called a 'medium bomber' and 'glory machine' by B-24 crews. The ETO was called 'the big league' and other air forces, the 15th AF in Italy among them, considered themselves to be 'junior league' players in comparison.

Improving morale
United Service Organization shows such as the all-soldier show, *Skirts*, which played 212 times in the UK to a total audience of 260,000, entertained troops. On base, 'clubmobiles' and US Red Cross 'doughnut wagons' helped considerably to remind them of the joys of home. So too did the arrival of V-mail and letters from home, although 'Dear Johns' (letters from an airman's sweetheart or wife, ending their relationship) had the reverse effect on morale. Chaplains administered to all faiths, especially before a mission. Sport and recreation time were cherished. If a group recorded 100 or 200 missions flown, they were rewarded with a party and a stand-down from combat of one or two days respectively.

Medals and awards

Service awards, and Distinguished Unit Citations (created by executive order, 26 February 1942, to honour occasions when a unit displayed 'such gallantry, determination and esprit de corps in accomplishing its mission as to set it apart from and above other units participating in the same campaign') were awarded for the purpose of improving morale. Often they had the reverse effect. 15th AF personnel pointedly suggested that it might be a good idea to stamp their conservatively awarded DFCs with the number '15' in order to distinguish them from 8th AF DFCs. However, between August 1942 and 29 December 1944, one of the heavy bomb groups in the 15th AF distributed a total of 15,544 Air Medals and Oakleaf Clusters!

This is the full list of awards and decorations made to the 8th AF, 17 August 1942–15 May 1945:
Medal of Honor – 14;
Distinguished Service Cross – 220 (plus Oakleaf Cluster – 6);
Distinguished Service Medal – 11 (plus Oakleaf Cluster – 1);
Legion of Merit – 207 (plus Oakleaf Cluster – 2);
Silver Star – 817 (plus Oakleaf Cluster – 47);
Distinguished Flying Cross – 41,497 (plus Oakleaf Cluster – 4,480);
Soldier's Medal – 478 (plus Oakleaf Cluster – 2);

Distinguished Service Cross
Authorized by Act of
Congress approved
9 July 1918

Distinguished Service Medal
Authorized by Act of
Congress approved
9 July 1918

Silver Star

Purple Heart
Authorized by Act of
Congress 2 July 1926

Soldier's Medal

Air Medal

Distinguished Flying Cross
Act of Congress approved
2 July 1926

Air Gunner Staff Sgt. Maynard 'Snuffy' Smith (wearing RAF 1941-pattern gloves, A-6 boots, B-6 jacket, and B-3 life preserver), 306th BG, who was awarded the Medal of Honor for his actions on 1 May 1943. EM Medal of Honor winners also received $2 per month extra pay. Tradition has it that a Medal of Honor wearer is entitled to a salute from another serviceman or woman regardless of rank. Although this is neither custom nor regulation, 'Snuffy' Smith is reputed to have insisted on this practice. He also adopted the British fashion of having his award printed after his name. 'Snuffy' flew only a few more missions before being transferred to a ground job. (Richards Coll.)

Purple Heart 6,845 (plus Oakleaf Cluster – 188);
Air Medal – 122,705 (plus Oakleaf Cluster – 319,595);
Bronze Star – 2,972 (plus Oakleaf Cluster – 12);
Unit Citation – 27;
Meritorious Service Unit Plaque – 19.

Morale in the 7th and 12th AFs slipped when approval of recommendations for the Air Medal took as long as six months – men wanted to receive their medals while they were still alive. In the NAAF, fighter crews accused the bomber crews of taking more medals than them, and vice versa. The Bronze Star Medal in 1944 promised to fill the gap between the Legion of Merit and the Good Conduct Medal, and was hailed as 'a means of rewarding the ground crews for the wonderful work they had been doing'. Battle stars were worth five discharge points and counted towards battle-participation credits.

Awards of decorations

Decorations were awarded by the War Department acting on behalf of the President, except that the commanding general of a separate army of a higher unit in the field in time of war could award all decorations other than the Medal of Honor (sometimes referred to incorrectly as the *Congressional* Medal of Honor, a gold medal awarded by Congress to military and civilian personnel for outstanding achievements; recipients have included Charles A. Lindbergh and Hyman G. Richover★) and the Distinguished Service Medal. A decoration was presented in recognition of an outstanding act of heroism or an especially noteworthy service performed by an individual.

Medal of Honor

This is the highest and most rarely awarded decoration conferred by the USA, and was established by Act of Congress on 12 July 1862. It is awarded in the name of Congress to an officer or enlisted man who, in actual conflict with an enemy, distinguishes himself conspicuously by gallantry and intrepidity at the risk of his life, and above and beyond the call of duty. In all, 37 were awarded to the AAC during the Second World War, 23 of which (62 per cent) were awarded posthumously.

The medal consists of a five-pointed star, surrounded by a laurel wreath, suspended from a bronze bar, and bearing the inscription 'For Valor'. The ribbon is light-blue, with thirteen white stars.

United States Air Force Medal of Honor recipients, 1942–5

★ indicates posthumous award

1942

18 April	Doolittle, Lt.-Col. James H. Tokyo, Japan
7 August	Pease★, Capt. Harl Jr, 19th BG/5th AF, Rabaul, New Britain
8 November	Craw, Col. Demas T., Port Lyautey, French Morocco Post (killed on ground)
8 November	Hamilton, Maj. Pierpont M., Port Lyautey, French Morocco

1943

5 January	Walker★, Brig.-Gen. Kenneth N., 5th Bomber Command, Rabaul, New Britain
18 March	Mathis★, 1st Lt. Jack, 303rd BG/8th AF, Vegasack, Germany
1 May	Smith, Staff Sgt. Maynard H., 423rd BS, 306th BG/8th AF, St. Nazaire, France
16 June	Sarnoski★, 2nd Lt. Joseph R., 3rd BG/5th AF, Buka, Solomon Islands
16 June	Zeamer, Maj. Jay Jr., 43rd BG/5th AF, Buka, Solomon Islands
26 July	Morgan, Flt. Officer John C., 92nd BG/8th AF, Kiel, Germany
1 August	Baker★, Lt.-Col. Addison E., 93rd BG/8th AF, Ploesti, Romania
1 August	Hughes★, 2nd Lt. Lloyd D., 389th BG/8th AF, Ploesti, Romania
1 August	Jerstad★, Maj. John L., 93rd BG/8th AF, Ploesti, Romania
1 August	Johnson, Col. Leon W., 44th BG/8th AF, Ploesti, Romania
1 August	Kane, Col. John R., 98th BG/9th AF, Ploesti, Romania
18 August	Cheli, Maj. Ralph, 38th BG/5th AF, Nr. Wewak, New Guinea (died as a PoW, 6 March 1945)
11 October	Kearby, Col. Neel E., 348th FG/5th AF, Wewak, New Guinea (killed in action 5 March 1944, Wewak)
10 October–15 November	Bong, Maj. Richard I., 49th FG/5th AF, south-west Pacific (killed 6 August 1945, Burbank California)

★ *America at War 1941–45*, Norman Polmar and Thomas B. Allen (Random House, NY, 1991)

Brig.-Gen. Leon Johnson, CO, 14th Combat Wing, wearing the Medal of Honor presented to him at an awards ceremony in September 1943 at Shipham, Norfolk, for his actions at Ploesti on 1 August, when he led the 44th 'Flying Eightballs' over the refineries. His medal is actually the third style, being authorized on 23 April 1904. The Medal of Honor is the only US military decoration hung from a ribbon (in this case, light-blue moire with thirteen white stars) around the wearer's neck. The fourth style Medal of Honor, which appeared in 1944, had an additional pad of pale-blue ribbon bearing thirteen white stars. (Bill Cameron Coll.)

Lt.-Col. Leon Vance, awarded the Medal of Honor for his actions on 5 June 1944, is seen here with his daughter, Sharon, who gave her name to her father's Liberator. Vance underwent the amputation of his right foot, and was later invalided home in a C-54. Somewhere between Iceland and Newfoundland, the Skymaster with its crew and patients disappeared without trace. (USAF)

Col. (later Lt.-Gen.) Jimmy Doolittle (left) on USS *Hornet* with Vice-Admiral Marc A. Mitscher, prior to the Tokyo raid, 18 April 1942, for which he received the Medal of Honor. (USAF)

2 November	Wilkins★, Maj. Raymond H., 8th BS/3rd BG, Rabaul, New Britain
20 December	Vosler, Technical Sgt. Forrest L., 303rd BG/8th AF, Bremen, Germany

1944

11 January	Howard, Lt.-Col. James H., 356th FS, 354th FG/9th AF, Oschersleben, Germany
20 February	Lawley, 1st Lt. William R., 305th BG/8th AF, Leipzig, Germany
20 February	Mathies★, Sgt. Archibald, 351st BG/8th AF, Leipzig, Germany
20 February	Truemper★, 2nd Lt. Walter E., 351st BG/8th AF, Leipzig, Germany
11 April	Michael, 1st Lt. Edward S., 305th BG/8th AF, Brunswick, Germany
5 June	Vance, Lt.-Col. Leon R. Jr, 489th BG/8th AF, Wimereaux, France (killed 26 July, near Iceland)
23 June	Kingsley★, 2nd Lt. David R., 97th BG/15th AF, Ploesti, Romania
9 August	Lindsey★, Capt. Darrell R., 394th BG/9th AF, Pontoise, France
9 July	Puckert★, 1st Lt. Donald D., 98th BG, 15th AF, Ploesti, Romania
26 October	Carswell★, Maj. Horace S. Jr, 308th BG/5th AF, South China Sea

2 November	Femoyer*, 2nd Lt. Robert E., 711th BS, 447th BG/8th AF, Merseberg, Germany
9 November	Gott*, 1st Lt. Donald J., 729th BS, 452nd BG/8th AF Saarbrücken, Germany
9 November	Metzger*, 2nd Lt. William E., 729th BS, 452nd BG/8th AF Saarbrücken, Germany
24 December	Castle*, Brig.-Gen. Fred W., 4th BW/8th AF

1945	
11 January	Shomo, Maj. William A., 82nd Tactical Reconnaissance Squadron, Luzon, Philippines
12 April	Erwin, Staff Sgt. Henry E., 29th BG/20th AF, Koriyama, Japan
25 April	Knight*, 1st Lt. Raymond L., 346th FS, 350th FG, Po Valley, Italy
25/26 December	McGuire, Maj. Thomas B., 475th/5thAF, Luzon, Philippines (killed in action 7 January 1945, Los Negros, Philippines)

Distinguished Service Cross

Instituted by Congress in 1918, this medal is awarded to persons who, while serving in any capacity, distinguish themselves by extraordinary heroism in connection with military operations against an armed enemy.

The medal is a cross of bronze with an eagle in its centre. The ribbon is broad band of blue, bordered on both edges by narrow bands of red and white.

Silver Star

Established for the Army in 1932 and instituted in 1935, this medal is awarded to persons serving in any capacity cited for gallantry in action which does not warrant the award of the Medal of Honor or the Distinguished Service Cross.

The medal consists of a silver star imposed on a bronze star. The ribbon has stripes of blue, white, blue, white, red, white, blue, white, and blue.

Purple Heart

This award was originally established by Gen. George Washington in 1782 (at that time it was called the Badge of Military Merit). After the Revolution it was not used, but it was re-established in 1932, and is now given to anyone wounded in action while serving in the US Armed Forces. A posthumous award of the Purple Heart is also made to the next of kin of officers or enlisted men killed in action or who die of wounds received in action.

The medal is a purple enamelled heart within a bronze border, with the profile head of Gen. George Washington. The ribbon is purple with white edges.

Distinguished Flying Cross

This is awarded to any person who, while serving in any capacity with the AAFs subsequent to 6 April 1917, has distinguished himself by heroism or

Col. James R. Luper, CO of 457th BG until he was shot down and taken prisoner on 7 October 1944. He wears the 'bird colonel' badge on his garrison cap and epaulette and the AAF branch of service wings and propeller below the letters 'US' (to confirm identification if shot down) on his lapel. Below his Pilot's Wings and medal ribbons (DFC, Purple Heart, Air Medal, American Defense Medal and ETO Medal), he wears the AAF Marksmanship Badge (Expert) with five silver bars, for rifle, machine-gun, pistol, aerial gunner and small-bore. (USAF)

extraordinary achievement while participating in an aerial flight. In wartime, it is also awarded to members of allied armed forces.

The medal takes the form of a four-bladed propeller on a bronze cross patee. The ribbon's stripes are blue, white, blue, white, red, white, blue, white and blue.

Air Medal

Authorized by Executive Order of the President in 1942, this medal is awarded to any person who, while serving in any capacity, subsequent to 8 September 1939, has distinguished himself by meritorious achievement while participating in airborne action. This decoration is awarded in those cases where the act of meritorious service does not warrant the award of the Distinguished Flying Cross.

The medal, which takes the form of a pendant on a ribbon striped with the Air Corps colours of blue and gold, is a fleur-de-lis which surmounts a compass rose. In relief on the rose is a swooping US eagle with lightning bolts clutched in its talons.

Soldier's Medal

This decoration, established on 2 July 1926, is awarded to military personnel for heroic, voluntary risk of life not involving actual conflict with an armed enemy.

```
                        HEADQUARTERS
                  NINTH U. S. AIR FORCE

                                    APO 696, c/o Postmaster,
                                    New York, New York,
                                    16 September 1943.
    GENERAL ORDER)
                   :
    NO.      89)
                          EXTRACT

              AWARDS TO THE 389TH BOMBARDMENT GROUP (H) .

                      SECTION I I I

    *    *    *    *    *    *    *   ¼   *    *    *    *    *    *
```

3. By direction of the President, under the provisions of the Act of Congress approved 2 July 1926, (Bull. 8. W. D., 1926), and in accordance with authority delegated by the War Department, a Distinguished Flying Cross is awarded to each of the following-named officers and enlisted men:

For distinguished and meritorious performance of duty while participating in aerial flight against the enemy in operations against the Ploesti Oil Refineries of Romania on 1 August 1943. In this mission of extraordinary importance and danger, these officers and men, crew members of the 566th Bombardment Squadron, 389th Bombardment Group(H), performed their duties with such brilliance and skill as to bring lasting honor to their organization. Undaunted by the tremendous length of the mission, by the assaults of hostile aircraft(fighters), or by the concentrated and deadly gunfire of some of the heaviest anti_- aircraft fire and installations in Europe, they fought their way to the target, and bombed and strafed it with such highly destructive force that it was largely destroyed. Their part in this mission, which was one of the most daring and difficult in aviation history, was such as to bring high honor, not only to themselves and their organization, but to the United States Army Air Forces.

```
    *    *    *    *    *    *    *    *    *    *    *    *    *    *

    LEONARD D. BOISCLAIR      11096859    S/Sgt West Warwick, Rhode Island
    WILLIAM J. BOUR           16073706    S/Sgt Chicago, Illinois
    CHARLES A. BURKE          35267609    T/Sgt Quinwood, West Virginia
    ERNEST J. COX             15104032    S/Sgt Muncie, Indiana
    MARCUS A. DECAMP          19088359    T/Sgt Clear water, Nebraska
    GEORGE B. FARRELL         36347095    T/Sgt Oaklawn, Illinois
    RUSSELL D. HAYES          37418412    S/Sgt Waterloo, Iowa

    *    *    *    *    *    *    *    *    *    *    *    *    *    *
              By command of Brigadier General STRAHM:

    OFFICIAL:                              CLAIRE STROH,
                 C.M. SEEBACH,             Colonel, Air Corps
                 Colonel, AGD,             Acting Chief of Staff.
                 Adjutant General.
```

The medal is a bronze octagon on which the words 'Soldier's Medal, For Valor' and the recipient's name are inscribed. The ribbon bears two outer stripes of blue, with its centre carrying thirteen white and red stripes of equal width.

Distinguished Service Medal

This medal, which dates from 1918, is awarded to persons who, while serving in any capacity, distinguish themselves by exceptionally meritorious service to the government in a duty of great responsibility,

A technical sergeant gunner in Service Dress, or 'Class A' uniform, receives his Air Medal from a lieutenant-colonel. Sergeant stripes consisted of three chevrons pointing upwards over the 'rockers' and were OD on black for winter wear and brown or khaki for summer. (USAF)

and to all enlisted men to whom the Certificate of Merit had been granted, on or before 9 July 1918, under the provisions of previously existing law.

The medal consists of the coat of arms of the USA in bronze, surrounded by a circle of dark-blue enamel, with the inscription: 'For Distinguished Service'. The ribbon carries bands of scarlet, a stripe of dark-blue, a band of white, a stripe of dark-blue and a band of scarlet.

Legion of Merit

This decoration stems from the Badge for Military Merit, the USA's oldest decoration, established by George Washington in 1782. It is awarded to outstanding officers and enlisted men of the armed forces of the USA or of friendly foreign nations who have distinguished themselves by exceptionally meritorious conduct in the performance of outstanding services.

Developed from the Great Seal of the United States, the medal is a five-pointed US star of heraldic form, in red and white enamel, with a constellation of the thirteen original stars on blue in its centre. US personnel who win the Legion of Merit also wear a 'V' on the ribbon.

Good Conduct Medal

This decoration is awarded to those enlisted men who, on or after 27 August 1940, honorably completed three years of active federal military service, or

Lt.-Gen. Carl A. Spaatz attaches a Battle Streamer, awarded for their part in the attack on Ploesti, 1 August 1943, to the 389th BG's guidon at Hethel, England. (USAF)

who have completed one year of continuous, active federal service since 7 December 1941, and who are recommended for the award by their commanding officers for exemplary behaviour, efficiency, and fidelity.

The medal takes the form of an eagle with its wings displayed and inverted, standing on a sword which rests on a closed book; an encircling design is formed by the words: 'Efficiency, Honor, Fidelity'. The ribbon is scarlet, with three white stripes on each side.

Oakleaf Clusters

None of the decorations described above is issued more than once to any individual (except a posthumous award of the Purple Heart), but for each succeeding achievement sufficient to justify an award, a bronze Oakleaf Cluster may be awarded. A silver Oakleaf Cluster may be worn in lieu of five bronze Oakleaf Clusters for the same decoration.

Theatre Campaign Medals

These are awarded for 30 days consecutive or 60 days non-consecutive service in the following theatres: European-African-Middle Eastern; Asiatic-Pacific, and for service within the US theatre outside the continental USA.

Battle Streamers

AAF Battle Streamers – bunting attached to unit flags – were awarded to units that served in the Second World War. Stars marking participation in these actions were worn on personnel campaign ribbons.

CHAPTER FOURTEEN

War Diary

1941

1 September Air War Plan (AWPD/1) approved by Secretary of War Henry Stimpson. President Franklin D. Roosevelt endorses the plan on 11 September.

7 December Japanese attack on Pearl Harbor. Of 146 aircraft in commission before the attack, 83 remained in action afterwards. Six AAC pilots shoot down four enemy aircraft during attack.

8 December The USA declares war on Japan. Japanese air strikes on Clark and Iba airfields, Philippine Islands.

11 December Germany declares war on the USA.

1942

23 February 8th AF arrives in England.

February 10th AF activated for combat in the CBI theatre.

2 April Andaman Islands attacked by B-17s in first mission by 7th BG from India.

18 April Sixteen AAF B-25B Mitchells with crews hand-picked from the 17th BG and 89th Reconnaissance Squadron, under Lt.-Col. James Doolittle, launch from the carrier *Hornet* 800 miles east of Tokyo and attack Tokyo (13 aircraft), Nagoya, Kobe and Yokohama) with 500 lb bombs; 15 aircraft crash-land in China, 1 in Siberia. Of the 75 fliers down in China, 3 die accidentally, 8 are captured by the Japanese, and after 'trials', 3 are executed; 1 dies in prison. Intended as a morale boost, the raids push forward Japanese plans to invade Midway to prevent further carrier attacks on Japan, and as a result, two carriers are unable to join the invasion force.

23 April Brig.-Gen. Ira C. Eaker appointed Chief, VIII Bomber Command in Europe.

7–8 May Battle of the Coral Sea. Japanese seaborne threat to southern New Guinea thwarted.

4–6 June Battle of Midway reverses Japanese tide in the Pacific. Enemy fleet loses four aircraft carriers. 7th AF B-17s and torpedo-carrying B-26s help in repulsing invasion fleet.

11 June 11th AF bombers make first attack on Kiska, main Japanese air base in the Aleutians.

12 June US heavy bombers bomb a European target for the first time.

	Thirteen B-24Ds commanded by Col. Harry H. Halverson, part of the HALPRO force en route to join the 10th AF to bomb Tokyo from the Chinese mainland, use their staging base at Fayid on the Great Bitter Lake, near the Suez Canal, to attack the oil fields at Ploesti, Romania; 10 bomb through solid cloud cover, 1 blasts port of Constanta, 2 release their bombs on unidentified targets. Seven Liberators land in Iraq as planned, but two others are interned in Turkey.
4 July	US crews take part in joint USAAF/RAF raid on enemy targets in Europe for the first time when six crews in the 15th (Light) Bombardment Squadron join in attacks on four airfields in Holland using A-20 aircraft. Two US-crewed planes shot down.
3 August	In their first combat action, 11th AF P-38s shoot down two Japanese flying boats.
8 August	Pacific Offensive begins with landings on Guadalcanal, Solomon Islands. AAF B-17s attack nearby Japanese stronghold at Rabaul to divert enemy.
17 August	First American heavy bomber raid against railyards at Rouen, France, by B-17s of the 97th BG.
August –September	Allied Air Forces, SWPA, renamed 5th AF, help repulse Japanese thrusts at Buna in New Guinea. Operations feature airlift of troops into and within the theatre.
October	US aircraft in the Pacific start sowing mines in narrow waters, river mouths and harbours in the Malay Peninsula, Japanese-occupied areas of the south-west Pacific and the China coast, and in the inland seas around Japan itself.
14 August	First German aircraft shot down by a USAAF fighter when two P-38s from the 27th Squadron of the 1st FG and a P-40, destroy an FW 200 Condor near Iceland.
20 October	Brig.-Gen. Asa N. Duncan, Chief of Air Staff, issues a revised set of objectives to be carried out by VIII Bomber Command. In part, it states: 'Until further orders every effort of the VIII Bomber Command will be directed to obtaining the maximum destruction of the submarine bases in the Bay of Biscay.' The limited number of Fortresses available prevents VIII Bomber Command hitting submarine yards inside Germany.
8 November	Operation TORCH: invasion of North Africa. US 12th AF take part.
November	IX Bomber Command activated under the command of Gen. Lewis Brereton.
December	South-eastern New Guinea secured.
1943	
23 January	Casablanca Conference. Ira C. Eaker, acting Commanding General, 8th AF, makes a case for continued daylight bombing.

Churchill has obtained an agreement from Roosevelt for the 8th AF to cease daylight bombing and join the RAF in night bombing. Eaker sees Churchill and convinces him otherwise. Churchill particularly likes the phrase 'round-the-clock bombing', and although not totally convinced, is persuaded that day and night bombing should be continued for a time. Directive marks the beginning of the Combined Bomber offensive in Europe by the USSAF and RAF Bomber Command.

27 January To demonstrate that daylight precision bombing can triumph over area bombing by night, Eaker orders the first US attack on Germany (U-boat construction yards at Wilhelmshaven); 91 B-17s and B-24s despatched, but bad weather reduces the attacking force to 53 B-17s, which drop their bombs on the shipyards from 25,000 ft through a German smoke screen (2 others bomb Emden). Despite heavy fighter opposition, only three bombers shot down.

3 March US bombers intercept 8 Japanese transports and 8 destroyers moving reinforcements from Rabaul to Lae, New Guinea. In two days, air action sinks all the transports and four destroyers. Some 3,000 enemy troops, half the force, are lost at sea.

18 April P-38G Lightnings of the 339th Fighter Squadron, 13th AF, intercept and shoot down over Bougainville the Mitsubishi transport carrying Admiral Yamamoto, the architect of the Pearl Harbor raid. The interception, 550 miles from their base at Guadalcanal, is made possible by the use of long-range drop tanks.

1–2 May Battle of the Bismark Sea: 3,000 Japanese troops lost as twelve enemy ships are sunk by 5th AF planes.

13 May Axis surrender in North Africa.

June Operation POINTBLANK, an intermediate priority objective aimed at the German fighter strength, is finally published. Primary objectives listed are the 'German submarine yards and bases, the remainder of the German aircraft industry, ball bearings and oil'; secondary objectives: 'synthetic rubber and tyres and military motor transport vehicles'. The objective concludes: 'It is emphasized that the reduction of the German fighter force is of primary importance: any delay in its prosecution will make the task progressively more difficult.' The CBO plan calls for 2,702 heavy bombers in 51 groups to be in place before the Allied invasion, planned for mid-1944.

22 June First really deep penetration of Germany, to the synthetic rubber plant at Huls, producing approximately 29 per cent of Germany's synthetic rubber and 18 per cent of its total rubber supply; 235 B-17s despatched, and most of the route is flown without escort. One of the three diversionary raids planned to draw enemy fighters away from the Huls

force only succeeds in alerting them; 16 B-17s are lost and 170 damaged; 183 Fortresses bomb plant so effectively that full production is not resumed for six months.

July	13th AF supports ground forces in the reduction of Rabaul in Operation CARTWHEEL.
10 July	Allied invasion of Sicily.
17 July	A record 322 8th AF bombers are despatched to Hanover.
24 July	'Blitz Week' begins with an attack by 324 B-17s from the 1st and 4th Wings on targets in Norway, with one force flying a 2,000 mile round trip to Bergen and Trondheim, the longest US mission over Europe to date; 167 bombers from the 1st Wing bomb Heroya and completely devastate a factory complex, while 41 bombers bomb shipping at Trondheim. 'Blitz Week' costs the 8th AF about 100 aircraft and 90 combat crews, which leaves fewer than 200 heavy bombers ready for combat.
1 August	Raid on Romanian oil refinery at Ploesti by 177 B-24D Liberators from five groups: 44th, 93rd, 389th of the 8th AF, and the 98th and 376th BGs of the 9th BC. Operation TIDAL WAVE. Malfunctions and accidents en route reduce the effectiveness of the force. Navigational errors cause

B-24D Liberators over the burning oilfields at Ploesti, 1 August 1943. (USAF)

severe problems in the target area, forcing some groups to bomb each other's assigned targets. Delayed-action bombs from preceding groups damage or destroy Liberators in the following groups; 167 actually attack their targets and drop 311 tons of bombs on the refineries; 54 B-24Ds are lost over the targets, and 3 more crash at sea. Seven B-24D crews are interned in Turkey, while 19 land in Cyprus, Sicily or Malta. Of the 92 that return to North Africa, 55 have varying degrees of battle damage. However, 42 per cent of the plant's refining capacity and 40 per cent of its cracking capacity are destroyed. Most of the refineries are repaired and, within a month, are operating at pre-mission capacity again. (The USAAF would lose in excess of 200 more bombers and over 2,000 further aircrew in raids on the Ploesti refineries before the end of the war in Europe.) All five groups receive Presidential Unit Citations, while five Medals of Honor are awarded (three posthumously). At the end of August, after more raids from Benghazi, the three 8th AF groups are ordered back to England. The two 9th Air Force groups, the 98th and 376th, are transferred to the 12th AF after Ploesti.

15 August	STARKEY deception plan created to make Germany believe that an invasion of the French coast is imminent.
17 August	376 Fortresses bomb the Schweinfurt ball-bearing plant and the aircraft plants at Regensburg, which are estimated to produce 200 Me-109s a month, or approximately 25–30 per cent of Germany's single-engine aircraft production: 60 B-17s are shot down (36 from the 1st Wing at Schweinfurt and 24 from the 4th Wing at Regensburg); 27 B-17s are so badly damaged they never fly again; 60 B-17s of the 4th Wing, which continue to North Africa, have to be left behind in North Africa for repair.
September	5th AF assists Army forces in capture of Lae, Finschhafen, in New Guinea.
9 September	Allied invasion of Italy. Italy surrenders.
1 October	15th AF begins strategic bombing of German and Austrian targets from Italy.
14 October	Second Schweinfurt raid: 291 B-17s attack, 60 aircraft lost, and damage sustained to 138 B-17s that return to England.
2 November	Devastating US raid on Japanese main base at Rabaul.

1944

1 January	Establishment of US Strategic Air Forces in Europe Command to control operations of 8th and 15th AFs.
19–26 February	'Big Week' series of sustained raids on German aircraft industry. Total losses amount to 226 US bombers.
Spring	7th and 13th AFs concentrate on Japanese bases in eastern Caroline Islands, Truk and Ponape.

4–6 March	31 B-17s of the 8th AF bomb Kleinmachnow area, south-west of Berlin, becoming the first US bombers to attack the German capital. On 6 March, 730 heavy bombers and almost 800 escort fighters are despatched by 8th AF to Berlin.
March–June	Interdiction campaign to isolate north-western France, the area of Operation OVERLORD.
19 March –11 May	Operation STRANGLE: interdiction campaign to choke off German rail supply in Italy.
2 June	First FRANTIC shuttle mission. Lt.-Gen. Ira C. Eaker leads a 15th AF shuttle force of 130 B-17s and 70 P-51s from Italy to Poltava and Piryatin, Russia, bombing the Debrecen railyards in Hungary en route. On 6 June the force bombs Galatz, Romania, returning to Soviet bases. On 11 June it bombs Foscani airfield, Romania, on return to Italy.
5 June	First B-29 mission of the war. Landing fields in China are used as staging posts to refuel and re-arm 98 B-29s for 2,000 mile round trip to bomb rail targets in Bangkok: 14 abort and 5 crash on landing. Only eighteen bombs land on target area.
6 June	Operation OVERLORD, the invasion of north-west France: 8,722 AAF aircraft over France in support of the operation. Altogether, 2,362 bomber sorties involving 1,729 B-17s and B-24s are flown on D-Day, dropping 3,596 tons of bombs. VIII Fighter Command fly 1,880 sorties and claim 28 enemy fighters shot down; 742 B-26 sorties are flown by the 9th AF. Total losses: 3 B-24s (including 2 that collide).
11 June	First shuttle raid between the USSR and Italy. 15th AF bomb the Romanian airfield at Foscania.
15/16 June	From China 47 B-29s conduct first raid on Japanese home islands with a night raid on the Imperial Iron and Steel Works at Yawata on the island of Kyushu; 7 B-29s lost. 5th and 13th AFs come under control of new FEAF command.
18-19 June	Battle of the Philippine Sea: naval aviators shoot down over 300 enemy planes in an action dubbed the 'Marianas Turkey Shoot'.
21 June	Second FRANTIC shuttle mission. 8th AF shuttle force to Russia involves 114 B-17s of the 13th and 45th Wings, 3rd Bomb Division, who bomb a synthetic oil refinery just south of Berlin and then fly on to landing fields in the Ukraine, escorted all the way by 61 P-51s of the 4th and 352nd FGs; 144 B-17s land in the Ukraine; 73 at Poltava, remainder at Mirgorod; 64 P-51s land at Piryatin. A German raid on Poltava on 21/22 June destroys 47 B-17s and damages 29 others. On 26 June, 72 Fortresses fly home, bombing a target in Poland and staging through Italy, then bombing a target in France en route to England on 5 July. The entire tour covers 6,000 miles, ten countries and 29¼ hours of operational flying.

June	Guam, Saipan and Tinian secured for bases for staging B-29 raids on Japan from late 1944. Operation MATTERHORN: B-29s begin operations from Chengtu against Japanese home island targets, starting with the steel works at Yawata. Logistical difficulties limit the success of the operation, and the effort tails off by March 1945.
14 July	Operation CADILLAC: mass drop by 322 8th AF B-17s of 3,780 supply containers to the French Forces of the Interior.
6 August	76 Fortresses in the 95th and 390th BG, 8th AF, and 64 P-51s fly shuttle mission to Russia, bombing the Focke Wulf plant at Rahmel, Poland, en route. They fly a raid to the Trzebinia synthetic oil refinery and return to Russia before flying to Italy on 8 August, bombing two Romanian airfields en route. On 12 August they fly back to Britain on the last stage of their shuttle, bombing a French airfield en route.
10 August	Mariana Islands secured. US heavy bomber bases within range of Japanese home islands. By November, over 100 new B-29s arrive on Guam.
August	Longest B-29 mission of the war; 3,950 mile flight from Ceylon to Palembang in Sumatra.
11 September	Final FRANTIC mission: 75 B-17s and 64 P-51s of the 8th AF attack Chemnitz and fly on to the Soviet Union. On 13 September the B-17s bomb a steel works at Diósgyör, Hungary, and land in Italy.
18 September	117 B-17s of the 8th AF drop 1,284 containers of ammunition, guns and supplies to Poles in beleaguered Warsaw, but only 130 fall into the right hands.
10 October	FEAF B-24s strike former Dutch oil refinery at Balikpapan, Borneo.
25 October	Invasion of Leyte: US forces return to the Philippines.
24 November	B-29s of Brig.-Gen. Emmett 'Rosie' O'Donnell's 73rd Wing, operating from the Marianas, bomb Tokyo for the first time. Musashima aircraft factory raided.
1945	
January	US tactical air forces help defeat German forces engaged in the Battle of the Bulge, the last enemy offensive in the west.
February	Raids on Berlin: bombing offensive continues through to the last days of the war. In the Pacific, 7th AF bombers support US Marines in fighting for Iwo Jima.
13–15 February	8th AF and RAF Bomber Command raze German city of Dresden. HE and firestorms cause 35,000 civilian deaths.
9/10 March	First low-level (4,500–9,200 ft) M69 incendiary bomb raids on Tokyo by over 300 B-29s flying from the Marianas destroys 16 sq. miles of the capital; 80,000 Japanese die; 14 B-29s lost and 14 damaged by flak.

1 April –25 June	FEAF and 7th AF operate against Japanese suicide fighter bases on the Japanese mainland and on Formosa as US Army and Marine ground forces take Okinawa. 7th AF transfers there to continue operations against Japan.
7 May	German representatives surrender in the west. War ends. VE Day proclaimed on 8 May 1945. Russians accept surrender on 9 May.
June	Co-ordinated US strategy for a massive amphibious invasion of Japan approved by President Truman. Operation OLYMPIC will be the code-name for the invasion of Kyushu, the southernmost of the main Japanese islands, by 767,000 troops in November 1945, and CORONET the invasion of Honshu, the largest of the Japanese islands, in March 1946.
16 July	Scientists test-explode the first atomic device at Alamogordo, New Mexico. President Truman authorizes the use of the atomic bomb against Japan, and a mission directive is sent to Gen. Carl A. Spaatz, commander of the newly formed US Strategic Air Forces in the Pacific. A top secret squadron is ready with 15 specially-modified B-29s in the 313th Wing, XXI BC, on Tinian, ready to deliver the first atomic bomb, code-named 'Little Boy', after 3 August 1945, as soon as weather will permit visual bombing.
6 August	XXI Bomber Command B-29 *Enola Gay*, flown by Col. Paul Tibbets from Tinian, releases atomic bomb 'Little Boy' (a uranium device) from 31,600 ft on Hiroshima: 48,000 buildings are destroyed; 71,379 Japanese die immediately and 68,023 are injured (19,691 seriously) in the explosion.
9 August	'Fat Man', a plutonium device and the only remaining atomic device in existence, is dropped on Nagasaki from B-29 *Bock's Car*. An estimated 35,000 die immediately in the conflagration; 5,000 are missing, 60,000 are injured.
14 August	A record 804 B-29s bomb targets in Japan. Japanese Government surrenders.
2 September	Japanese surrender aboard USS *Missouri* in Tokyo Bay. VJ Day declared. On this date, US Air Forces total 243 groups.
30 September	Demobilization. On this date, the AAF has 1,895 installations, including 1,333 in the US ZOI. A total of 1,992,960 personnel (310,443 officers, 1,682,517 EM) are in the service. (The AAF reached peak strength in military personnel in March 1944, when 306,889 officers and 2,104,405 EM made up a force of 2,411,294 in total.)

Appendix I

8th Air Force Group and Squadron Codes

2C	838thBS	487thBG	B6	363rdFS	357thFG
2G	836thBS	487thBG	B7	374thFS	361stFG
2S	834thBS	486thBG	B9	554thFS	496thFG
2U	785thBS	466thBG	B9	436thFS	479thFG
30	601stBS	398thBG	BG	334thBS	95thBG
3L	391stBS	34thBG	BK	546thBS	381stBG
3Q	852ndBS	491stBG	BN	359thBS	303rdBG
3R	832ndBS	486thBG	BO	368thBS	306thBG
4F	837thBS	487thBG	BX	338thBS	96thBG
4N	833rdBS	486thBG	C	862ndBS	493rdBG
4R	844thBS	489thBG	C5	364thFS	357thFG
4Z	791stBS	467thBG	C7	555thFS	496thFG
5E	385thFS	364thFG	CG	38thFS	55thFG
5E	1st Scouting Force (until 2.45)		CH	365thFS	358thFG
5Q	505thFS	339thFG	CI	576thBS	392ndBG
5Y	384thFS	364thFG	CL	338thFS	55thFG
5Z	856thBS	492ndBG	CL	3rd Scouting Force	
6A	789thBS	467thBG	CP	367thFS	358thFG
6K	730thBS	452ndBG	CQ	708thBS	447thBG
6L	787thBS	466thBG	CS	370thFS	359thFG
6N	504thFS	339thFG	CT	712thBS	448thBG
6X	854thBS	491stBG	CV	368thFS	359thFG
7D	731stBS	452ndBG	CY	343rdFS	55thFG
7Q	850thBS	490thBG	D7	503rdFS	339thFG
7V	752ndBS	458thBG	DC	577thBS	392ndBG
7W	848thBS	490thBG	DF	324thBS	91stBG
8I	18thBS	34thBG	DQ	551stFS	495thFG
8R	846thBS	489thBG	DR	452ndBS	332ndBG(M)
9A	858thBS	492ndBG	DS	511thBS	351stBG
9B	436thFS	479thFG	E2	375thFS	361stFG
9H	857thBS	492ndBG	E3	732ndBS	453rdBG
9H	1st Scouting Force (from 3.45)		E8	734thBS	453rdBG
9Z	728thBS	452ndBG	E9	376thFS	361stFG
AG	330thBS	93rdBG	EC	578thBS	392ndBG
AN	553rdBS	386thBG(M)	EE	565thBS	389thBG
AV	335thFS	4thFG	EI	714thBS	448thBG
AW	339thBS	96thBG	EP	351stBS	100thBG
AX	107thRS	67thRG	ER	451stBS	332ndBG(M)
B	861stBS	493rdBG★	ES	13thPS	7thPG

B-17Gs of the 388th BG, which was unique in England in that the group carried no squadron identification letters or markings. The two parallel black bands on the wing and tail began to appear on 338th BG aircraft from late January 1945. (USAF)

*B-17 Squadrons (no codes used on			HN	705thBS	446thBG
B-24s)			HO	487thFS	352ndFG
ET	336thBS	95thBG	HP	567thBS	389thBG
F8	733rdBS	453rdBG	HR	551thBS	385thBG
FL	704thBS	446thBG	HV	61stFS	56thFG
FO	527thBS	379thBG	HV	27thFS	1stFG
FR	525thBS	379thBG	IA	366thFS	358thFG
FW	556thBS	387thBG(M)	IE	709thBS	447thBG
G4	362ndFS	357thFG	IG	713thBS	448thBG
GC	579thBS	392ndBG	IJ	710thBS	447thBG
GD	534thBS	381stBG	IN	613thBS	401stBG
GJ	506thBS	44thBG	IO	715thBS	448thBG
GL	410thBS	94thBG	IR	711thBS	447thBG
GN	427thBS	303rdBG	IS	703rdBS	445thBG
GO	328thBS	93rdBG	IV	369thFS	359thFG
GX	5458thBS	385thBG	IW	614thBS	401stBG
GY	367thBS	306thBG	IY	615thBS	401stBG
H6	735thBS	453rdBG	J2	435thFS	479thFG
H8	835thBS	486thBG	J2	435thFS	479thFG
HL	308thFS	31stFG	J3	755thBS	458thBG
HL	84thFS	78thFG	J4	753rdBS	458thBG

J6	406thBS			QI	361stFS	356thFG
JD	545thBS	384thBG		QJ	337thBS	96thBG
JJ	422ndBS	305thBG		QK	66thBS	44thBG
JU	707thBS	446thBG		QP	2ndFS	52ndFG
JW	326thBS	92ndBG		QP	334thFS	4thFG
K8	602ndBS	398thBG		QW	412thBS	95thBG
KI	55thFS	20thFG		R2	7thBS	34thBG
KS	557thBS	387thBG(M)		R4	803rd(P)	/36thBS
KX	558thBS	387thBG(M)		R5	839thBS	487thBG
KY	366thBS	305thBG		RD	423rdBS	306thBG
L2	434thFS	479thFG		RE	329thBS	93rdBG
L2	434thFS	479thFG		RG	552ndBS	386thBG(M)
LC	77thFS	20thFG		RJ	323rdBS	323rdBG(M)
LD	418thBS	100thBG		RN	700thBS	445thBG
LF	526thBS	379thBG		RQ	509thBS	351stBG
LG	322ndBS	91stBG		RR	566thBS	389thBG
LH	350thFS	353rdFG		RT	706thBS	446thBG
LL	401stBS	91stBG		RU	554thBS	386thBG(M)
LM	62ndFS	56thFG		S	860thBS	493rdBG★
LM	71stFS	1stFG		S3	851stBS	490thBG
LN	350thBS	100thBG		S4	845thBS	489thBG
M3	729thBS	452ndBG		SC	612thBS	401stBG
MC	79thFS	20thFG		SG	550thBS	385thBG
MD	336thFS	4thFG		SI	814thBS	482ndBG
MI	812thBS	482ndBG		SO	547thBS	381stBG
MK	701stBS	445thBG		SS	451stBS	332ndBG(M)
MS	535thBS	381stBG		SU	544thBS	384thBG
MX	82ndFS	78thFG		SX	352ndFS	353rdFG
MX	307thFS	31stFG		T4	847thBS	489thBG
MZ	413thBS	96thBG		T8	853rdBS	491stBG
N2	383rdFS	364thFG		T9	784thBS	466thBG
N7	603rdBS	398thBG		TQ	559thBS	387thBG(M)
N8	600thBS	398thBG		TS	333rdBS	94thBG
NB	67thBS	44thBG		TU	510thBS	351stBG
NG	660thBS	493rdBG		U8	786thBS	466thBG
NM	34thTCS	315thTCG		UA	43rdTCS	315thTCG
NV	325thBS	92ndBG		UN	63rdFS	56thFG
OC	359thFS	356thFG		UN	84thFS	1stFG
OE	335thBS	95thBG		UX	327thBS	92ndBG
OR	323rdBS	91stBG		V2	855thBS	491stBG
OS	357thFS	355thFG		VE	532ndBS	381stBG
P	863rdBS	493rdBG★		VF	5thFS	52ndFG
PC	813thBS	482ndBG		VF	336thFS	4thFG
PE	328thFS	352ndFG		VK	358thBS	303rdBG
PI	360thFS	356thFG		VM	552ndFS	495thFG
PN	450thBS	332ndBG(M)		VP	533rdBS	381stBG
PU	360thBS	303rdBG		VT	453rdBS	323rdBG(M)
PY	407thBS	92ndBG		VX	109thRS	67thRS
PZ	486thFS	352ndFG		W8	849thBS	490thBG
Q2	790thBS	467thBG		WA	524thBS	379thBG
Q6	4thBS	34thBG		WD	335thFS	4thFG
QE	331stBS	94thBG		WD	4thFS	52ndFG

WF	364thBS	305thBG		XN	654thBS	25thBG(R)
WQ	68thBS	44thBG		/802ndRG(P)		
WR	2nd Scouting Force			YA	555thBG	386thBG(M)
WR	354thFS	355thFG		YU	455thBS	323rdBG(M)
WT	456thBS	323rdBG(M)		XR	334thFS	4thFG
WV	702ndBS	445thBG		XR	349thBS	100thBG
WW	369thBS	306thBG		YB	508thBS	351stBG
WX	653rdBS	25thBG(R)		YF	358thFS	355thFG
/802ndRG(P)				YJ	351stFS	353rdFG
WZ	84thFS	78thFG		YM	409thBS	93rdBG
WZ	309thFS	31stFG		YN	652ndBS	25thBG(R)
X4	859thBS	492ndBG		/802ndRG(P)		
X7	788thBS	467thBG		YO	564thBS	389thBG
XA	549thBS	385thBG		Z5	754thBS	458thBG
XK	365thBS	305thBG		ZM	12thRS	67thRG
XM	332ndBS	94thBG		ZS	153rdRS	67thRS

9th Air Force Group and Squadron Codes

AJ	356thFS	354thFG		E4	377thFS	362ndFG
AN	533rdBS	386thBG		E5	62ndTCS	314thTCG
AX	107thTRS	386thBG		E6	402ndFS	370thFG
A6	389thFS	366thFG		FT	353rdFS	354thFG
A7	359thFS	368thFG		FW	556thBS	387thBG
A8	391stFS	366thFG		F4	492ndFS	48thFG
A9	380thFS	363rdFG		F5	428thFS	474thFG
A9	160thTRS	363rdTRG		F6	670thBS	416thBG
B2	390thFS	366thFG		GQ	355thFS	354thFG
B3	381stFS	363rdFG		G4	362ndFS	357thFG
B4	387thFS	365thFG		G8	378thFS	362ndFG
B6	363rdFS	357thFG		G9	509thFS	405thFG
B8	379thFS	362ndFG		H2	49thTCS	313rdTCG
CH	365thFS	358thFG		H5	392ndFS	367thFG
CJ	71stTCS	434thTCG		H9	586thBS	394thBG
CM	78thTCS	435thTCG		IA	366thFS	358thFG
CN	73rdTCS	434thTCG		IB	77thTCS	435thTCG
CP	367thFS	358thFG		ID	74thTCS	434thTCG
CU	72ndTCS	434thTCG		IH	1stPFS	(TCC)
CW	76thTCS	435thTCG		I6	30thPS	10thPG
C2	396thFS	368thFG		I7	493rdFS	48thFG
C3	382ndFS	363rdFG		J7	303rdTCS	442ndTCG
C3	162ndTRS	363rdTRG		J8	92ndTCS	439thTCG
C4	388thFS	365thFG		KS	557thBS	387thBG
C5	364thFS	357thFG		KX	558thBS	387thBG
DR	452ndBS	322ndBG		K4	511thFS	405thFG
D3	397thFS	368thFG		K5	584thBS	394thBG
D5	386thFS	365thFG		K6	430thFS	474thFG
D6	642ndBS	409thBG		K9	494th,BS	344thBG
D8	94thTCS	439thTCG		L3	512thFS	406thFG
ER	450thBS	322ndBG		L4	91stTCS	439thTCG

Code	Unit	Group	Code	Unit	Group
M2	88thTCS	438thTCG	ZM	12thTRS	67thTRG/10thPRG
M6	309thTCS	315thTCG	ZS	12thTRS	67thTRG
NM	34thTCS	315thTCG	Z4	301stTCS	441stTCG
N3	47thTCS	313rdTCG	Z7	48thTCS	313rdTCG
N3	496thBS	344thBG	Z8	84thTCS	437thTCG
N5	111thTRS	69thTRG	2A	669thBS	416thBG
O7	514thFS	406thFG	2L	302ndTCS	441stTCG
O8	575thBS	391stBG	2N	81stFS	50thFG
PN	449thBS	322ndBG	2R	50thTCS	314thTCG
P2	572ndBS	391stBG	2W	33rdPS	363rdTRG
QL	22ndTRS	69thTRG	2Z	510thFS	405thFG
Q7	90thTCS	438thTCG	3A	53rdTCS	61stTCG
Q8	23rdTCS	349thTCG	3B	93rdTCS	439thTCG
Q9	61stTCS	314thTCG	3D	82ndTCS	436thTCG
RG	552ndBS	386thBG	3F	313thTCS	349thTCG
RJ	454thBS	323rdBG	3I	14thTCS	61stTCG
RU	554thBS	386thBG	3J	99thTCS	441stTCG
R3	410thFS	373rdFG	3T	22ndFS	36thFG
SH	75thTCS	435thTCG	3X	87thTCS	438thTCG
SS	451stBS	322ndBG	4A	310thTCS	315thTCG
SW	33rdPRS	10thPG/67th	4C	44thTCS	316thTCG
S2	32ndTCS	314thTCG	4J	305thTCS	442ndTCG
S6	79thTCS	436thTCG	4K	506thFS	404thFG
S9	34thPS	10thPG	4L	574thBS	391stBG
TQ	559thBS	387thBG	4N	394thFS	367thFG
T2	83rdTCS	437thTCG	4P	513thFS	406thFG
T3	45thTCS	316thTCG	4T	585thBS	394thBG
T5	10thFS	50thFG	4U	89thTCS	438thTCG
T6	573rdBS	391stBG	4W	406thFS	371stFG
UA	43rdTCS	315thTCG	5C	671stBS	416thBG
U2	598thBS	397thBG	5D	644thBS	410thBG
U5	81stTCS	436thTCG	5H	668thBS	416thBG
U9	411thFS	373rdFG	5I	643rdBS	409thBG
VT	453rdBS	323rdBG	5K	86thTCS	437thTCG
VX	109thTRS	69thTRG	5M	15thTRS	61stTCG
V4	304thTCS	442ndTCG	5X	29thTCS	313thTCG
V5	412thFS	373rdFG	5W	587thBS	349thBG
WT	456thBS	323rdBG	6B	599thBS	397thBG
W3	313rdFS	50thFG	6C	14thLS	
W5	640thBS	409thBG	6E	36thTCS	316thTCG
W6	97thTCS	440thTCG	6M	494thFS	48thFG
W7	37thTCS	316thTCG	6Q	647thBS	410thBG
XX	34thPS	69thTRG	6V	53rdFS	36thFG
X2	596thBS	397thBG	6Z	96thTCS	440thTCG
X5	59thTCS	61stTCG	7D	80thTCS	436thTCG
YA	555thBS	386thBG	7F	485thFS	370thFG
YC	10thTRS	69thTRG	7G	641stBS	409thBG
YU	455thBS	323rdBG	7H	306thTCS	442ndTCG
Y5	495thBS	344thBG	7I	497thBS	344thBG
Y8	507thFS	404thFG	7J	508thFS	404thFG
Y9	15thTCS	61stTCG	7U	23rdFS	36thFG

7X	645thBS	410thBG	8Y	98thTCS	440thTCG
7Y	429thFS	474thFG	9D	401stFS	370thFG
8C	100thTCS	441stTCG	9E	312thTCS	349thTCG
8L	393rdFS	367thFG	9F	597thBS	397thTCG
8N	405thFS	371stFG	9O	85thTCS	437thTCG
8R	153rdLS		9Q	404thFS	371stFG
8U	646thBS	410thBG	9S	14thLS	
8V	31stPS	10thPG	9X	95thTCS	440thTCG

Appendix II

Leading USAAF Aces (air-to-air)

Maj. Richard I. Bong	40	35th/49th/475thFG	5thAF	killed 6 Aug. 1945
Maj. Thomas B. McGuire Jr	38	475th	5thAF	
Col. Francis S. Gabreski	28	56thFG	8thAF	
Col. Robert S. Johnson	27	56thFG	8thAF	
Col. Charles H. MacDonald	27	475thFG	5thAF	
Maj. George E. Preddy	26.83	352ndFG	8thAF	
Col. John C. Meyer	24	352ndFG	8thAF	
Col. David C. Schilling	22½	56thFG	8thAF	
Lt.-Col. Gerald R. Johnson	22	49thFG	5thAF	
Col. Neel E. Kearby	22	348thFG	5thAF	
Maj. Jay T. Robbins	22	8thFG	5thAF	
Capt. Fred J. Christensen	21½	56thFG	8thAF	
Capt. Ray S. Wetmore	21¼	359thFG	8thAF	
Capt. John J. Voll	21	31stFG	15thAF	
Col. Walker M. Mahurin	20¾	56thFG	8thAF	
Lt.-Col. Thomas J. Lynch	20	35thFG	5thAF	

Col. Francis S. 'Gabby' Gabreski, 56th FG, 8th AF, who finished the war as the top-scoring fighter ace in Europe, with twenty-eight victories. (USAF)

'Kit' Carson's Mustang, *Nooky Booky IV*, 357th FG, being warmed up by his groundcrewman on the steel matting at Leiston. (via Merle Olmsted)

Lt.-Col. Robert B. Westbrook	20	18th/347thFG 13thAF	KIA 22 Nov. 1944
Capt. Donald S. Gentile	19.83	4thFG 8thAF	
Col. Glenn E. Duncan	19½	353rdFG 8thAF	
Capt. Duane W. Beeson	19.3	4thFG 8thAF	PoW 5 Apr. 1944
Capt. Leonard K. Carson	18½	357thFG 8thAF	
Col. Glenn T. Eagleston	18½	354thFG 9thAF	
Maj. Walter C. Beckham	18	353rdFG 8thAF	
Maj. Herschel H. Green	18	325thFG 15thAF	
Lt.-Col. Hubert Zemke	17¾	479th/56thFG 8thAF	
Maj. John B. England	17½	357thFG 8thAF	
1st Lt. John F. Thornell	17¼	352ndFG 8thAF	
Lt. Henry W. Brown	17.2	355thFG 8thAF	
Col. Gerald W. Johnson	17	356th/56thFG 8thAF	PoW 27 March 1944
Capt. James S. Varnell Jr	17	52ndFG 15thAF	
Capt. Clarence E. Anderson	16½	357thFG 8thAF	
2nd Lt. Ralph K. Hofer	16½	4thFG 8thAF	
Capt. John T. Godfrey	16.33	4thFG 8thAF	
Maj. George S. Welch	16	8thFG 5thAF	
Lt.-Col. William D. Dunham	16	348thFG 5thAF	
Lt.-Col. Bill Harris	16		
Col. Don J.M. Blakeslee	15½	4thFG 8thAF	
Capt. Donald M. Beerbower	15½		
Maj. Samuel J. Brown	15½	31stFG 15thAF	
Capt. Richard A. Peterson	15½	357thFG 8thAF	
Lt.-Col. John C. Herbst	15	23rdFG 14thAF	
Maj. William T. Whisner Jr	15	352ndFG 8thAF	

Col. James A. Goodson	15	4thFG	8thAF	PoW July 1944
Lt.-Col. Jack T. Bradley	15	328thFG	9thAF	
Maj. Edward Cragg	15	8thFG	5thAF	
Maj. Robert W. Foy	15	357thFG	8thAF	
Capt. Cyril F. Homer	15	8thFG	5thAF	
Maj. Daniel T. Roberts Jr	15	4475thFG	5thAF	
Lt.-Col. Donald H. Bochkay	14.84	357thFG	8thAF	
Lt.-Col. John D. Landers	14½	49/357/55/78FG	8thAF	
Capt. Joe H. Powers Jr	14½	56thFG	8thAF	
Capt. Robert M. DeHaven	14	49thFG	5thAF	
Capt. Arthur F. Jeffrey	14	479thFG	8thAF	
Maj. Robert C. Curtis	14	52ndFG	15thAF	
Capt. John F. Hampshire	14	23rdFG	14thAF	KIA 2 May 1943
Lt.-Col. Edward O. McComas	14	23rdFG	14thAF	
Lt. Donald J. Strait	13½	356thFG	8thAF	
Lt. George Carpenter	13.33	4thFG	8thAF	
Lt. Donald S. Bryan	13.33	352ndFG	8thAF	
Lt. Willard W. Milikan	13	4thFG	8thAF	
Lt. Felix D. Williamson	13	56thFG	8thAF	
Lt. Glennon T. Moran	13	352ndFG	8thAF	
Lt. Robin Olds	13	479thFG	8thAF	
Capt. Harry A. Parker	13	325thFG	15thAF	
Capt. James L. Brooks	13	31stFG	15thAF	
Col. Robert L. Scott Jr	13	23rdFG	14thAF	

Select Bibliography

B-24D Source & Instruction Manual.

Bell, Dana *USAF Colours 1942–45 Inc., European & Med Theatres of War*, Squadron/Signal Pubs, 1980.

Bombardiers' Information File AAF: The Official Guide to the Army Air Forces, Pocket Books, New York, 1944.

Bowman, Martin W. *Fields of Little America*, PSL, 1983.

—— *Castles in the Air*, PSL, 1984.

Carter, Kit C. and Mueller, Robert *The Army Air Forces in WWII: Combat Chronology*, Albert F. Simpson Historical Research Centre, Air University & Office of Air Force History HQ USAF, 1973.

Davis, Richard G. *Carl A. Spaatz and the Air War in Europe*, Centre for Air Force History, Washington DC, 1993.

Department of Armament, 'Fundamental Physics of Modern Bombsights: Automatic Computing Sights Sperry Type K (.50 calibre)', *Operating Bulletin* No. 14-227A, 1 July 1942.

Ferguson, Aldon P. *RAF Burtonwood: 50 Years in Photographs*, Airfield Publications, 1989.

Freeman, Roger A. *The Mighty Eighth*, MacDonald, 1970.

—— *The Mighty Eighth War Diary*, Macdonald.

—— *The Mighty Eighth War Manual*, Macdonald.

—— *The US Strategic Bomber*, MacDonald Ill. War Studies, 1975.

—— *Airfields of the 8th Then and Now*, After The Battle, 1978.

Hansell, Brig.-Gen. Hayward *The Air Plan That Defeated Hitler*.

HQ, 2nd AF *Pilot's Safety File*, Colorado Springs, Colorado, 1944.

Lhote, Gilles and Clyman, Jeff *Cowboys of the Sky*, Avirex, 1988.

Maguire, Jon A. *Gear Up*, Schiffer Publishing, 1944.

—— *Silver Wings, Pinks & Greens: Uniforms, Wings & Insignia of USAAF Airmen in WWII*, Schiffer Publishing, 1944.

Mills Link, Mae and Coleman, Hubert A. *Medical Support of the Army Air Forces in WWII*, Office of the Surgeon General, USAF, Washington DC, 1955.

Nalty, Bernard C., Shiner, John F. and Watson, George M. (Alfred M. Beck, chief editor) *With Courage: The USAAFs In WWII*, Air Force History & Museums Program, Washington DC, 1994.

Newby, Leroy W. *Target Ploesti: View from a Bombsight*, Arms & Armour Press, 1983.

Polmar, Norman and Allen, Thomas B. *WWII: America At War 1941–1945*, Random House, New York, 1991.

Price, Alfred *WWII Fighter Conflict*, MacDonald & Janes, 1975.

Rottman, Gordon and Chin, Francis, Osprey Military Elite Series, *US Army Air Force 1 and 2*, 1993 and 1994.

Rust, Kenn C. *Air Force in WWII Histories*, Historical Aviation Album, 1973.

Swanborough, Gordon and Bowers, Peter M. *US Military Aircraft Since 1909*, Putnam, 1963.

Sweeting, C.G. *Combat Flying Equipment: US Army Aviators Equipment 1917–45*, Smithsonian, 1989.

The Officer's Guide, Military Service Publishing Co., Harrisburg, Pennsylvania, July 1943.

USAF Warrior Studies Office of Air Force History *Strategic Air Warfare*, Washington, DC, 1988.

Wesley Frank Craven and James Lea Cate *Air Force Combat Units of WWII*, *The Army Air Forces in WWII*, Vols I–VII (edited by Maurer Maurer), US Government Printing Office, Washington, DC, 1961.

Windrow, Richard and Hawkins, Tim *The WWII GI: US Army Uniforms, 1941–45*, Windrow and Greene, 1993.

Yeager, Gen. Chuck and Janos, Leo *Yeager – an autobiography*, Bantam Books, 1985.

Index